HOMICIDE
Murders and manslaughter in
21st century Ireland

HOMICIDE
Murders and manslaughter in 21st century Ireland

John Burke &
Eoghan Rice

MERLIN
PUBLISHING

First published in 2006 by
Merlin Publishing
Newmarket Hall, Cork Street,
Dublin 8, Ireland
Tel: +353 1 4535866
Fax: +353 1 4535930
publishing@merlin.ie
www.merlinwolfhound.com

£14,933.

10-Digit ISBN 1-903582-68-7
13-Digit ISBN 978-1-903582-68-8

A CIP catalogue record for this book is available from the
British Library.

10 9 8 7 6 5 4 3 2 1

Typeset by Gough Typesetting Services
Cover Design by Artwerk Design
Printed and bound in Denmark by Nørhaven Paperback A/S

Acknowledgements

To tell the story of homicide in Ireland is to tell the story of calculated assassination and hot-blooded revenge. It is to tell of young people who left their homes for a night's socialising, never to return, and of elderly people who died violently when the homes they considered safe were invaded. It is a story of loss and of grief for countless families. And it is also the story of the killers themselves and their varied paths to taking the life of another human being.

As news reporters with *The Sunday Tribune* we have directly covered many of the cases dealt with in this book – over 60 violent deaths in total are contained in these pages. We owe a large debt of gratitude to the members of the Gardaí, victims' families, and lawyers connected to these tragic killings, who shared their stories and vital information with us over a long period of time.

The figures on murder and manslaughter detailed in this book are based on a cross-reference of officially published homicide data, alongside An Garda Síochána's internal 'violent death list' and our own research in the National Library – giving the analysis contained in this book a level of unprecedented accuracy. We are grateful to Garda Superintendent Kevin Donohoe and the Garda Press Office for providing us with this data.

We are also particularly grateful to Dr. Ian O'Donnell and his colleagues at the UCD Institute of Criminology. The Institute has led the way in the study of crime patterns in Ireland and deserves enormous credit. In particular, 'Crime and Punishment in Ireland 1922 to 2003', edited by Ian O'Donnell, Eoin O'Sullivan and Deirdre Healy, was an invaluable source of information when writing this book. It is our hope that statistics uncovered by *Homicide* can add to the public debate surrounding violent crime, just like research carried out by the Institute.

To accurately analyse and track the trends in murder and manslaughter in 21st century Ireland required us to examine over 360 homicides since the start of the decade. This would not have been possible without the catalogue of work produced by countless journalists, court reporters, archivists, opinion pollsters and national library staff who, over time, have produced a wealth of research material in which we immersed ourselves for over 12 months.

Thanks also to our colleagues in *The Sunday Tribune*, in particular award-winning *Tribune* photographer Mark Condren and Pictures Editor Maureen Gillespie.

Much thanks also goes to the team at Merlin Publishing, Aoife Barrett, Noelle Moran and Chenile Keogh, who kept us busy with deadlines and whose enthusiasm for the project made it possible.

Last, but by no means least, we would also like to thank our families, friends and girlfriends, Dee and Sorcha, who were a tremendous source of encouragement and support and who put up with our long hours, toiling away at this project in temporary preference to better company.

John Burke and Eoghan Rice

Contents

Introduction

The Rise of Violent Death

The country awoke on Saturday January 1, 2000, having celebrated the New Year like never before. The dawn of a new Millennium had led to a total shut-down, with the Government sanctioning a once-off four-day-long weekend.

Army Sergeant Tommy O'Brien was working while most of the country was out partying. The 35-year-old completed a 24-hour shift at McKee Army Barracks in Dublin and immediately returned to his home in Ashbourne, Co. Meath. He arrived home at 10 am on New Year's Day.

O'Brien withdrew money from an ATM machine and went straight to his local pub, where he stayed into the evening. It is believed that he drank as many as 12 pints before returning to his mother's house in the Milltown Estate. He did not remain in the house for long, however. Instead, he called into a neighbour. When he was leaving the neighbour's house, he came across Dermot McKeever.

McKeever was one of a number of new tenants in a house on the estate that had attracted much local comment and idle speculation. A rumour, which later proved to be entirely baseless, had circulated the area that the occupants were involved in the drugs trade. While complaints of this nature had been made to Gardaí in Ashbourne, there was no evidence to actually substantiate the rumour.

Regardless of this, the rumours were to the fore of O'Brien's intoxicated mind. As he stood on the pavement close to his home, the army Sergeant confronted McKeever about his supposed involvement in the illegal drugs business.

The situation turned violent almost immediately. In the fist-fight that followed, McKeever struck O'Brien in the face, knocking him to the ground.

O'Brien walked away. He was bruised and angry. He made the short trip back across the estate and returned to his home. He picked up a legally-owned shotgun and quickly returned to McKeever's house. He discharged one shot, hitting McKeever. Having fired once, O'Brien turned on his heels and returned home. He reloaded the weapon with cartridges and went back to McKeever's house again. He proceeded to fire off more shots outside the house, almost fatally wounding a second man.

Gardaí, responding to an emergency call, arrived on the scene within minutes. When the squad car pulled up, Tommy O'Brien turned the weapon on the local officers. At great personal risk to himself, Garda Sergeant Paul Tennanty confronted the armed and drunk man. The brave Garda managed to persuade O'Brien to put the gun on the ground. When O'Brien complied he then arrested the army Sergeant.

Despite attempts to save him, Dermot McKeever died two hours later in James Connolly Memorial Hospital.

The trial of Tommy O'Brien was as open-and-shut a case as a court is ever likely to hear. He had been caught by Gardaí standing near the body of Dermot McKeever holding the murder weapon.

Gardaí told the court that O'Brien believed the occupants of the house, including the deceased, to be involved in the drugs trade. However, although there had been complaints made to the Gardaí regarding the activities of the occupants, a search of the property following the shooting dead of McKeever had uncovered no illegal substances. Furthermore, nobody who lived in the house had ever been charged with drugs-related offences.

The jury of seven women and five men did not take long

in their deliberations. It took them just over two hours to unanimously convict Tommy O'Brien of murdering Dermot McKeever. Speaking after the verdict had been delivered, Justice Patrick Smith noted that O'Brien had been a man of "exemplary character" prior to the incident and had served 19 years in the army, including six tours of duty in the Lebanon. He added, however, that alcohol had been a "huge contributory factor" in the murder of Dermot McKeever. Although O'Brien had sought treatment for an alcohol problem, this had not had the desired effect. Justice Smith also noted that a psychiatric report pointed to a "short-fuse personality". Coupled with the large quantity of alcohol consumed over many hours before the shooting, this had led to a rapid escalation of events following McKeever's physical assault on O'Brien.

Tommy O'Brien was sentenced to life imprisonment, the mandatory term for anybody convicted of murder.

* * * * *

Dermot McKeever was the first person to be killed violently in Ireland this decade. His murder came just 18 hours into the new century. It was tragically fitting that the first day of the new Millennium dawned with bloodshed on the streets of Ireland. The 21st century has already been marked with a dramatic increase in the number of homicides in this country.

This book, for the first time, seeks to analyse the homicide rate in Ireland. It uses the 336 homicides which occurred between January 1, 2000, and December 31, 2005, in order to generate a detailed breakdown of the 'Who, How and Why' of homicide in modern Ireland. The authors will show the dramatic rise of violent death and attempt to answer some of the compelling questions about the shocking level of homicides which, in recent years, have affected all members of Irish society – young and old, Irish and non-Irish, rich and poor.

In *Homicide*, the authors have compiled never-before seen statistics – based on cross-referenced material, such as the Internal Provisional Garda Violent Deaths lists, from 2000 to

2005, data from the Department of Justice, and from a detailed analysis of court records and published media reports. This material has allowed us to deliver an unprecedented level of accurate data, which forms the basis for this analysis into the growing phenomenon of violent death in Ireland.

A total of 336 people were victims of homicide in Ireland during the first six years of the new century – an average of 56 people each year, which translates into more than one person killed every week over a six-year period. More people are killed violently in Ireland today than at any time during the last half century.

In 1960, just six people were victims of murder or manslaughter in Ireland – the same number of people were killed during a 16-day period in April 2002. Throughout the 1960s, there was an average of 12 people killed violently each year. That figure rose dramatically the following decade, as violent deaths more than doubled. In 1972, there were 28 killings. In the 33 years since that watershed, the homicide rate has never again fallen below 20.

The high number of deaths in the 1970s has often been partially attributed to the outbreak of the Troubles in Northern Ireland and the associated criminality that spread into the Republic. The hostilities brought with them a culture of violence and the "normalisation" of violent death. Indeed, a bloody blip occurred in 1974 when 57 people were recorded as having been violently killed – 33 of these died during the Dublin and Monaghan bombings.

The homicide rate rose in the 1980s, when an average of 29 people were killed each year, and rose again the following decade. Throughout the 1990s there was an annual average of 40 homicides. But the level of murder and manslaughter still had some way to go before reaching the levels experienced today.

In 2005, 60 people were violently killed. As recently as ten years ago that figure that would have seemed an impossible end of year tally. The figure is also way out of line with population growth. In the 1980s Ireland experienced 0.84 violent deaths per 100,000 population. This figure rose to an average of 1.1 per

100,000 throughout the 1990s. It now stands at 1.4 per 100,000. While the population of Ireland has risen, its growth has not been as fast as our willingness to resort to extreme violence.

Indeed, such figures represent a growth of 27% in the Irish homicide rate over the last ten years. Not only is this figure remarkable within the context of Irish society, it is totally against the trend internationally. While Ireland has been experiencing a massive growth in violent death, Europe, on average, experienced a decrease.

Comparing international data on homicide gives a fascinating insight into the problems now faced in respect of violent death in Ireland. The United Nations 'Survey of Crime Trends and Operations of Criminal Justice Systems' covering the years from the 1990s and into the early 2000s shows that the level of homicide, in the pre-accession EU, declined over that period.

At an average of just under 3 deaths per 100,000, the EU's homicide rate declined consistently from the mid-1990s onwards. While Ireland's homicide rate remains lower than many of its European neighbours, what is truly startling is the rate at which it is growing.

Never before has Ireland experienced such affluence as its inhabitants presently enjoy in the 21st century. Never before has the rate of employment been so high. Ordinary Irish people now own large property portfolios at home and often abroad also. The affluence and economic strength of Ireland's workforce has achieved an unprecedented high. Yet, for all these tremendous developments over the past decade, Irish society has still managed to produce a landmark number of homicides. That such an unprecedented figure of murders and manslaughters could occur today raises major questions about the Irish attitude to violence, about law enforcement and the challenges that lie ahead for Irish society.

While homicide rates in Ireland remain below those of countries such as America or Britain, the speed at which the figures are rising is a major concern. Over a relatively short period Ireland has essentially changed from a country where murder was rarely committed to one where it is a weekly occurrence. Just a matter of years ago the discovery of a body would have transfixed the entire country. Today we don't bat an eyelid while glancing over headlines of shootings, stabbings and brutal assaults that have extinguished life on this island.

Ireland is a country that has seen a huge growth in the willingness of people to use extreme violence, even against family and friends.

In certain parts of Ireland, the homicide rate is now on a par with the major urban centres of Europe and America. New York, for example, recorded a homicide rate of 4.7 per 100,000 in the year 2002. That same year, there were five people killed in Co. Waterford, a county with a population of just over 100,000 people. While the actual numbers killed in New York were clearly much greater than the equivalent figure in Waterford, statistically the areas now have near-identical homicide rates. Comparing New York to Waterford may seem fanciful on one level, but it illustrates a culture of violence that has become engrained in Ireland, and the massive problems we face in tackling it.

Some of the blame for Ireland's growing homicide rate must fall on successive governments, who presided over the planning decisions which have come back to haunt modern Ireland. Murder and manslaughter rates are at their highest in a number of clearly identifiable urban areas. The sprawling housing estates of west Dublin, both north and south of the River Liffey, have driven much of the rise. Together with areas such as Moyross in Limerick and Ballybeg in Waterford, huge tracts of west Dublin suffer from a culture of lawlessness which is directly linked to decades of government neglect.

In a recent interview with *The Sunday Tribune*, Minister of State Noel Ahern admitted that the State was presently spending €160 million a year rectifying the planning mistakes of the past. He commented that it is now "an uphill battle" to rid certain urban areas of violence and anti-social behaviour due to these mistakes.

"The thinking back then [the 60s and 70s] was to find a

green field and build 400 houses in it," said Ahern. "These estates were mass-produced and there were no facilities or amenities built. They were too big and too many people with social problems were put in together… We can build youth centres and community centres now but we're making up for lost time. At this stage, a problem has developed and a culture has developed amongst some people who don't abide by the law."

It was a remarkable admission from a senior member of one of the political parties who stood over many of these alarmingly poor planning decisions, from the 1960s onwards.

Opposition politicians have been constantly critical of the state of decay in which many estates were left to rot. Labour TD Roisin Shortall, who represents Dublin North West, says that violence and drug use have taken a hold of large chunks of the west of Dublin.

"Many housing estates that are soulless and deprived, and as a result many people see no future," she said. "We are now paying the consequence for years of under-investment and we have reached a situation where the rule of law no longer applies. We allowed ghettos to develop and there is now a climate of lawlessness."

Shortall blames school absenteeism for much of the social problems facing certain areas of the city. It is a viewpoint backed-up by the National Education Welfare Board (NEWB), who, in a recent submission to the Government, said that pupils in west Dublin have absenteeism levels from primary school that are almost twice that of other areas of the city. The submission also pointed to the low number of staff employed as Education Welfare Officers (EWO), who monitor levels of absenteeism in schools nationwide. The ratio of EWOs to school population is "significantly below the international norm", the report said.

There are, undoubtedly, other factors behind Ireland's growing homicide rate. Even a casual glance of the list of those killed in Ireland over recent years points to an obvious link with alcohol consumption. Fuelled by the Celtic Tiger, alcohol consumption rates in Ireland have spiralled over recent years. Official estimates put at 480,000 – or 12% of the population – the number of Irish people who are either addicted to or abusive of alcohol. Not only does this place a huge burden on the health service, it is placing an increasing burden on the courts service. As this book shows, alcohol abuse plays a role in a shocking number of murders and manslaughters in modern Ireland.

The dramatic rise of violent death in recent years was recently alluded to by Mr Justice Barry White, one of Ireland's most experienced trial judges, after he had officiated over the appeal of a murder conviction in Co. Wexford. The case in question, which saw a man charged with the fatal stabbing of his sister's boyfriend, was typical of the sort of homicide cases coming before the courts today – a concoction of drink and drugs, followed by a late-night row and a fatal stabbing.

During sentencing, White commented: "We live in an increasingly more and more violent society. Less than 50 years ago, you could count the number of unlawful killings in this country on one hand. Now, it is almost a daily occurrence."

Dr. Ian O'Donnell, Director of the UCD Institute of Criminology, concurs with White. O'Donnell, the leading expert on crime trends in Ireland, notes that, in just 50 years, Ireland has gone from being a very safe country to one where murders are commonplace. In the middle of the last century, "the population was almost on first-name terms with every victim and perpetrator," he says, which is in stark contrast to today's public reaction to individual homicides.

Despite the dramatic growth of homicide in Ireland, there remains little public debate about the growing number of people being killed in violent circumstances. We continuously discuss individual crimes but rarely examine the data for underling trends. One explanation for this is that there is a paucity of officially-funded research into murder and manslaughter in contemporary Ireland. In some senses, the media has also contributed to this situation. Some media outlets have too often given vast columns of space to high-profile murders, particularly those involving women, without examining the context or trends behind the rising number of killings.

Indeed, how unprepared Ireland has been for the rise in

violent crime is perhaps best illustrated by the lack of centrally collated data by official sources. Separate homicide figures obtained by the authors, from both the Department of Justice and the Gardaí, were at times in direct conflict with each other. The figures could only be properly distilled into accurate data by cross-referencing them with other sources and archives. For instance, according to official Garda figures, there were 58 homicides in 2005. However, the authors identified 60 victims of homicide over that 12 month period. In addition, official publications from the Central Statistics Office (CSO) quote historical homicide figures that only count murders but seemingly ignore manslaughter cases. Likewise, crucial Department of Justice statistics are based entirely on sometimes incomplete Garda figures. There remains a remarkable lack of information on the actual trends underlying violent death in Ireland. A major effort on behalf of the State is needed to provide accurate and up-to-date data and major research into the stories behind the raw figures. To date, much of what we know about homicide in Ireland has been provided by the ground-breaking work of the UCD Institute of Criminology and its Director, Dr. Ian O'Donnell.

We would all benefit hugely as a society to know who is killed, how and, most importantly, why. In order to maintain our values as a society, we need to face the truth about violence in this country. As *Homicide* shows, Ireland is facing a new challenge in terms of trying to contain levels and types of violence which have never been experienced before. It is crucial that we all have access to the information that will equip us to be best prepared to face that battle.

The challenge An Garda Síochána faces in probing cases of homicide has changed dramatically over recent years. New and entirely different types of murder and manslaughter cases are now coming before detectives. An overwhelming number of homicides in modern Ireland arise out of late night or domestic disputes and are often carried out in front of witnesses and without any attempt on behalf of the perpetrator to remove forensic evidence. In such cases, convictions often follow swiftly. However, the force achieves remarkably differing levels of success identifying perpetrators who carry out different categories of killing. So-called 'gangland' killings present massive difficulties for the Gardaí, as the force struggles to crack this most modern of policing problems.

Internationally, however, the Gardaí's record remains impressive. Their success rates, in bringing the perpetrators of horrific crimes to justice, remain above many of their foreign colleagues.

Homicide examines why Irish conviction rates relating to 'gangland' killings, in particular, remain low compared to some other jurisdictions. Fundamentally, we question assumptions about the public's attitude to 'gangland' crime – in the context of the spiralling consumption of illegal drugs by young, and not-so-young, Irish people, in tandem with an ambivalence to the violent deaths of young men from socially disadvantaged backgrounds.

Remarkably, one in ten victims of homicide in modern Ireland is of non-Irish birth. We take a seminal look at the trends in the violent deaths of foreigners on Irish soil, showing why some nationalities are more likely to die in bloodshed than others. We also analyse the killing of women, children and young men, as well as revealing Ireland's most dangerous county.

Homicide is a chilling analysis of Ireland's growing phenomenon of violent death, offering a unique and unprecedented insight into a problem many thought we would never see.

John Burke and Eoghan Rice
Autumn 2006

One

Suffer the Innocent

Baby Jack Everitt Brennan was just 17 months old when he was choked to death. The last minutes of his life were shockingly brutal. The amount of physical force used to extinguish the last breath from the tiny infant's body was sufficient to kill an adult man. But even more unbelievable than the violent attack was the connection between the child and his killer.

At the trial of the infant's killer, Judge Paul Carney would describe the story of the infant's last moments of life as "distressing for everybody that was in any fashion connected" to it. For little baby Jack's family, the comment could be described as a remarkable understatement.

The details of how Jack's killer planned the homicide were tremendously harrowing for the tiny victim's family, as they sat in the Central Criminal Court and listened to the most agonising story that any parent and grandparent could ever endure. The family would have to sit and listen to the story of how a man had planned and executed the killing of their baby. They would hear disturbing evidence about the premeditated nature of the murder. How the man removed Jack from the place where the little infant slept. How he loaded the child into a buggy and then located a brick and some orange clothesline rope to use as tools in the wicked enterprise.

But baby Jack's mother Barbara and the little infant's grandmother Patricia had an extra pain to endure. The brutal murder was carried out by Patricia's 18-year-old son and Barbara's beloved brother, David – baby Jack's uncle.

That the man who killed the child was the baby's own uncle is a horrifying truth for any parent who ponders the safety of his or her children. Most parents have concern for their children's safety in the company of strangers, but David Brennan was not a stranger to his young victim. It is a tragic fact, however, that an analysis, carried out for this book, of child homicides since 2000, shows that most killings are carried out by a close family relative of the victim. It is not a bogeyman nor a child-predator who carries out the unthinkable act, but invariably a member of the child's own family who is blighted themselves by psychiatric illness.

In this case, the young man lived in the same house as the little infant. Baby Jack slept in the bedroom that had once been David's when he was a young child.

Jack and his mother Barbara lived with Barbara's mother Patricia at Marsh Road in Drogheda. David Brennan had been raised in the same house. David was Patricia's youngest child and he had a history of troublesome conduct, involving substance addiction and volatile behaviour. His mother had briefly barred him from living at her house in October 1999 but she later relented and he was allowed back home to live with her. By the time he returned to live at his mother's house in early 2000, his nephew Jack was occupying his old bedroom.

Patricia Brennan had coped admirably for years, trying to help her troubled son. She had provided him with love and support and had welcomed him back to her house in the hope that it would allow him to get help for his many problems. However, it was while he was living with his mother, sister and newborn nephew Jack that David's strange behaviour was to take a tragic and brutal turn for the worst.

During his four-day trial at the Central Criminal Court

in January 2002, Patricia's evidence to the court portrayed a family under tremendous pressure due to the fluctuating state of her son's mental health. She said that the family had endured insurmountable obstacles to getting David a level of care that would protect his life and those around him.

Patricia Brennan said she felt her son was "running out of time" and that his behaviour had become frighteningly volatile and irrational in the final days of February 2000. Patricia desperately wanted to commit her son to a mental institution for his own safety. As other cases of child murders will show, a family's belief that something terrible is about to occur, however professionally unqualified, is at times not heeded by those capable of providing that care.

Patricia Brennan told the court that on the evening of February 29, 2000 she took her then 18-year-old son David to visit her GP, Dr Howard Barry. She hoped that the doctor could suggest some course of action to deal with the young man's increasingly strange behaviour.

Dr Barry referred David Brennan to Saint Brigid's psychiatric hospital in Ardee. At 6 pm on February 29, Patricia Brennan and her sister, Adeline Curran, drove the troubled young man to the psychiatric hospital.

There, both women spoke with the house officer at the hospital, Dr M.S. Das. The two women told the doctor that the young man's behaviour was wildly erratic. Patricia believed her son was in a state of rapid deterioration. She would later inform the jury that she told the doctor that she could not bring him home that night.

"I felt David was running out of time," she later said in court. The young man spent a short period in the doctor's office, she said, before emerging again. Dr Das told her that he was "not going to take him in".

When she was asked in court by her son's defence counsel, Sean Moylan SC, how she felt after hearing this news, she replied: "I was totally devastated." Patricia Brennan was asked in court whether she had considered signing a committal order for her son on that evening in February 2000 but she said that it had not come up in her discussion with Dr Das. This was a claim that would later be disputed.

Patricia Brennan again insisted that David should not return home with her that night and that she was deeply distressed over his state of mind. But, after failing to have him committed to the psychiatric hospital, Patricia brought David back to her home at Marsh Road at around 7.20 pm that evening. After arriving home, David went over to his father's house at Pitcher Hill. After a brief time there he returned to the Marsh Road house and seemed to be settling in for the night.

Patricia Brennan was out of the house with her sister-in-law when David rang her later on that night. "I said: 'David, are you all right?' and he said, 'Yes' but he sounded agitated. He asked me would I be long," she later recounted in court.

Baby Jack's mother Barbara had put the infant to bed at around 7.30 pm. She checked the child in his room at around 9 pm. It was around midnight that she noticed that her brother David had left the house. Some time after midnight, Barbara rang her mother Patricia and told her that David had gone. The young man's mother returned home and went out to search for her missing son. She spotted him near the Marsh Pub, with a dog. It was around 1.30 am in the early hours of March 1. There were muck splatters on both sides of his cheeks. His runners were muddy and the rear of his trousers was covered in dirt.

When Patricia Brennan found her son he appeared totally distressed, but she had no idea that her dishevelled son had just carried out the most unthinkable act. Neither Patricia nor her daughter Barbara were aware that baby Jack had been taken from his bed.

Patricia Brennan was deeply worried about her son. That night, she lay awake in bed concerned about David's growing detachment from reality and the necessity for urgent care that she felt he now needed.

At around 10.20 am the following morning, Patricia's daughter Barbara rang her at work. "She [Barbara] was distressed because she could not find Jack," the infant's grandmother later said.

Patricia Brennan sensed that something was terribly wrong. She considered her son's distressed state on the previous night and guessed that he had hurt his little nephew. She returned home where she confronted her son. Patricia asked him if he had harmed baby Jack. "I repeated: 'you killed baby Jack'. David answered one word: 'yes'", Patricia would later tell the court during David's trial.

The troubled young man's mother then asked her son where the baby was. Again, he said just one word: "quarry."

Minutes later Barbara Brennan rang the Gardaí, hoping still that the fateful words spoken by her brother were the reflections of a troubled mind and were not true. Drogheda-based Garda John Yorke arrived at the Brennan home at 10.35 am. Garda Yorke immediately questioned David about the disappearance of the infant. At first the young man would not reply to the questions. Then he said in a low voice that the baby was, "in the quarry".

David Brennan initially refused to get into the squad car with the Gardaí but after a short time he eventually agreed to show the officers where the quarry was located. At the quarry, Garda Yorke asked David where the baby was. "He pointed to the left towards the viaduct. I saw the body of a baby lying face down in the water," Garda Yorke subsequently related to the court.

Later, in custody at Drogheda Garda Station, David Brennan told Gardaí the gruesome details of what he had done in the early hours of March 1. He confessed that he had taken the baby from his bed at 12.55 am. He said that he placed Jack in a buggy which he took from the house, and which would later be found nearby at the Carmelite cottages near the quarry. David recounted how he brought the child to the viaduct. There, he took the infant from the carrier and placed his hands around baby Jack's fragile neck, squeezing tight until his breath stopped. It took little time for the young man's forceful hands to end the toddler's life. He then trussed the baby's limp body up with rope which he brought from the garden shed at his mother Patricia's house. David said he tied the brick to the rope before dropping the infant's body over the edge into the water below.

Later, while under care at the Central Mental Hospital in Dundrum, David Brennan told the facility's medical director, Dr Charles Smith, that he killed baby Jack to relieve his sister Barbara from a bad future in relation to the child.

The court heard that David Brennan had been diagnosed as suffering from paranoid schizophrenia and that his mental illness was central to his actions in the hours of February 29 into March 1, 2000. He frequently went into a psychotic state during which he would experience delusions and hallucinations. Dr Smith told the court that it was under this state of confusion that David Brennan had acted on that fateful night.

The court heard how David Brennan had been barred from his mother's house for four months in October 1999 and that when he returned, the infant was occupying David's old bedroom. "In an abnormal way, he would have felt resentful about that," Dr Smith told the court.

The then Deputy State Pathologist Professor Marie Cassidy, told the court that Jack died from asphyxia caused by manual strangulation.

At the beginning of the January 2002 trial, David Brennan's defence team read a statement on behalf of their client. In the statement, David Brennan made a full admission of the entire details of the child's death. Nonetheless, David Brennan pleaded not guilty to the murder. The state's prosecuting counsel, Michael Durack SC, told the jury that they had to decide whether at the time of the killing the accused man before them was of sound or unsound mind.

On January 7, 2002, the jury at the Central Criminal Court found David Brennan guilty but insane of the charge that he murdered his nephew.

After the verdict was delivered, the family of David Brennan issued the following statement through a solicitor: "The past two years have been a most harrowing and difficult time for the family. They are relieved that there is now some closure. Nothing will bring Jack back... However, the family takes some comfort in the knowledge that David is at last receiving, and will continue to receive, the medical treatment which sufferers of his condition so require," the statement concluded. Patricia Brennan said that Barbara Brennan still loves her brother, despite the fact that he took her child's life. "She still loves her brother. She knows he was ill," Patricia said.

David Brennan was admitted to the Central Mental Hospital in Dundrum on March 3, 2000, two days after the brutal death of his young nephew. At first the young man did not respond well to the course of treatment which doctors set for him. Some months after he was admitted to the hospital he made a crude attempt to flee from the facility but to no avail. The Central Criminal Court was told that David

Brennan would certainly require medical treatment for the rest of his life.

There is little doubt that David Brennan fell through the cracks in the mental health system. Following the trial, a panel of three experts was assembled by the then North Eastern Health Board, now subsumed into the larger Health Service Executive (HSE), to examine where the problems lay in the treatment of David Brennan prior to the killing of his nephew.

The panel spent months analysing the treatment that had been available for David Brennan. The facts contained in the report made for compelling reading. The experts' conclusions pointed to serious deficiencies in the mental health services in the south Louth area where the Brennan family lived.

The experts said that persons with mental disturbance had to endure an "unacceptably long" waiting period before they could make an initial appointment to obtain help. At the time David Brennan killed his nephew there was a waiting period of up to nine months for persons seeking a first appointment with the south Louth mental health services. At the same time, there was a less than six-week waiting period to make a similar appointment in other areas within the county, the report noted.

It emerged that David Brennan had been in contact with two separate arms of the Health Board which did not communicate with each other and which had no system of mutual referral. He was first referred to the mental health services in October 1999 by a local GP, but it was not until February 15 the following year that he was given an appointment for an outpatient consultation. He missed that appointment and he was issued with a new date, as is standard practice, for the following month. By the time the second appointment came around, he was on remand for the murder of his nephew Jack.

The report also found that Brennan had been receiving treatment for drug addiction. He had been referred on December 14, 1999 by the Probation and Welfare Service and was seen on January 17, 2000 but the report noted that, crucially, there was no communication between the addiction and mental health services in relation to his case.

The experts also examined the circumstances of the evening of February 29, 2000, when Patricia Brennan had brought David to Saint Brigid's psychiatric hospital in Ardee, in the hope that he would be admitted. The expert panel was told that Dr Das, the senior house officer at Saint Brigid's, had offered David Brennan voluntary admission but that David refused it. Dr Das told the reporting team that it was his understanding that the family were aware of his offer. The report made no criticism of Dr Das or of the hospital procedure at Saint Brigid's psychiatric hospital.

The expert report cast a fascinating light into the life of a troubled young man and the shortcomings in the treatment of his mental illness. As Catherine Cleary, the *Sunday Tribune's* then Security Correspondent put it: "the murder of a child and all the emotion that surrounds his horrific death means that Brennan's treatment had to be examined. Had the young man hanged himself or thrown himself off the side of the quarry, as so many untreated disturbed young men have done, there would have been no expert group, no panel, no oral briefings in hotel rooms from experts to compile a corporate review of systems and procedures."

Furthermore, after the report was published, it emerged that the Brennan family had not been offered any counselling to cope with the death of baby Jack. No one in the mental health services contacted them between the time of the fatal incident and the report's conclusion two years later, in September 2002.

David Brennan remains in the care of the Central Mental Hospital.

* * * * *

The death of baby Jack Everitt Brennan is not unique among the profile of child-homicides in Ireland since 2000. Many perpetrators are naturally loving and ordinarily decent people who at some time fall victim to psychiatric illness that tragically obscures their judgement and reasoning.

Nine-year-old Jennifer Palmer and her six-year-old sister Louisa wanted to go to Leisureland swimming pool in Salthill, which was a short drive away from their Galway City home. The girls had been promised an excursion but their father Roy, a scientist and fish pathologist at the National University of Ireland Galway, had a head cold. Roy's wife Catherine said that she'd take them instead.

Roy Palmer felt uneasy about his wife taking the girls to the pool. Catherine had been under considerable mental duress, as a result of frequent and severely irrational delusions about her own physical health. She and Roy were trying hard to cope with the problems that her psychiatric illness presented and Roy tried in every way manageable to support his wife. Accepting her assurances that she could cope, he saw Catherine off with the couple's two daughters in the car. It was a bright March morning as the trio set off at 11.30 am. Roy Palmer would not see his beloved wife, or his little girls, alive again.

Later that afternoon Roy Palmer went over to visit a property he owned in Maunsell Road in the City. From there he rang the couple's home on Lower Canal Road a number of times. There was no reply. He became concerned that there was nobody at home. He drove around to the homes of a number of people whom he hoped would have some idea where Catherine and the girls had gone. He thought they might have called into someone's home for refreshments. Along the way he drove to his wife's parents' house and also to the home of a friend of Catherine's, but none of them had seen the trio. At around 4 pm he finally made it back to the couple's home. There was no sign of where his wife or the girls had gone since they had left that morning.

Roy Palmer was at home for about an hour when the phone rang. On the line was his sister-in-law Patricia, who was living in Dublin. Patricia had heard on the radio that a woman and two young girls had been involved in some sort of accident at Kinvara. Roy Palmer would later say, "I knew then it was them, but I prayed that it wasn't."

At Tarera pier, between Ballinderreen and Clarenbridge, on a spot overlooking Galway Bay, commercial diver Eugene Houlihan was alerted that someone had gone into the water in a car. He grabbed some diving gear and rushed to the scene. The car had plunged into nine feet of murky water and was on its roof. He dived into the dark. Houlihan peered into the upside-down vehicle but could see nobody in the front. He returned to the surface to get some rope.

He dived again and managed to bring two bodies to the surface. The front door of the car was not locked but both back doors were firmly closed and could not be opened. Houlihan struggled to get his hands on the bodies inside. He slowly carried out the limp frames of Catherine Palmer and her nine-year-old daughter, Jennifer. The two bodies rose slowly from the depths and it was already too late for the woman and her daughter. The body of the youngest victim, six-year-old Louisa, would later be taken from the back of the car after the vehicle had been hauled to the surface. She remained secured by a seat belt in a child's booster seat. It could not be established whether the two girls had been awake or asleep at the time that their mother drove the car off the pier edge and into the water. The diver's bravery in attempting to save the woman and the two girls would later be singled out for special praise at the inquest into the three deaths.

Shortly afterwards, Gardaí delivered the news to Roy Palmer that his wife and two girls had drowned. It was March 6, 2000, a date which would be forever etched in his mind.

Three months later, on June 15, 2000, the Galway West coroner, Dr Ciaran McLoughlin, convened an inquest into the deaths of thirty-six-year-old Catherine Palmer and her two young daughters.

The inquest would reveal some of the details of Catherine Palmer's tragically disturbed mind at the time she drove her two daughters into the water at Kinvara. Local Garda Michael Harte was at the scene when Catherine Palmer's body was taken from the water. The personal effects that Garda Harte found on the woman's clothing were illustrative of her anguish.

He recovered a small piece of red notepaper from the 36-year-old woman's trouser pocket. On it Catherine Palmer had written: "this is hell" a total of nine times. Also scribbled on the other side of the sheet was written: "a disgusting waste of two beautiful girls, two human beings", and the words "waste" and "destroy".

Roy Palmer had lost his wife and two little girls in an instant but the problems that the family had endured had stretched back to a year before the tragic events at the Galway pier. Catherine Palmer's mental disturbance had been of great concern to her husband and family. But it would be four years before the full facts surrounding her fragile mental state would emerge publicly. In the end, it took a High Court action for Roy Palmer to inform the public of his wife's illness.

Roy Palmer issued legal proceedings against the Western Health Board and against Professor Thomas Fahy, the former Head of the psychiatric unit at University College Hospital in Galway. Counsel for Roy Palmer, James Nugent SC, told the High Court in January 2004 that five years previously Catherine Palmer had developed a fixation in her mind that she was deeply unwell. She had insisted that she was going to die. Medical tests could find no sign that she was physically sick, but Catherine remained convinced that she was terminally ill. Moreover, she was certain that the death she would endure would be horribly painful and that she had infected her two daughters with some sort of mysterious illness.

The High Court was told that Catherine Palmer had been admitted to the psychiatric unit at University College Hospital, under Professor Fahy's care. But to the annoyance of her husband, she was released from the hospital after just one week. The court action was settled for €110,000 after Professor Fahy withdrew his denial of liability. The case against the hospital and the Health Board were struck out. Approving the settlement plus costs, Judge Richard Johnson described the case as heart-rending.

In a statement issued on behalf of the families of Roy and Catherine Palmer, they said they had struggled to make people aware of what had led to the deaths. They had endured the fact that the tragic loss of Catherine, Jennifer and Louisa was clouded in half-truths that were not properly or publicly made known for a long time after the tragedy. It was totally unacceptable, the families insisted, that there had been no mandatory full inquiry into such deaths. "We believe that a public understanding of their circumstances would aid other individuals and families in the future," the statement said. "This case was taken for the memory of Catherine, Jennifer and Louisa." The statement added that all damages awarded in the case were to be donated to charities for mental health, women's health and children's care.

The deaths of the two Palmer girls were sadly similar to

a significant number of other child killings that have taken place in Ireland since 2000. Many of the deaths were inflicted by a close family relative of the victim, often suffering from a mental disorder, who did not get the help they needed in time.

Thirty-year-old Jacqueline Costello came remarkably close to getting some treatment for her deteriorating psychiatric condition. The mother-of-three lived with her young sons at a rented home at Mullinavat in Kilkenny. Jacqueline had lived in her hometown of Waterford with her long-term partner Stephen O'Keeffe for several years. But the couple had gone through a difficult period in their relationship and Jacqueline moved with her three small children to the Kilkenny town in late September 2000.

Jacqueline brought her eldest boy Robert, aged eight, to live with her in Mullinavat, as well as her three-year-old son Martin and her 22-month-old baby Stephen. Although struggling to cope with difficulties in their relationship, Jacqueline and Stephen O'Keeffe remained close. He visited her at the rented house three weeks after she had departed from their previous home together. But when Stephen O'Keeffe called to the house in Kilkenny he was shocked at what he found.

He would later recount that he became "very concerned" about Jacqueline and the circumstances that his former girlfriend and her three small children were living in. O'Keeffe immediately contacted Costello's GP and a social worker.

But over the following days O'Keeffe noticed that Costello's mental state was deteriorating rapidly. She was becoming more erratic and odd in her behaviour. Stephen believed that Jacqueline was heading for a mental breakdown.

On the morning of October 28, 2000 Stephen convinced
Jacqueline to accompany him to Waterford Regional
Hospital. But when they got to the hospital, she became
"quite upset".

"She was seen by a doctor and a nurse but she panicked
and refused to go in and ran off," Stephen O'Keeffe later
recounted. Stephen pleaded with Jacqueline to return to the
hospital but she refused. He was deeply concerned for her
welfare. He later admitted that he was absolutely "worn out"
trying to reason with his distressed former girlfriend. He felt
he had no option but to bring her back to the house where
she lived with her three sons.

Stephen O'Keeffe was not the only one who noticed
that Jacqueline's behaviour was becoming deeply erratic
and volatile in the days and weeks leading up to the end of
October 2000.

John and Maria Ramshaw were Jehovah's Witnesses
who had befriended the young woman. They had remained
in touch with her since she moved to her new home. On
October 21 the elderly couple visited her and the children in
Mullinavat. What she told them disturbed them considerably.
Jacqueline insisted that she had been hearing voices. She
believed that God was talking directly to her.

A week later, on the evening of October 28, the couple
returned to visit Jacqueline and made a grim discovery.
When Maria Ramshaw and her husband called they found
Jacqueline in the garden of the property. She was shouting and
crying loudly. When she became aware of the elderly couple's
presence, she calmed slightly. She turned to them and said:
"Come in then, you might as well see the evidence."

Maria Ramshaw spotted a dark form lying on the floor
of the living room. She later recounted that Jacqueline was
relatively calm at this stage. She was sufficiently within her

wits to warn the Ramshaws not to let her three-year-old son Martin see the scene that lay before their eyes. Jacqueline then left the house and attempted to lock herself into the garage.

Maria Ramshaw peered further into the living room. What she saw shocked her. A little boy lay motionless on his back on the floor. It was Jacqueline's eldest son Robert. Sitting on his chest was a tiny kitten. "It made me feel terrible. He was lying very still, his legs spread out and his arms up… with bubbles of froth coming from his mouth," the woman later recounted.

Maria Ramshaw tried to resuscitate the child but to no avail. She could find no trace of a pulse on his body. Scattered around the room were a large quantity of tablets and bottles of 7-Up. Before running from the house, Jacqueline had told the couple not to drink from the bottles of the fizzy drink, as she believed them to be poisonous.

Jacqueline continued to act erratically. She dashed in and out of the house, threatening to kill herself. John Ramshaw quickly found the phone and summoned an ambulance and the Gardaí.

Gardaí arrived immediately and found Jacqueline Costello still in a distressed state. The disturbed young woman would later tell Gardaí that she had wanted her eight-year-old son Robert to take some tablets to calm him down. "I just wanted him to take the sleeping tablets. He said 'no fucking way', so I caught him by the throat and killed him," she told Gardaí.

The statement that Jaqueline gave to Gardaí was illustrative of her mental trauma. In that statement she said how she had been cleaning the house on the morning of October 28 and her children were laughing at her. "They were running around me. I had no rest at all. I just wanted to clean up and be normal," she said. The young mother recounted that she said to Robert: "You know what has to be done, take some sleeping tablets. He said: 'I don't want them, I want to live, I want to live'." She again told her son to take the tablets, telling the boy: "you'll be doing us all a favour."

"I don't know what happened. I don't know where I got the strength. I put my hand around his throat; I just made sure he died. I couldn't look. I felt so sick. I just couldn't believe what happened to me," Jacqueline told Gardaí.

Jacqueline Costello was tried in the Central Criminal Court in April 2002 for the murder of her eldest boy. State Pathologist Professor Marie Cassidy gave evidence that Robert had died primarily from asphyxiation, partial suffocation and compression of the neck as well as inhalation of gastric contents. Jacqueline had no recollection whatsoever of placing her hand over her child's mouth.

Such was the state of mind of Jacqueline Costello when she took her son's life, that her actions bore no relationship to the character her family and friends had known. Stephen O'Keeffe told the jury at her trial that as a mother to the three boys Jacqueline was "second to none". He said that it was his belief that when she committed the murder of little Robert "she wasn't there," as he described it. Put simply, he did not believe that the normal Jacqueline, whom he knew and loved, was the same person mentally as she became in the final days and weeks prior to the tragedy.

Her brother Patrick said it was the last thing imaginable that his sister would ever harm any of her sons if she were in a rational state of mind. Patrick was contacted at his family home in the early hours of the day following the killing of his nephew. He was told that he would have to accompany a Garda to a medical unit to identify a deceased person, but he was not informed immediately of the victim's identity. His first reaction was to presume that his sister had done something to harm herself.

In the hours leading up to the tragedy Patrick had received

phone calls from Jacqueline who was clearly in a distressed state. He had spoken to Robert just hours before he was killed. While he was on the phone to his sister, Jacqueline had handed the boy the phone. Patrick realised that his sister was speaking in a very distressed tone. Her son Robert also realised that his mother was acting strangely. Patrick Costello assured his nephew that he should not worry. He said everything would be fine and that he'd be down to visit him and his mother that night.

Patrick Costello did not get a chance to speak to his nephew again. The next contact he had was from the Gardaí, informing him that a terrible tragedy had occurred at the Mullinavat home.

The roots of the trauma that the Costello family were enduring, in actuality, extended back for many years. Jaqueline's volatile psychiatric state, and the difficulties that such a condition brought, had been a considerable strain on her family. There was a clear pattern of psychiatric instability in Jacqueline's history and much of the burden had fallen on the shoulders of her parents, Thomas and Irene. Their daughter had tried to take her own life once in 1995 when she took an overdose of pills. On another occasion, she tried to cut herself.

Her erratic condition became an unmanageable problem for the elderly couple but there would be one further bitter twist in the story for them. In early September 2000, a visibly disturbed Jacqueline called to their home in Waterford. After years of problems dealing with their daughter's behaviour, they were, in the words of her father Thomas: "wrecked from it all. We couldn't go through it again." He turned his daughter away from the house. It was a decision that he said he regretted dearly, although he could not have known what calamitous and horrifying event would occur just seven weeks later. He described it as his "biggest mistake".

The Costello family could not have been expected to see that their daughter posed a danger to her children. They had simply endured years of suffering and had reached a threshold which they could not pass. But the fatal incident of October 28 was by no means inevitable. R149,933

It emerged in court that Costello had been briefly treated with medication for schizophrenia after a suicide attempt and had responded well. However, this treatment was discontinued. Dr Helen O'Neill, Consultant Psychiatrist at the Central Mental Hospital in Dundrum, told the court that at the time of the murder, Costello believed that Robert was the "evil incarnation of her deceased brother".

Dr Brian McCaffrey, an independent consultant psychiatrist, gave evidence that since the mid-1990s, she had been treated primarily for depression and not for schizophrenia. When counsel for the defence asked Dr McCaffrey whether he believed that Costello should have been diagnosed as a schizophrenic he replied: "I just don't know.

The jury took just 20 minutes of deliberation to find Jacqueline guilty but insane in relation to the murder of her child.

The presiding judge, Mr Justice Butler, did not spare strong words in his comments at the conclusion of Jacqueline Costello's trial. "Poor Robert was the prime victim, but the accused [Jacqueline] too is a very real victim," the Judge said. Justice Butler added that there had been a number of "missed chances" that could have saved the life of Robert Costello. Butler said Robert was a bright boy who had clearly realised the suffering that his mother was going through. She was sent to the Central Mental Hospital following her conviction.

* * * * *

The true number of cases in which psychiatric illness played a factor in the violent deaths of children since the beginning of the decade cannot be fully known. This is primarily due to one simple fact: in several cases the perpetrator also took their own life at the same time, or shortly after, taking the life of their young victim.

For Barry Grace, the most difficult part of his grief over the death of his two daughters, Abby and Mikahla, is the fact that they were drowned by his beloved former wife. Sharon Grace brought her two daughters into the water at Kaats Strand on the edge of Wexford town, on the second weekend in April 2005. The distressed mother extinguished her own life and that of her two girls in the shallow waters at the edge of the strand. Their bodies were later discovered by local fishermen.

For Sharon's estranged husband, the unanswered questions remain the toughest part of coping with the trauma of losing his two girls. But he is certain of one thing: though the deaths will remain classified as a double homicide, his deceased wife should not be seen as a killer. Sharon Grace is a victim on an equal level, Barry Grace insists.

He is adamant that ascribing reasons to such an unreasonable act is the ultimate insult to the memory of his late wife: "There isn't any rational explanation for it. If Sharon was thinking and acting normally that day, then she would never have done what she did."

Barry Grace was away for a weekend with his friends on a card-playing trip to Cork when he got a phone call from a relative to say that there was something wrong with Sharon. He immediately travelled home to Wexford. But awaiting him was news of the tragedy that had unfolded in his absence.

Sharon and Barry had become estranged in the months prior to the deaths. Barry said that the couple's estrangement was inflamed because of failures in the family law system:

"There was no way of settling things out with simple mediation. It wasn't possible for Sharon and I to sort out arrangements for the girls' future together, like we should have been able to do. I think it drove us both to despair. The system works in a way that throws both parents into battle with each other. I wanted access to visit Abby and Mikahla but when I sought that access, then Sharon got frightened maybe, because she didn't allow me to see them like I had been doing after we split."

But Grace does not believe that this combat was in any way a factor in Sharon's fateful actions in mid-April 2005: "I will keep saying this forever. Sharon was a loving and kind mother who cherished the two girls above all else. There is no way that anything like a row between us would have driven her to harm the girls. There's just no way she would have done something like that if she was thinking normally."

Barry Grace says that he cherishes his memories of the two little girls, who had distinct characters: "I will always treasure my memories of Mikahla and Abby. Mikahla was very sensitive, like her mum. Little Abby was full of fun and energy. On Saint Patrick's Day, I had helped them for the full day and I brought them to see the parade in Wexford town. A week before, they had helped me assemble a play swing at the rear of Sharon's home. Mikahla would run away when I'd be hammering loudly and little Abby was standing there handing me my tools and laughing."

But in the weeks before Sharon Grace took her own life and the life of her two girls, her attitude towards her estranged husband altered dramatically. Barry said: "In the last six weeks everything just changed and I wasn't allowed to see the children. I don't know why. I went from seeing my girls three times a week for a few hours each time to not being able to call them on the phone. I'll never know why that happened."

Some media coverage of the deaths hurt Barry Grace immeasurably. One newspaper included Sharon in a list of notorious female killers, coupling her with Myra Hindley and other women who were famed for their involvement in violent murder.

And the triple deaths of Sharon Grace and her two young daughters almost claimed a fourth life. Barry Grace confesses that he considered taking his own life. Despite strong support from his family and especially his brother Vincent, he looked for solace in the bottom of a bottle: "I drank a lot. Bottles and bottles of vodka. I hit rock bottom. I had lost everything and I had no answers to explain where it all went wrong or why this had happened."

The true motive for why Sharon Grace took her young daughters' lives, as well as her own, will never be fully known. But there are some clear patterns in the homicides of children in Ireland since 2000. Twenty-six young people under the age of 16 have been the victim of homicide in that period. That number represents just over seven per cent of all the violent deaths that occurred in the State over the six years. One recurring fact remains consistent in the profile of child-homicides: more young victims are violently killed by one of their parents than at the hands of any other type of perpetrator. Sixteen of the 26 victims were killed by either their mother or by their father.

Insofar as the data can be regarded as sufficient to extract patterns, there is a suggestion that mothers and fathers take their child's life in distinctly different ways. Ten of the 16 killings carried out by a parent were perpetrated by fathers. Six of the killings were carried out by the children's mother. In nearly all of the cases in which a mother took the life of her child, it was by a means that could be described as primarily non-violent. In five out of the six deaths at a mother's hand, the victim or victims were drowned. In one other case, that of young Robert Costello, the child was choked to death. But analysis shows that fathers who kill do so with considerably more force and bloodshed. While three of the ten children killed by their father were drowned, the remaining seven deaths were considerably more brutal and bloody.

Six-year-old Deirdre O'Sullivan was shot in the face by her father. Christopher Crowley had taken the girl from the care of her mother, his estranged partner, and hid out in Tipperary. Fearing Gardaí were closing in on him in August 2001, he brutally shot Deirdre at close range. The little girl was the only child to have been shot to death over the six years.

A further four children were stabbed to death by their fathers. Amongst the most disturbing of these was the murder of nine-year-old Trevor Fox and his six-year-old brother Cillian. They were killed by the boys' father, Gregory, at the family's home in Castledaly in Co. Westmeath. The then-36-year-old had earlier attacked his wife Debbie with a broken beer bottle, a knife and a hurley stick at the couple's home because he thought she was having an affair. The couple had been having difficulty in their marriage of eleven years.

Fox then entered his eldest son's bedroom and stabbed the child 31 times before moving to the room in which the youngest boy slept. He stabbed Cillian 16 times with the same weapon. Fox told Gardaí after his arrest in July 2001 that he had taken the life of the two children because he didn't want them to wake up and find their mother dead. Fox, who is originally from Dublin, received three life terms after being convicted at the Central Criminal Court, in 2003.

In June 2001, David Hickey was sentenced to life for a similar crime, the murder of his three-and-a-half-month-old baby daughter, the details of which were among the most shocking to be told to any jury at the Central Criminal Court.

Twenty-seven-year-old Hickey shared a flat with his girlfriend, Sinead Smullen, and their baby girl in Newbridge town in County Kildare. It was outside this home, on Edward Street near the town's Grand Hotel, that passers-by spotted a wounded and bleeding woman in the early hours of Sunday April 30, 2000. Sinead Smullen had been stabbed in the neck and the back. She evaded death only by the good fortune that the knife had narrowly missed her lungs and arteries.

There had been a "domestic dispute" between the couple and Hickey had become ferociously violent. He took a knife into his hands and lashed at his girlfriend. She ran from the flat, desperate to avoid the blows.

Gardaí arrived at the scene and went immediately to the couple's flat with the intention of taking Hickey into custody for questioning in relation to the serious assault on Sinead Smullen. The officers on duty did not expect to findwhat awaited them inside the small flat. Baby Leilah's body was blood-soaked. Hickey had turned the knife on the infant, stabbing her to death as she lay in her small cot. A doctor pronounced the infant dead at 4 am.

The remaining cases where a child was killed by their father were similarly violent, with beatings administered by hand or, in one case, involving the use of a lump hammer.

But while parents can be identified as the most frequent perpetrators in the violent deaths of children in the six years from 2000 onwards, ten of the 26 young victims met their deaths at the hand of someone other than a parent.

Three young children died in acts of arson in which they were almost certainly not the intended victim. Adam Lieghio was just a month short of his second birthday when he died of smoke inhalation at a fire at the home in which his family lived in Darndale in July 2000. Seventeen months later, 36-year-old Gregory Redmond, from Fairfield in Coolock, admitted at his trial in relation to the child's death, that he had thrown a petrol bomb into the family's home to "get back" at Steffano Lieghio, a member of the dead child's family. Redmond and other witnesses told the court that 19-year-old Lieghio had assaulted the accused the evening before the fire attack. Redmond spent the remainder of the night drinking before going home and assembling a crude but effective petrol bomb, using a petrol container and a child's sock. After he had consumed several pints of lager, two vodkas and had smoked a joint of cannabis as well as having taken "a few lines of cocaine", he would later set a flame to the end of the sock before throwing the device through the kitchen window of the Lieghio home. The intended target of the petrol bomb was not even in the house when Redmond struck.

Redmond pleaded not guilty to the charge of murder. His defence counsel, on behalf of the accused, told the Central Criminal Court that the father-of-six admitted that he had committed the act of arson that led to the toddler's death but he said that he did not want to be branded a murderer for the rest of his life. However, Redmond was fortunate he was not facing multiple homicide charges. Five people, including the child's grandmother, a teenage boy, and two children aged ten and three, had managed to escape the flame-engulfed house.

On January 26, 2002, Redmond was sentenced to ten years with the final three years suspended, after being found not guilty of the child's murder but guilty of manslaughter.

Four-year-old Limerick girl Katelyn Ryan was also killed in a maliciously started fire at her home in April 2003. The homicide bore remarkable similarities to the killing of Adam Lieghio three years earlier. Again, it was a dispute completely unconnected to the young victim which escalated and which was to prove fatal to this most innocent of victims.

The little girl had been unable to escape the flames that engulfed the house on the night of April 8. The girl's mother

Jackie had managed to jump to safety from a bedroom window with her 16-month-old baby in her arms, narrowly avoiding being subsumed in flames and choking smoke. It proved impossible to get back into the house for firefighters and locals. Katelyn was found lying unconscious on the ground of her parents' bedroom, between the bed and a wardrobe. She had suffered extensive burns and was rushed to Limerick Hospital before being transferred to Crumlin.

Katelyn lost her battle for life at Crumlin's children's hospital two days after the firebomb attack at her family's home.

Investigating Gardaí were quickly alerted to the involvement of 23-year-old local man Patrick Slattery in the arson attack and arrested him. Officers found traces of partially evaporated petrol on his clothing, although Slattery initially denied having any involvement in the incident. But he later admitted his role in full. In a statement to Gardaí, Slattery claimed that the Ryan's 14-year-old son had been terrorising both of his younger brothers and also his mother. He claimed that windows in his mother's house had been smashed repeatedly. He insisted that he had been personally assaulted in his own home by associates of the 14-year-old youth. Darragh Ryan had been "at everyone in the area" Slattery said in his statement, which was later read out in court during Slattery's trial for the little girl's murder. The accused man said he had reached a point where he could tolerate it no more and decided to take matters into his own hands. Slattery acknowledged that he, and he alone, was responsible for little Katelyn's death.

Slattery told the court that on the night that he launched the fire attack on the Ryan house, he had been drinking with friends. He had been talking about how he felt about Darragh Ryan allegedly making life hard for him and his family. "It all just built up," he said. Slattery returned to his home at

Ballincurra Weston in the City and filled a container with petrol, which he had stored for burning rubbish, before going over to the Ryan's home. There, he poured the petrol in the letterbox and lit it with his cigarette lighter. He walked away from the Ryan's house and didn't stop to look back.

Slattery said that if he could turn the clock back and bring the girl back to life he would do all that he could to make it happen. He insisted that he was deeply remorseful over the loss of an innocent child's life.

On February 5, 2004, Patrick Slattery was jailed for the child's murder, for which he received a life sentence.

While the courts have provided some solace, however scant, for the families of Adam Lieghio and Katelyn Ryan, there has been no such closure for Elizabeth Hughes, the mother of 12-year-old Stephen Connor-Hughes. The boy was burned to death when the makeshift camp that he and a playmate had constructed was the brunt of an arson attack.

Stephen had built a play area along with some young friends close to his home at Rossfield Park in Tallaght. The fifth-class student at Saint Thomas's National School in Jobstown was camping overnight in this small hut, when flames engulfed it. He died from smoke inhalation. Stills taken from CCTV footage near the scene showed a man close to the point where the fire erupted.

Speaking to the media over three years after her son's death in 2001, Elizabeth Hughes described the Garda investigation into the killing as a shambles. Despite strong evidence, including new information that the family had uncovered after hiring a private detective, there had been no arrests made a full three years after the boy's death.

At the time Elizabeth Hughes spoke to the media, she insisted that there was an urgent need for a senior officer, from a division outside the area in which the homicide occurred, to conduct a review of the case. The dead boy's mother was supported at a senior political level: the leader of the Labour party, Pat Rabbitte TD, raised the issue of the Garda investigation in the Dáil with the Minster for Justice, Michael McDowell. Rabbitte said that, based on his understanding of the case, the entire details of which could not be made public, the case represented an "extraordinary circumstance" where there were serious questions to be answered about the conduct of the force.

Elizabeth Hughes's pressure worked. The following November, the investigation into Stephen's death was effectively reopened, though Gardaí had said it was never formally closed. The case file was moved to the remit of the force's cold case unit. Over 300 people were re-interviewed. A man in his 40s was arrested in April 2006 and a file was sent to the office of the Director of Public Prosecutions (DPP) in relation to Stephen's death.

Of all the 26 children whose lives have been ended violently in the six years since the start of 2000, the story of one boy's death has remained the most talked about, the most contentious and the most divisive of all. The death of Cork schoolboy Robert Holohan has been ingrained in the memory of anyone who takes even a cursory interest in events in Irish society. At 2.30 pm, on January 4, 2005, Robert cycled out of the driveway of his family's home at Ballyedmond, Middleton. It was the last time that the boy's mother, Majella Holohan, would see her son alive.

An hour later, the boy called to the home of his friend, 20-year-old local Wayne O'Donoghue. O'Donoghue was considered by many who knew him in the community as a model young man. He was a good son and brother, he was studying to be an engineer at Cork Institute of Technology, and had a long-term girlfriend. He would later claim in court that, after refusing to bring Robert for a drive, the boy threw stones at his car, whereupon O'Donoghue told the court that he became angry and grabbed the child. He squeezed Robert in a strangle-hold. He insisted that the incident occurred in a moment of rage, not knowing the force would be sufficient to take the child's life.

Sometime between an hour and an hour-and-a-half later, O'Donoghue drove to Ballintra East in the proximity of Inch and dumped the child's body in thick undergrowth. He later tried to retrieve it but failed.

Later in the evening, the Holohans became worried that Robert had not returned home. A search was mounted for the missing boy. But while the Holohan family were hoping against hope that their child was not hurt, Wayne O'Donoghue was busy reassuring Majella that Robert would soon be located.

Over the following three days, O'Donoghue pretended to assist in the search for the missing child. Not once did he supply even an anonymous tip-off to the Gardaí or to the family of the missing child to end their search.

On January 12, Robert's body was located in the thick undergrowth where O'Donoghue had discarded him. A day later a post-mortem revealed that the child had died from asphyxia caused by compression of the neck. Four days later, after first telling his father Ray what had happened on the day that Robert called to the house, Wayne O'Donoghue made a seven-hour statement to Gardaí before being arrested and charged with the murder of Robert Holohan.

O'Donoghue's murder trial was set for mid-December 2005. Behind the scenes, events in the Garda investigation were unfolding apace. Information leaked to several journalists in the weeks leading up to the trial indicated that a shocking discovery had been made in the process of the forensic examination of the dead child's body. But to the surprise of most journalists, the leaked evidence that the prosecution's lawyers were expected to deliver in court did not materialise.

On December 14, Wayne O'Donoghue was acquitted of the murder of Robert Holohan but was found guilty of manslaughter. His parents, Teresa and Ray, wept openly in the back of the public gallery at Courtroom 2 in the Central Criminal Court in Cork. Robert Holohan's parents showed no reaction as they exited the court. Mr Justice Paul Carney remanded O'Donoghue to custody pending sentencing three weeks after Christmas. Nobody expected the explosive events which followed.

On January 24, Majella Holohan delivered her victim impact statement, in which she was given an opportunity to address the court about the impact of her son's killing, at the discretion of the Judge. The contents had been agreed with the defence lawyers for Wayne O'Donoghue. In it she would speak of her anguish at the killing of her precious son and the pain and suffering that the loss had brought to her family, which could never be diminished.

But Majella Holohan then diverged from her script. She asked just a handful of questions. The most provocative of these stunned the courtroom into silence. "Our doctors have told us to get on with our lives. But how can we, knowing that there was semen found on my son's body?" the visibly shaken mother asked.

Majella Holohan was correct. Semen had indeed been detected on her son's body. But it later emerged that the discovery had presented a tangled and complex problem for the Director of Public Prosecutions.

Chief State Pathologist, Professor Marie Cassidy, had taken the semen sample from Robert's hand. Gardaí immediately prioritised the shocking find. The sample was sent to Britain for a full analysis. In the UK, a specialist team under the lead of Dr Jonathan Whittaker at the FSS laboratory in Yorkshire tested the sample. The scientists were using a new technique pioneered by Dr Whittaker's group called low copy numbering DNA (LCN-DNA), which permits forensic data to be extracted from minute samples of tissue.

Dr Whittaker's initial conclusion was as shocking as the find itself. His team concluded that there was a one-in-70 million chance that the semen sample had originated from anyone other than Wayne O'Donoghue. It was as a consequence of this initial report that the DPP brought a charge of murder against Wayne O'Donoghue.

But further items taken from the O'Donoghue house were sent to the lab, including a bathroom mat on which Wayne O'Donoghue told Gardaí that he had laid out the body of the boy, in an attempt to resuscitate him after choking him. After carrying out tests on the bathroom mat, Dr Whittaker's team made a revised report in which they diminished the likelihood that the semen found on the child matched Wayne O'Donoghue's at all.

The emotive and heartrending questions that Majella Holohan had made during her victim impact statement presented a great many questions for the public. A child had been killed and semen had been found on the dead boy's body. Wayne O'Donoghue was now public enemy number one. Inferences that Wayne O'Donoghue had subjected Robert Holohan to a sexually inappropriate act were made in open and, at times, heated public discourse even though such a contention had never been tested or even addressed in a court of law. But crucial information was yet to be revealed in relation to the forensic débâcle. Three months after the courtroom drama, details of one further forensic test emerged in an exclusive report by *Sunday Tribune* journalist Conor McMorrow.

A forensic scientist, Emma Lynch from the British firm

Hayward Associates, had been commissioned to examine the forensic data on behalf of the defence team. O'Donoghue's father and two brothers had submitted swabs to generate DNA profiles. Lynch had examined the profiles of all the O'Donoghue family who lived in the house and shared the bathroom from which the mat was taken. She compared the profiles with the sample taken from the child and the initial sample from the floor mat itself.

Lynch's examination revealed that there was a complete match between the sample on the mat and a sample taken from one of the O'Donoghue family. Her analysis indicated that the semen found on the boy's hand was not Wayne's. It had been transferred onto Robert's body from contact with the floor mat when Wayne laid him down on the bathroom floor in a futile effort to resuscitate the boy.

But to argue over where the semen found on Robert's hand originated undoubtedly misses the most important question of all. Should an accused person be tried in the court of public opinion on the basis of evidence that the state's prosecutors have deemed unusable – even if the victim is a defenceless child? And does the emotional delivery of that information outside of the boundaries of an agreed statement, even by a victim's heart-broken mother, render it any more reliable?

There is only one fair answer to such a question. That answer is 'No'. Nonetheless, there is little doubt that the public and press fascination with the death of Robert Holohan will continue long after Wayne O'Donoghue's release from the Midlands Prison sometime in late 2007 or early the following year.

Two

Loved, Honoured but Betrayed

The pub was bustling with late-night drinkers, but the voice of one man seemed to stand out. Eighteen-year-old Jonathan Kepple was visibly drunk. He seemed hyper and was swaying slightly. But it was not Kepple's actions that were attracting the attention of his fellow drinkers – it was his words. People standing beside Kepple and his friends tried not to overhear what he was saying but his extraordinary boasting kept attracting their attention.

He was bragging to his friends about how he had killed a man, hours earlier. He claimed he had beaten him to death following a row on the street. He was boasting, showing his knuckles to his embarrassed friends, as revellers standing nearby nervously listened in.

"Shut up, you're making a show of us," urged Thomas Higgins, a friend of Kepple's, who was conscious of the attention he was drawing onto them.

But Kepple persisted. He told them that he had met a man on the street and had begun a fight with him. He had beaten him so badly that the man had died. Small bloodstains on his clothes appeared to back up his claim.

The story was only partially true. While there had been no man and no street fight, there was a dead body. Not far from where the men stood drinking, the lifeless remains of their friend, 17-year-old Rachel Sandeman, lay covered by a bush on a patch of waste ground.

The popular girl from the Mahon area of Cork City had been brutally beaten and strangled to death by Kepple. The two friends had become embroiled in an argument and Kepple had responded with overwhelming and terrifying force. He savagely beat his female companion before strangling the life from her body.

Kepple had not even arranged to meet Rachel on the night that would prove to be her last. They had been socialising separately when they bumped into each other outside a Chinese takeaway in Cork city centre.

Rachel had been at a local disco and was on her way to the home of Alice O'Connor, an old friend who also lived in Mahon. The route to her friend's house was familiar as Rachel had lived in Mahon all her life. She attended the nearby Ursuline Convent in Blackrock and was working part-time in a local Abrakebabra restaurant, where she hoped to save up enough money to go on a summer holiday.

Rachel had left the disco with a number of friends but had become separated from them. She was alone when she bumped into Kepple in the early hours of February 5, 2000.

Although she was already late for her friends, Rachel was happy to become further delayed. She had known Jonathan only a matter of weeks, but she liked him. He was new on the scene, only having moved into the area a short while previously, and there was a mutual attraction between the pair.

Jonathan Kepple was both a native and a stranger. Although he was born in Cork, he had spent almost half his life in London. He had moved there with his family when he was 10 years old. Although back in his native city, Kepple was adjusting to life in his new surroundings. He spent a lot of time in the company of his cousins, who had lived and grown up in Cork, but he had made some friends of his own too.

Although of tender years himself, 18-year-old Kepple's return to Cork meant that he had to move away from his two children, whom he had fathered during his time in England. He had a reputation as something of a party animal, a reputation he did nothing to counter following his move to Ireland.

By the time he met Rachel on that February evening, Kepple was already highly intoxicated. Not only had he been drinking, he had also consumed two ecstasy tablets.

Rachel and Kepple continued talking on the street, but were soon interrupted. Sinead Holbrook, a friend of Rachel's, had been waiting for her in Alice O'Connor's house and had become concerned that Rachel had not yet arrived. She walked down the road and spotted Rachel talking to Kepple, whom she did not know.

Sinead Holbrook would later break down in court as she recalled her friend telling her not to worry and that she would follow her up to O'Connor's house in a few minutes. Rachel wanted to be alone with Kepple and urged her friend to go back to the house and wait for her there. Sinead agreed and walked back to the house, leaving the pair alone.

A few minutes later, Kepple offered to walk Rachel to her friend's house and the two set off on their way. However, their attraction towards one another soon got the better of them. They diverted off the road and went to a patch of waste ground near Nutley Road, where they began kissing. The couple were hidden from public view.

However, while relations between the pair had developed quickly, they were to sour with equal speed. As they were preparing to leave, Rachel began to enquire about Kepple's life in England, and specifically the two children he had left behind. She asked him why he had moved away from his children and accused him of being a bad father. Kepple would later claim that Rachel began to taunt him over his relationship with his children, alleging that at one point she slapped him.

Kepple clenched his fist and punched Rachel with full force to her face. She fell to the ground, clutching her face and screaming. Kepple leaned over her and continued his assault.

"She was going on about my kids in England," Kepple would later tell Gardaí. "I just flipped…I punched her into the face with my right fist and knocked her to the ground. I punched her four times into the nose and put my hands around her neck. She couldn't scream because of the way I was holding her throat."

Kepple had already subjected Rachel to a ferocious beating and was now strangling her to death. She attempted to scream, hoping to alert the attention of a passer-by. However, the shielded area that Rachel had sought in order to be alone with Jonathan Kepple would now ensure that nobody could help her. Kepple's hands drowned out her silent screams and ensured that nobody could hear her last sounds. He pressed down on her throat, using his thumbs to push down hard on her windpipe, until Rachel made no more noise.

There was silence in the air as Kepple checked Rachel's body to see whether she was still alive. She wasn't.

Having killed the 17-year-old girl, Kepple's first instinct was not to panic or run for help. Instead, he looked for an area where he could conceal his victim, dragging Rachel's lifeless body to some nearby bushes and pushing her further from public view.

Having concealed her body, Kepple made his way to the house of his cousin, Maurice Kepple, who lived locally. Although he had just taken a life in the most brutal of circumstances, Kepple did not act out of character. Even when pressed by his cousin about the blood on his clothes and knuckles, Kepple maintained enough composure to make up the story of how he had supposedly got into a fight with a man down the road.

As the night wore on they went to a pub and his mask of calmness began to slip. Kepple kept talking about the fight and claimed that he had killed the man. His cousin and friend were becoming increasingly embarrassed by his loud boasts and urged him to keep quiet.

Later that night, however, Kepple took his cousin to the waste ground where Rachel Sandeman's body was lying covered by bushes. Maurice Kepple was stunned. He, too, knew Rachel. He couldn't believe that he was looking at her dead body.

It was Maurice Kepple who would alert Gardaí to the crime. At 4 pm the following day, Maurice led Gardaí to the gruesome discovery.

Jonathan Kepple was arrested immediately but initially denied all knowledge of the incident. When pressed by detectives on the identity of the teenage girl found dead off Nutley Road, Kepple said that he did not know.

However, as officers continued their questioning, Kepple realised that the game was up. Suddenly, he changed his story and dramatically confessed to the brutal slaying.

"Her name is Rachel Sandeman," he said through a veil of tears. "I didn't mean to do it, I just lost it. I took two Es on top of a lot of drink … Rachel hit me. I snapped. I lost my temper."

Detective Garda Paul Lynch would later tell the court that Kepple was sobbing uncontrollably and shaking, as he confessed to killing the young girl.

While Jonathan Kepple was confessing, the community of Mahon was struggling to come to terms with the horrific killing in the early hours of February 5. Gardaí went door-to-door in the usually quiet neighbourhood, informing residents of the discovery of Rachel's body and appealing for any eye-witnesses.

Friends and neighbours left floral tributes at the scene where Rachel's life had been so cruelly snatched away. At her funeral service at Mahon's Church of the Holy Cross, former classmates formed a guard of honour, while friends tried desperately to console Rachel's mother and older sister and brother, Susan and Daniel.

Although Rachel's murder had not been witnessed by anyone other than Jonathan Kepple, eye-witnesses were not to be needed. The confession was enough to ensure a manslaughter conviction, but Gardaí wanted Kepple to go down for murder. To achieve this, prosecution lawyers would have to prove that he intended to kill his victim.

Kepple admitted killing Rachel Sandeman but denied her murder. The defence team claimed that he had snapped under provocation and did not mean to kill her. The prosecution, meanwhile, insisted that Kepple knew what he was doing when he began choking the life from Rachel.

In an attempt to explain the savagery of the events, defence lawyers argued that Kepple was still suffering from the effects of a road accident 13 years earlier. His mother, Anne Kepple, told the court that her son had not been the same since he was rendered temporarily unconscious after being knocked down as a six-year-old child. Counsel for the defence argued that this incident had led to Kepple suffering brain damage, which, they said, led to serious mood swings and loss of temper.

However, these claims were blown away by the prosecution team. A medical report written after Kepple was knocked down was produced in court. The report showed that he had suffered just two cuts to the face and no bone injuries. The car crash did not change Keppel's behaviour, they insisted, and could not be used as an excuse for the brutal murder of Rachel Sandeman.

The jury agreed with the prosecution and found Kepple guilty of Rachel's murder. Friends and family of the young woman hugged each other as the mandatory life sentence was handed down.

* * * * *

Rachel Sandeman was the first Irish female homicide victim this century. A further 57 women would meet their deaths violently over the course of the next six years – one woman being killed in Ireland every five weeks.

Although fewer women are victims of homicide in Ireland than men – 17% of homicides are women – there is a disturbing level of conformity amongst many female murder cases. Some of Ireland's most shocking cases have involved women. Two-thirds of women killed in Ireland between the years 2000 and 2005 – a total of 39 women – were killed in their own homes. This alarming figure illustrates the domestic nature of so many female killings in Ireland. While men frequently die outside pubs and late-night restaurants, the vast majority of women killed in Ireland die in the sanctuary of their homes.

Of the 58 female murders relevant to this book, 21 women were strangled to death and a further 15 died as a result of a physical attack. Like Rachel Sandeman, well over 90% of women homicide victims are killed by people they know.

All but five female homicides over the last six years have led to charges being brought. In every single case where a conviction has been brought the killer was a man. While a handful of women have been convicted of murder in Ireland over recent years, no woman has been found guilty of the murder of another female.

The tragic murder of Rachel Sandeman is just one in a growing list of women killed by somebody they were in some way romantically involved with. Boyfriends and husbands account for 21 of the 53 men convicted – 40% – for the murder of women in Ireland during the first six years of the decade. Many of these cases are marked by years of brutality towards the woman. While couples often try to mask their abusive relationships, presenting a normal front to the rest of the world, in some cases the abuse has gone so far that this is not possible.

David Hughes and Janet Chaney had this type of relationship. The couple had been together since the mid-1980s but had slipped into a life of chronic drink and drug abuse.

Hughes' assaults on his partner were both frequent and brutal. The relationship was in such a state of chaos that their two young children were living in care. Defence lawyers for Hughes would later tell the court that the couple had reached "the depths of dysfunctionality".

Hughes was born in Dundalk but like thousands of other young men had left these shores in the early 1980s to seek employment in Britain. He was only 20 years old when he left Ireland in 1982, in search of a better life.

But Hughes was a drifter. He worked on and off in the building trade but struggled to hold down jobs. Like so many Irish immigrants in Britain, alcohol abuse became a problem. His growing addiction was not helped by his relationship with Englishwoman Janet Chaney. Five years his elder, Janet also drank excessively.

While in England, Hughes had recorded a number of convictions for violent assault. Janet, too, had a number of past convictions and the couple's relationship became marked by heavy drinking and regular drug abuse. It was also a relationship punctuated by violence.

The couple lived together in England until 1999, when they decided to move back to Ireland. Inisbofin was their first port of call, although they soon moved back to Hughes' native Dundalk, where they lived in a house in Oakland Park.

On April 13, 2004, Janet Chaney visited her local Dunnes Stores in Dundalk and purchased 12 cans of Guinness, 12 cans of larger and a bottle of vodka. She returned to the house she shared with Hughes at Oaklands Park and the couple began a day of heavy drinking.

The court would later hear that Janet seemed to get drunk very quickly, which made Hughes suspect that she was either hiding drink from him or that she was taking drugs without telling him. They began to argue and it was not long before the argument had descended into the usual violence.

Hughes slapped his partner of 18 years and she fell to the floor. Lying on the ground, she began screaming and kicking. He grabbed her by the hair and pulled her to her feet. The couple continued shouting at each other, but that did not stop them drinking large quantities of alcohol well into the night.

At one point, Janet pulled out her mobile phone to call a friend. She told Hughes she would get someone to come around to the house and assault him. He grabbed the phone from her hand and started hitting her with it. Janet escaped the clutches of her violent partner and stormed upstairs. Hughes was not finished yet, however. He chased her up the stairs and once again punched her in the face. He looked around for an implement to use on his partner. He picked up a television remote control and struck her in the face with the makeshift weapon.

Janet was screaming hysterically. Her screams were

loud enough to alert the attention of their neighbours, but they were used to hearing loud arguments from the house. Neighbours would not have thought it unusual to hear Janet's voice coming through their walls.

Janet pointed to the mark on her face and screamed at her partner that she would go outside and let everyone see what he had done to her. She rushed down the stairs and towards the front door but, once again, she could not outpace Hughes.

He grabbed her forcefully and pulled her to the ground. Tearing at her arms, Hughes began to drag his screaming partner back up the stairs. But she was struggling violently and he lost control, causing his partner to fall back down to the ground floor of their home.

Before she had time to stand up, Hughes raced back down the stairs and grabbed her once again. Putting his hands underneath her arms, he dragged Janet up the stairs and threw her onto the bed.

Janet Chaney was extremely intoxicated and badly beaten. As she lay on the bed, Hughes went into a separate bedroom and closed the door behind him.

A short time later, however, just after 3 am, he was awoken by a loud bang. Hughes rose from his bed and went to the stairway, where he saw Janet lying at the bottom of the stairs. He cursed her and again dragged her upstairs, step-by-step, and put her back into bed.

At 8 am, Hughes awoke. He wanted to go to the local shop but did not trust his partner not to injure herself in his absence. The only way to ensure that she did not once again fall down the stairs was to keep her in bed, and so Hughes tied her to the bed.

Hughes went to the shop and returned half an hour later. When he re-entered the bedroom, however, he noticed that Janet had not moved since he left. He untied her and called out her name. There was no response. He gently slapped her on the cheek to wake her up, but again there was no response.

Janet's eyes were closed and she looked pale. Hughes began to panic. He realised that this was not the usual drink-induced heavy sleep. He knew that this time Janet was seriously ill. He propped her up but she vomited all over herself. Hughes was now shouting and attempted to administer the kiss of life to his dying partner. Again, however, she got physically sick.

Hughes grabbed the telephone and quickly dialled for the emergency services, screaming for an ambulance. In the minutes between the telephone call and the paramedics arriving, Hughes again attempted to wake Janet up, who was now showing no signs of life.

The ambulance sped towards the couple's house. Driving the ambulance was Brendan Matthews, a medical technician with the North-Eastern Health Board. He would later tell an inquest into the death of Janet Chaney that when he pulled up outside 58 Oakland Park, he saw a man in a highly agitated state standing outside the house.

The paramedics went upstairs and found Janet lying on a double bed. She had no pulse but she was still warm. They lifted her off the bed and commenced CPR with the aid of a defibrillator. However, while the paramedics had first suspected a heart attack, they instantly saw the bruising on Janet's face and the blood around her mouth. Janet was rushed downstairs and into the ambulance, which sped off towards Louth County Hospital, where a medical team was on standby at the A&E unit.

Doctors immediately placed her on the critical list and rushed her to Intensive Care. At the same time, such was the level of bruising to her body that doctors informed Gardaí of the situation. Gardaí arranged for the house at Oakland Park to be preserved pending an examination.

David Hughes was taken to Dundalk Garda Station, where he began giving a statement to Garda Conrad McGuinness. Hughes was told that his partner was in a critical condition in hospital. He was shaking and in a state of total shock.

Midway through giving his statement to Gardaí, Sergeant Bill Piper entered the room. Standing over the table, he looked Hughes in the eye and told him that Janet Chaney had just died.

Hughes was dumbstruck. Although he had abused his partner for years, he never dreamt that any serious harm would come to her. He was shaking and crying as he gave Gardaí a full statement, outlining the events of April 13.

Hughes told Gardaí everything that had happened that night. After he was charged, he refused bail, saying that he deserved to be in prison for what he did.

State Pathologist Professor Marie Cassidy conducted a post-mortem on Janet and concluded that she had died as a result of brain injuries sustained after a prolonged session of drinking and rowing with David Hughes.

The post-mortem showed the horrific extent of the injuries to Janet's body. Aside from injuries to her legs and arms, she also had severe markings on her face, head, neck and trunk, as well as four broken ribs. Dr Cassidy gave her opinion that the victim had been struck by a blunt object at least eight times, most likely when she was lying face down.

Despite confessing to assaulting his partner prior to her death, Hughes was not charged with manslaughter but instead faced a charge of reckless endangerment. It is likely that a more serious charge was not brought due to the fact that Janet had fallen several times of her own accord. This fact was highlighted by Judge Patrick McCartan when he noted that not all the injuries on her body were inflicted by the accused.

Representing Hughes, Derek Kenneally said that his client "expressed remorse for his actions on that fateful day and was in a genuine state of mourning at the death of his partner". Kenneally pointed out that his client had pleaded guilty to the offence, had fully co-operated with Gardaí and had voluntarily refused bail. Hughes had a history of alcohol and drug addiction, which was a major factor behind his violent outbursts, he said. The incident that claimed Janet Chaney's life had finally made Hughes realise that he must clean up his act and make something of his life, it was argued.

Judge McCartan noted that Hughes had several convictions for violence, some of which involved assaults on his partner. However, none of these convictions had led to custodial sentences. Perhaps if Hughes had been sent to jail on one of these occasions he might have changed his ways and Janet would still be alive, remarked the Judge.

The law allowed for a maximum sentence of seven years on a charge of reckless endangerment but Judge McCartan said he believed this offence to be within the lower range of that type of conduct, given the fraught nature of the relationship and the amount of alcohol consumed on the day. He sentenced Hughes to 18 months imprisonment, back-dated to the time of arrest.

The fact that alcohol consumption can be factored into sentencing goes against the wishes of Women's Aid, the country's largest women's support group. They argue that the level of drunkenness should not affect sentencing.

According to Margaret Martin, Director of the organisation, alcohol does not cause domestic violence, even if it does increase its severity. "It is important to point out that there is a common misconception about the connection between alcohol and domestic abuse," says Martin. "Although there is often a strong link between the two, we see no evidence of a causal link between alcohol and domestic violence. Our experience suggests, however, that alcohol abuse by a partner greatly increases the risk of severity and frequency in the abuse, especially of physical and sexual abuse."

A report by the National Crime Council in 2005 found that most victims of domestic abuse claimed that incidents of violence were usually triggered by very minor events or, often, by nothing at all. However, 34% of victims of domestic abuse stated that alcohol was the trigger.

Nonetheless, while alcohol may increase the frequency or the level of the assault, women's groups argue that men who resort to violence against their partners are likely to carry out assaults, with or without the presence of alcohol. It was a combination of jealousy and alcohol that drove Declan Power, for example, to the edge and secured his place on a list of infamy – that of the double-killers.

Power, a mechanic from Ardmore, Co. Waterford, telephoned Gardaí at 3.45 am on the morning of March 9, 2002. He told them that a killing had taken place at his home.

As officers were arriving at his house 15 minutes later, two teenagers making their way home from a disco stumbled upon a body. It was that of Mossie Curran, a popular local man who was well known as the owner of the nearby Decies Bar.

The horrific events of a night of jealous rage were beginning to unfold.

The body of Joan Power (40) was discovered when Gardaí forced their way into the family home, shortly after 4 am. The mother-of-three had been stabbed and beaten to death in the hallway of her home. Declan Power, her husband, was nowhere to be found.

At the same time, a short distance down the road, Gardaí

were sealing off Main Street in the village of Clashmore, where Mossie Curran's body had been discovered. The father-of-three had been shot dead at point-blank range.

It soon became apparent that these two crimes were linked. Major roadblocks were put in place on main roads throughout east Cork and west Waterford, as Gardaí attempted to track down the missing husband of Joan Power.

They did not have to look far. Declan Power was driving aimlessly and in blind panic. He telephoned Gardaí from his mobile phone and admitted the gruesome double killing.

Gardaí pleaded with Power to surrender to them. He was still drunk and Gardaí worried that he might decide to end his own life rather than face the prospect of certain incarceration.

He refused to hand himself over or to tell Gardaí where he was. Instead, he continued driving along the back roads of west Waterford, evading Garda check points. An Air Corps helicopter tore through the night sky, frantically searching for Power's car.

After several hours of tense negotiations, however, Power eventually came to his senses and agreed to hand himself over to Gardaí at an arranged meeting point. Armed Gardaí were waiting to take Power into custody.

He was transferred to Dungarvan Garda Station and was formally charged with the killings of Joan Power and Mossie Curran.

Declan Power had been drinking in Decies pub earlier in the evening, and had even shared a game of pool with Mossie Curran. However, as Gardaí later testified, Power was an extremely jealous husband and was constantly accusing his wife of having affairs.

Joan Power had worked in Decies Bar for several years but had left the job three months earlier. She had been in Dublin two days before the incident, visiting her sister.

When her husband found out that Mossie Curran had also been in Dublin on business, at the same time, he became suspicious.

Power returned home to his wife and a furious row erupted. They were alone in the house and shouting soon filled the air. Power pushed his wife, screaming accusations that she was having an affair with her former boss.

It didn't take long for the argument to descend into violence. First, Power picked up a mallet and struck his wife viciously, knocking her to the ground. Next, he picked up a kitchen knife and thrust it into her body. He withdrew the knife, as his wife placed her hands over her wound. She fell to the ground in a pool of blood.

But Power's night was not yet finished.

He got back into his car and returned to Decies Bar to confront Curran. The pair argued verbally. Power then stunned Curran by producing a legally-held shotgun from the front passenger seat of his car. Before Curran could react, Power shot him three times in the head and chest.

When formally charged with the double-killing of his wife of 20 years and her former employer, Power responded: "I want to express how awfully sorry that I feel for his wife and family."

During his trial, a picture was painted of a good man overcome with jealousy. Investigating Officer Superintendent Michael Blake described the defendant as, "suspicious, jealous and possessive of his wife".

His defence lawyer said that his client was "devastated with remorse" and had been suicidal since the killings. He said Declan Power was "a loving father and a supportive father", as evidenced by the support he had received from his three children – Maria (20), Johnny (19) and Gemma (14) – throughout the ordeal.

The defence's pleas were not enough, however, and

Power was sentenced to two terms of life imprisonment. As sentence was passed, he sat composed in court. His children, however, cried – it was another parent lost.

* * * * *

Women are more likely to be killed by their husband or current partner than by any other category of killer. However, an average of one woman every year is killed by a spurned lover – an ex who cannot handle the collapse of the relationship. In some cases, the ex-partner is so distraught at the collapse of the relationship that he decides to take his own life and opts to take his former partner with him. Excluding cases involving minors, there were five murder-suicides in Ireland in the first six years of the decade. In each case it has been the man who has killed the woman before taking his own life.

International studies have shown that situations involving a couple account for roughly half of all murder-suicides. That figure is slightly higher than the Irish statistic: of the 11 murder-suicides to happen in Ireland between 2000 and 2005, four involved couples, six involved a parent and child and one – the killing of the Byrne family in Kilkenny – was a case of familicide, where the husband killed his entire family, before taking his own life.

While Geraldine Kissane was finishing up her shift at the Shannon Knights off-licence, Mark Sims, her ex-boyfriend, was laying his funeral clothes out on his bed and writing a goodbye note to his three young children.

Twenty-three-year-old Geraldine, the eldest of a family of nine, finished her shift in the Shannon off-licence shortly before 11.30 pm on October 7, 2001 and made her way to her mother's home nearby. From there, she planned to drop into her sister's house, which was just a couple of doors down the road.

However, Mark Sims was waiting. He knew her routine; he knew where and when to find her. As Geraldine walked alone towards her sister's house, he appeared out of nowhere.

Even his presence on the dark street would have been enough to frighten Geraldine. He had been pestering her ever since their relationship had ended and his behaviour had begun to scare her. The harassment had become so bad that Geraldine had contacted the Gardaí. Local officers had taken the complaint seriously and had spoken with Sims, warning him to stay away from his former girlfriend.

But he couldn't stay away. Now, Geraldine found herself face-to-face with Sims, alone on a darkened street. She was just yards from her sister's home but Sims was blocking her way. She screamed at him to move, but he refused. The argument attracted the attention of Geraldine's sister, Kerry, who was in her house. Kerry went outside to try to help her sister but, as she was nearing, Sims grabbed Geraldine by the arm and dragged her down a laneway beside the house.

Geraldine was struggling and trying to break free of Sims' grip. Kerry quickly moved towards the laneway, shouting at Sims to let go of her sister.

Suddenly, however, he produced a single-barreled sawn-off shotgun. Geraldine screamed and she frantically tried to escape the clutches of her ex-boyfriend. Kerry, too, screamed and ran back towards the house to get her brother, Adrian.

Tragically, there wasn't enough time. Sims pointed the weapon at Geraldine and pulled the trigger. A shot rang out and Geraldine collapsed silently to the ground.

She was already dead but Sims wanted to make sure. He pointed the gun downwards at her body and fired once more. By the time Kerry and Adrian reached the top of the laneway, Geraldine was already dead.

Sims stood over the body of his former girlfriend and, while looking at her, turned the weapon on himself. A third shot rang out and his body fell beside that of his former partner.

This killing had been meticulously planned – Sims had even taken time to polish his shoes, in advance of his own funeral. He had borrowed £200 from his employer and a further £200 from his sister to enable him to purchase a gun. Gardaí later discovered that the shotgun had been stolen during a robbery in Tipperary the previous August.

"It wasn't just a spontaneous thing where there was a row, the evidence indicates that it was very organised," said Inspector Tom Kennedy. "Everything else was arranged and the only thing that wasn't organised was the gun and he had to go and arrange that."

Wayne Roche would have understood what Mark Simms was going through. Roche was found dead after a separate incident in Bishopstown, Cork on Valentine's Night, 2003. Beside him was the body of Clíona Magner, his former partner, with whom he was still in love.

Like Sims, Roche had been unable to come to terms with the ending of his relationship. He had known Clíona Magner for many years, the pair's parents boasting an old friendship, but had been dating her for just one year. They had attended separate schools in Fermoy, but had both enrolled in the Cork Institute of Technology (CIT), Clíona to study mechanical engineering, Wayne to study catering. Here, the relationship bloomed and the couple began dating just a few months after arriving in CIT.

The pair were happy together until early in 2003 when Clíona ended the relationship, telling a devastated Wayne that she just wanted to be friends. He was deeply upset but Clíona thought he would get over it. So certain was she of this that she said there was no need for one of them to move out of the flat they had been sharing in Bishopstown since beginning their second year at college.

Roche, however, could not get over Clíona, and he could not handle living in the same flat as the woman who was rejecting him. In early February, Roche took an overdose of pills in an apparent suicide attempt. He received treatment and soon recovered. By mid-February he was back at his studies, as though everything was normal.

But things were far from normal. Five days before he would shoot and kill his ex-girlfriend before turning the weapon on himself, Wayne Roche asked a friend if he would help him repair his father's old 0.22 Winchester rifle.

Just two days before the pair were found dead, Clíona and Wayne enjoyed a drink together in a local pub. Friends who saw them that night said that Wayne was not acting out of the ordinary.

On Friday, February 14, just as couples all over Ireland were celebrating St. Valentine's night, Clíona's father, Pat Magner, called into the flat his daughter was still sharing with her former boyfriend in Bishopstown. He made the most shocking of discoveries – his daughter lying dead in her bed, a bullet wound to her head. Not far away lay the body of Wayne Roche, a gun beside him.

Both families were utterly devastated. For the family of Clíona, there was the knowledge that their young daughter had been brutally slain as she lay in her bed. At their home in Straw Hill, Fermoy, Pat Magner and Deirdre O'Grady tried to comfort their two other children. But how could they explain the sudden loss of their sister to Bronagh (14) and Darragh (10)?

The family of Wayne, however, were inconsolable in the knowledge that their son had suffered from such depression that he had decided not only to end his own life, but to also take the life of somebody he loved.

At the funeral service for Clíona, her devastated mother spoke of how her daughter, a promising showjumper, had been unlike other girls of her age, by showing no interest in clothes or make-up. Even before her school Debs, Clíona had not been interested in dressing up.

"About two weeks beforehand, she didn't have a dress, so we went off into town and I picked out a black one, Clíona's favourite colour," she told a packed church. "She tried it on in the dressing-room and then came out saying: 'It fits, it's fine, I'm gone, you pay,' That's the kind of girl she was."

Pat and Margaret Roche also had to comfort their three remaining children on the death of their brother. At the Requiem Mass for Wayne, held at St Patrick's Church, Fermoy, Wayne's older brother John, together with his younger siblings Devin and Darren, sat shell-shocked throughout the service. They were clearly unable to take on board the horrific events of Valentine's Night.

Addressing the crowd of over 3,000, Fr Gerry Coleman described Wayne Roche as a "gentle giant with plenty of goodness and love within him. We will never know what lay beneath the clouds that led him [Wayne] to lose his life so tragically on Friday last," said Fr Coleman.

Both sets of parents attempted to comfort each other following the services, each trying to deal with the tragedy.

While current or former partners account for the highest number of female killers in Ireland, blood relatives have also carried out some of the most horrific female murders over recent years.

The most shocking off all these cases are those which see mothers slain by their own children. Matricide – the killing of your mother – remains rare in Ireland. Yet the three occasions over recent years in which sons have been jailed for the murder of their mothers have repulsed the nation.

Two of the three men convicted of matricide – Kevin Bridgeman and Sean Fahy – face the prospect of never again being released back into society, such was the brutal nature of their crimes. The third, Damien Donnan, is already free but faces a lifetime of medical treatment and monitoring, to contain his complex mental difficulties. All three men were found to suffer from mental conditions, and the judges in each case accepted that the defendant was not sane at the time of the killing. A fourth man has been charged in connection with the killing of his mother, but the authors are precluded from discussing the details because the case has not yet been heard.

Kevin Bridgeman had not enjoyed a regular upbringing. His mother, Marie Bridgeman, was a well-known brothel-keeper in Dublin. She owned a number of properties across the City, which she staffed with girls who would entertain men for a good price. Much of the money earned by the girls would end up in Marie Bridgeman's pockets.

Her son, Kevin, was born in the mid-1960s when Marie was 21 years old. The pair lived in Santry, north Dublin for many years, the area where Marie was herself originally from. Kevin developed chronic paranoid schizophrenia whilst in his teens, a condition that got worse as the years went by.

In 2003, at the age of 35, he was still living with his mother due to his illness. At that stage, the Bridgemans had moved to Ratoath, Co. Meath. Marie's fortunes were on the wane. In 1999, she had been convicted of running a brothel on Wexford Street. Two years later she was again found guilty of the same offence. The Criminal Assets Bureau (CAB) had launched an investigation into her finances and seized more than €160,000 on behalf of the State.

At the same time Kevin's schizophrenia was becoming

increasingly problematic. Not only was he prone to mood swings, he was also deeply paranoid. He constantly complained that he was being followed by imaginary men, and at one stage told his mother that Lloyd's of London was monitoring his every move.

He was also showing a greater propensity for self-harm. In 1999, Kevin lay down underneath a bus in the hope that it would run over his legs. He later explained that he was convinced that worms had managed to crawl inside his body and were living inside his legs. His intention was to have his legs amputated in order to get the creatures out of his body.

On the evening of January 21, 2003, Kevin Bridgeman was at home alone watching television while his mother was in Dublin. She returned on the 103 bus to Ratoath at 11.30 pm, however, and telephoned Kevin, instructing him to walk down to the bus stop in order to walk her home.

Kevin Bridgeman did as he was told but it was to be the final time he would obey his mother's command.

As the pair walked back to their home, Marie told her son to go to bed upon their return. Kevin protested, but she would not listen.

Neighbours would later tell the court that they heard a commotion outside the Bridgeman's house. A neighbour telephoned the Gardaí, but it was too late for Marie Bridgeman. Kevin had knocked his mother to the ground with a punch. Before she could get up, he kicked her. As she lay on the ground attempting to regain her breath, he stamped on her head. She screamed, and so he stamped on her head again. Kevin Bridgeman kept stamping on his mother's head until she stopped screaming. After he had finished the assault, Kevin turned his back on his dead mother and calmly walked back into his house. It was here that Gardaí would find him just minutes later.

Kevin was arrested and taken in for questioning. He

gave Gardaí a full statement, admitting the killing of his mother. "I battered her to death with my fists," he told them. "I kept hitting her with my fists…I hit her and I gouged out her eyes."

He also claimed to have stabbed his mother, although like the boast about gouging out her eyes, this was not true.

When Gardaí asked Kevin whether he had meant to kill his mother, he replied, "No". When they asked him why he had killed her, he famously responded by saying that she was, "wrecking my head".

At his trial, the defence never disputed the fact that Kevin had killed his mother. The issue before the courts was whether he was sane at the time of the attack. Three psychiatrists testified that he was insane and could not have realised what he was doing when he began stamping on his mother's head and beating her with his fists.

Kevin Bridgeman was found guilty, but insane, and sentenced to the Central Mental Hospital, where he will be held at the pleasure of the Minister for Justice.

The killing of Marie Bridgeman bore a remarkable similarity to the murder of pensioner Margaret Fahy, 16 months previously. Although her personal background was a far cry from the criminal activities of Marie Bridgeman, Margaret Fahy knew what it was like to care for a son with a severe mental illness.

Her son, Sean Fahy, suffered from an extreme case of paranoid schizophrenia. It had not always been this way, however. Sean was a normal child until the late 1970s when, at the age of 17, he suddenly retreated completely from society. He spent long periods of time indoors and refused to leave the house.

Despite his illness, Sean met and fell in love with a girl, whom he married when he was 23 years old. The young couple had five children and everything seemed to be going alright, even if Sean did lapse into periods of paranoia.

After ten years of marriage, however, Sean became convinced that his wife was having an affair. He repeatedly accused her of cheating on him and would not listen to anyone telling him otherwise. He also believed that the IRA were after him and were attempting to kill him.

Although he had been prescribed medication to help him, Sean refused to take it. He believed that people were trying to poison him and accused doctors of trying to kill him.

Sean's marriage collapsed and it was not long before he was in need of serious psychiatric help. In July 2001, he was admitted to St. Brigid's Psychiatric Hospital in Ballinasloe, Co. Galway, but one month later he was released. On August 9, 2001, Sean Fahy left the hospital and returned to his mother's home.

While living with his mother, his belief that people were trying to poison him grew stronger. He travelled into Galway City to buy cigarettes from a machine because he believed that local shopkeepers were trying to sell him cigarettes dipped in poison. He also refused to eat anything his mother cooked for him. He believed that satellites were controlling his movements and that television presenters were telling him what to do.

Sean's bouts of paranoia became even more intense after drinking alcohol. On September 10, 2001, he went to the local pub for a few pints. When he returned home, he confronted his mother about what he claimed were her attempts to poison him.

What followed was a horrific attack on the 78-year-old grandmother. Sean Fahy kicked and punched his mother, breaking her fingers and her back in the process. He then picked up her walking stick and jammed it into her neck, causing massive blood loss.

Sean Fahy failed to comprehend his own actions. Having killed his mother, he went to bed, where he slept soundly for the night. It was only in the morning that he realised what he had done. After waking, Fahy went downstairs and saw the house covered in blood, with his mother's badly beaten body lying in the kitchen.

Reaching for his medication, Fahy decided to take his own life. He emptied the contents of his pill box into his mouth, hoping that the overdose would kill him.

At 10.15 am his brother, Michael Fahy, entered the house and uncovered the grotesque scene inside. Michael called for an ambulance and paramedics managed to save Sean Fahy's life. However, there was no saving his mother. She had died following a prolonged and horrific assault.

Investigating officer Inspector Tony O'Donnell told the court that it had been the worst case he had covered in his career. "Her back was broken in the lumbar area and there was an injury to her scalp consistent with a broken walking stick being driven into the scalp at least six times," he told the jury. "There was much blood on the floor, the walls and the radiators. A terrible violence had to be inflicted to cause this."

Psychiatrist Dr Brian McCaffrey told the court of Fahy's history of mental illness, saying that there was "no doubt" but that Sean Fahy was a seriously ill man. "He was so seriously ill that nothing would have stopped him killing his mother," he told the jury. "He felt he was doing the right thing to get rid of the evil [in his mother]. His reason for killing was not one of a reasonable man. The death of his mother was directly as a result of a disease of the mind, paranoid schizophrenia."

It took the jury just 10 minutes to find Sean Fahy guilty but insane of the murder of his mother. Like Bridgeman, he will probably spend the rest of his life at the Central Mental Hospital.

Damien Donnan was the first person to be charged with matricide this decade. The Limerick man was just 18 years old when he strangled his mother to death as she lay in her bed on the morning of April 17, 2000.

Donnan's case was truly remarkable. The youth admitted the brutal slaying of his mother, yet family members queued up in court to tell of their sympathy for a young man racked with complex mental problems.

Damien was a normal, healthy boy for much of his youth. However, things began to change after his parents separated. Along with his siblings, Damien lived with his mother in the Thomondgate area of Limerick, but the domestic situation was far from ideal. Damien's mother, Jennifer Donnan, began to drink and, although living apart, the relationship between his parents worsened.

Damien became reclusive, refusing to leave the house and suffered from uncontrollable bouts of depression. He also began to suffer delusions. In 1999, he attempted to strangle his younger brother, David, believing that it was the family dog he was choking, not his brother. Damien also attempted to take his own life on numerous occasions.

On the evening of April 16, 2000, Damien was at home. His father was visiting the house and, although his father and mother seemed to be getting on, Damien seemed agitated. He was depressed and acting in a restless manner.

Damien went to bed that night but could not sleep. He lay in bed for a few hours but he was restless and needed to get up. He felt like smoking a cigarette but he had none. Instead, he opened the door of his mother's bedroom and asked her could he take one of hers.

It was 3 am and Jennifer Donnan was asleep. She resented being woken up at this hour and told her son to go back to bed. Again, he asked her could he take one of her cigarettes. Jennifer rolled over in her bed and told her son that she would get his father to have words with him unless he went back to bed.

"She kept saying she was getting my father," he told Gardaí in a statement a few hours later.

Jennifer rose from the bed and, according to Damien's statement, tried to hit her son with her handbag. Damien caught her hand and she fell back.

Something inside of Damien Donnan snapped. Years of pent-up frustration and anger were about to be released. "I got her in a sort of a headlock and pulled her to the ground," he recalled. "I caught her by the throat with my two hands. I had one knee on each side of her body, leaning down on her throat...I realised what I was doing. I kept down on her throat until she stopped moaning...I realised she was dead. To me, she was dead...I have been getting her drink since I was seven. I just had enough. I had enough."

Damien took his hands away from his mother's throat and sat, one knee each side of her lifeless body. He stood up and walked out to the hallway, breathing heavily as he contemplated his actions.

Seconds later, he returned to the bedroom. Standing over his mother's corpse, he screamed, "Look what you made me do." In a fit of rage, Donnan again took to the floor and placed his hands around his mother's throat. Again, he strangled her. He told Gardaí he did this, "because I was angry".

Next he went into the bedroom of his brother, then aged nine. Shaking his brother awake, Damien bluntly told him, "David, I'm after killing Mam."

David Donnan began crying, but his brother told him to run to their grandparents' house, which was just doors away. David ran out of the house and began furiously knocking on his grandparents' front door. He was crying and screaming. His grandparents, Patrick and Frances Daly, got up from bed and urgently followed their grandchild back to his house.

They reached the home of their daughter at 3.15 am. Frances Daly testified that when she entered the house, Damien was standing in the hallway.

"What did you do?" she asked.

"She started it, Nana," he replied.

Damien Donnan's trial began in February 2002. However, from the outset, this was a highly unusual murder trial. The parents and sister of the deceased, as well as Damien's father, all told the court of his mental difficulties. Each witness said they did not hold Damien responsible for his actions.

Antoinette Riley, his mother's sister, described her nephew as "a lovely boy, very gentle". She said that Damien had been exposed to the conflict between his parents and had been badly affected by the disintegration of their marriage.

"Damien has been a victim of circumstance for far too long," she told the jury. "He's been mistreated for most of his life...[he] was like a pressure cooker waiting to go off...The family do not hold him personally responsible. Not at all."

Damien's grandfather, Patrick Daly, also told the court that his grandson was a good boy who suffered from an illness that he could not control. "I feel very sorry for him," said Daly.

Defence lawyers for Damien Donnan pleaded with the jury to acquit the young man of murder and to instead consider a manslaughter charge. Although Damien had admitted killing his mother, the circumstances surrounding the killing had to be taken into account, they said.

The jury found Damien Donnan not guilty of the murder of Jennifer Donnan, but guilty of her manslaughter. Sentencing for the case was repeatedly delayed while an adequate system of treatment was devised for Damien.

In July 2006, Mr Justice Paul Carney sentenced Damien to life imprisonment. However, Damien had already been in custody for six years and so Justice Carney suspended the rest of the sentence. Allowing for remission, Damien had already effectively served an eight-year sentence, which was the average length of imprisonment in manslaughter cases, said the Judge. He also said that Damien did not bear any moral culpability for the killing of his mother as he was clearly mentally ill at the time.

Damien's sentence was suspended on the condition that he complied with medical treatment.

"I do not want to impose any further punishment," said Mr Justice Carney. "I do want to protect Damien Donnan from himself and also protect the community as best I can."

Damien's family welcomed the Judge's decision. They had lost their daughter and sister, but recognised that Damien was severely ill when he killed her. For them, what was important was being able to help Damien get over his illness, even if it meant caring for the man who had killed their dear Jennifer. Some families, however, must cope with losing a loved one and then face the horrifying prospect of nobody being punished for the murder.

Over 90% of female murders have been solved, and of the 58 women killed in Ireland between 2000 and 2005, only five cases have not led to charges being brought. These five, each of which were extremely high-profile cases, have frustrated Gardaí for different reasons. Despite huge Garda resources being assigned to each case, the killers of the five women – Paiche Onyemaechi, Lynette McKeown, Rachel O'Reilly, Irene White and Emer O'Loughlin – have, at the time of writing, not been brought to justice.

Detectives investigating the brutal murder of college student Emer O'Loughlin are frustrated by the fact that they believe they know who killed the attractive 20-year-old, but have been unable to track him down.

Emer was a popular young girl from Tubber in Co. Clare. She was bright and could have found success in many fields, but she was following her dream of studying art. Emer had enrolled in an art course in a secondary school PLC in Galway City and was considered to be a very promising student. She lived in a caravan on a site just outside of Kinvara, Co. Galway. It wasn't very big, but Emer was happy to live there along with her boyfriend, Shane Bowe.

On April 9, 2005, a blaze broke out in the caravan next to Emer's and emergency services were called. Initially treating the incident as an accidental fire, they would soon discover that this was no accident. Inside the remains of the caravan was the body of a young girl. Emer O'Loughlin, the student who lived just yards away, had been in the caravan when the blaze broke out.

Tragically, Emer was not even supposed to be in Kinvara on the day she was murdered. Although her body was discovered on April 9, it is believed that she was killed the day before. On Friday April 8, Emer was due to be in classes all day, but her college was closed for the day due to the Pope's funeral. Her boyfriend, meanwhile, was at work.

Gardaí believe the killer struck knowing that Emer would be alone in her caravan.

The level of fire damage inflicted on her body meant that pathology experts were unable to say exactly how Emer died. Gardaí believe, however, that the attacker dragged her from where she was staying to the neighbouring caravan. Investigating officers have been unable to rule out the possibility that Emer was subjected to a horrific sexual assault before being murdered.

After killing his victim, the attacker set fire to the caravan in order to destroy all forensic evidence. It was not until the following morning that the remains of the missing student were discovered amid the charred debris. Although a post-mortem was inconclusive, Gardaí believe she was dead before the fire started.

Three days after the body of Emer O'Loughlin was discovered, Gardaí were called out to the Dun Aengus Fort on Inis Mór. A highly agitated man was throwing rocks at visitors to the cliff-top fort. When Gardaí arrived at the scene, the man began making threats, both against them and himself. Sporting highly distinctive dreadlocks and a beard, the man was screaming hysterically, as Gardaí attempted to persuade him to step away from the ledge. He said that he would jump off the cliff if they tried to arrest him.

For nine hours, a tense stand-off ensued. However, eventually, Gardaí managed to overpower the man during a violent struggle that took place just yards from the edge of the 300-foot-high cliff.

Officers took the man back to the mainland, where his identity was ascertained. He was a local man, originally from Carraroe, and had a history of violence and drug addiction. The 30-year-old had racked up a number of previous convictions, mostly for assault.

He was promptly admitted to the psychiatric hospital in Ballinasloe, where doctors examined him for five days. After this period, however, he was released.

Suspicions grew that this man was the killer of Emer O'Loughlin. Although there was no concrete evidence linking him to the murder, Gardaí were satisfied that he was the chief suspect.

On April 18 he was spotted boarding the ferry from Rossaveel to Inis Óirr. During his time in hospital, he had shaved off his dreadlocks and beard, and was now clean shaven and sporting a tighter hairstyle. However, despite radically altering his appearance, other passengers on board the ferry were later able to positively identify the man to investigating Gardaí.

He was alone when the ferry departed the Galway coast bound for the Aran Islands. When the ferry landed at Inis

Óirr, he remained on board as it then made its way to the larger island of Inis Mór.

It was to be the last time the man was ever seen.

The following day, tourists discovered a pile of clothing lying in a bundle at Dun Aengus. Gardaí were alerted and it was confirmed that the clothes were the same as had been worn by the suspect.

The discovery of a pile of clothes beside the cliffs clearly implied that the man had jumped to his death. However, no body was ever discovered in the water below Dun Aengus. Gardaí believe that this is because there was no suicide. Officers investigating the murder of Emer O'Loughlin believe the man left his clothes in a bundle in a bid to fake his own death.

In this act, it is believed that the suspect may have been inspired by media reports about the disappearance and subsequent re-arrest of Colin Whelan. The Meath man staged his own death after he murdered his wife, Mary, in February 2001. Whelan parked his car at Dublin's Howth Head and, using a fake identity, managed to board a flight to Mallorca. He appeared to have, literally, gotten away with murder. However, 16 months later, he was captured in Spain after Irish tourists identified him. Whelan was later sentenced to life imprisonment for his wife's murder.

While Gardaí investigating the murder of Mary Whelan got lucky when tourists tipped them off after returning to Ireland, officers investigating the murder of Emer O'Loughlin remain frustrated by their inability to track down their chief suspect.

Like most female victims of homicide, Gardaí believe that Emer knew her killer. They were not related or friendly, but investigating officers believe Emer knew the man to see. There is the terrifying prospect that he had planned the murder of the attractive young woman for some time. For the family of Emer O'Loughlin, justice will not be done until their daughter's killer is behind bars.

* * * * *

Although one woman has been killed in Ireland every five weeks over the last six years, it remains almost unheard of for a woman to be murdered during a random act of violence. Just four women were killed by strangers between 2000 and 2005.

The horrific murder of Bettina Poeschel stunned the country not only because she was a young woman chosen at random by her killer, but because she was a tourist visiting Ireland for just six days, when she was so brutally raped and murdered.

She had been planning the short break for months. The 28-year-old German journalist had always wanted to come to Ireland. When an old school friend moved to Dublin that gave her the perfect excuse to book the trip.

Bettina arrived in Dublin on September 20, 2001. Three days after she arrived, she sent her sister a text message. "She said she was on the beach and that everything was okay," recalled Cornelia Poeschel. "She said she was having a good time."

The young woman, 5 feet 10 inches tall and with shoulder-length blonde hair, had been staying in Dublin but had read about the famous Newgrange burial mound and it interested her greatly.

According to her father, Jorgen, she would have felt compelled to visit a site of such importance as Newgrange. Jorgen Poeschel would later recall that his daughter's interest in history and art was so great that it had sometimes precluded her from meeting men.

"I would see her as a girl who would like to meet a boyfriend as a companion but finds it hard as she expects so much," he said after he had arrived in Dublin shortly after her disappearance. "In this I mean she is so intelligent and into things like literature, art and history and she finds it difficult to meet somebody with the same interests."

Indeed, art was more than just an interest for Bettina. She worked for the music and cultural section of *Abendzeitung*, an evening newspaper based in Munich. Bettina loved Munich but also enjoyed seeing how people in other parts of the world lived. Ireland would have been considered a very short journey for a woman with such a passion for travel.

"[She travelled to] many countries on her own, like Ecuador and Puerto Rico," said Jorgen. "There are places we would have been afraid for her as she was on her own most of the time. I would describe her as a girl with no fear."

Bettina boarded the 9.35 am Enterprise train from Connolly Station to Drogheda, arriving in the Louth town at 10.05 am. CCTV footage would later show her leaving the town on foot. She walked the 10 km to Newgrange's Brú na Boinne Visitors' Centre.

Several locals remembered seeing her along the way. "She was on her own," said Mary McCabe, who was also in the area that morning. "She was wearing a mac jacket. She had a shoulder bag and glasses. I was thinking she didn't have an umbrella with her and it was raining and I was thinking 'she'll get wet'."

Moments after McCabe spotted Poeschel, local businessman Kenneth Martin also saw the young German walking along the Donore Road. It was 11.35 am. She would not be seen again for 22 days.

While Poeschel was making her way towards Newgrange, Michael Murphy, of Rathmullen Park, Drogheda, was working on the construction of a nearby motorway. At 10 am, instead of taking his usual tea break, Murphy told three work colleagues that he had to excuse himself in order to see the doctor.

Murphy did go to the doctor, but not until the following morning. Instead, while driving along the Donore Road, he forced the young German tourist into his car. He then brutally raped and murdered her.

After he had murdered Bettina Poeschel, Murphy drove his car to a laneway and hid her body in the undergrowth. He then returned to work, but his co-workers thought that he appeared agitated. Murphy kept excusing himself for periods of time and then returning once again. "He could be away for 20 minutes, half an hour or longer," said Pat McCahey. "He was away four or five times."

It is believed that Murphy returned to the body of his victim several times throughout the course of the day and night. On the evening of September 25, student Siobhán Byrne was sitting on a wall near Mullachrone Quarry with two friends when she noticed a black Honda Civic pull up outside a laneway, about 400 metres from where the body of Bettina Poeschel was eventually found.

"A lorry drove by and its lights shone on this figure, which we presumed was a man from his build," she recalled. "We saw a man going up into the laneway, he was running up it. Then we heard this car drive off in the Donore direction. We never saw it again."

It was not until October 17, 2001 that a search party, led by Detective Inspector Brendan McArdle, made the gruesome discovery.

"I came upon the body of a dead woman," he would tell the court. "She was lying face down and was naked from the waist down apart from black panties that were around the knees. The upper body was covered in a blue jacket and initially her head was not visible as it was separated from the trunk of her body."

So gruesome were the remains of Bettina that family members were not allowed to see the body. Instead, Gardaí presented Bettina's sister, Cornelia, with glasses, a mobile phone and a bag that were all found on her body.

A devastated Cornelia wept as she told Gardaí that the items all belonged to her only sister. It was a heartbreaking goodbye between sisters who had also been best friends. The two women shared an apartment together in Munich and were very close.

Gardaí soon became aware of Michael Murphy's suspicious actions on the morning of Bettina's disappearance. They knew that he had disappeared for periods of time; they knew he had been acting in an agitated manner; they knew that he had not attended the doctor's, as he said he had. Perhaps more importantly, and for reasons that would be revealed only after his trial, they knew about his past.

At 8.10 am on October 27, Murphy was arrested and, by 7 pm that evening, he was formally charged with the murder of Bettina Poeschel. Not only had Gardaí built up convincing circumstantial evidence against Murphy, forensic evidence was also piled against him. Experts had taken a sample of DNA from Murphy's hair and had matched it to DNA found on the victim's body. When Gardaí showed Murphy a picture of Poeschel, he claimed to have never seen her before. DNA evidence, however, indicated that Murphy had engaged in sexual relations with the woman either shortly before, or following, her death.

When Gardaí asked him to explain his whereabouts on the day in question, Murphy responded by saying, "I can't talk about this, just charge me with it."

In the course of the afternoon, Samantha Johnson, the suspect's girlfriend, came to Drogheda Garda Station. The following conversation was recorded:

Samantha Johnson: "Did you do it?"
Michael Murphy: "What do you think?"
SJ: "Tell me, did you do it?"
MM: "I'm sorry, Samantha."
SJ: "Did you do it, Michael? Tell me the truth."
MM: "Don't raise your voice."

When Johnson left the station, Gardaí continued to question Murphy, during which time the suspect broke down in tears and made what amounted to a confession of guilt:

Q: "Michael, will you tell us the full truth about what happened?"
A: "I'm sorry."
Q: "Tell us what happened."
A: "Just tell that girl's parents I'm sorry for taking her life and what I did to her. I'm so, so sorry."
Q: "How did you kill her, Michael?"
A: "I don't want to say anything else about it. I'm just so sorry about it."

In February 2004, Michael Murphy stood trial for the murder of Bettina Poeschel. The Poeschel family bravely sat in court throughout the trial, as Gardaí and doctors spared no detail in describing the state of Bettina's body when she was finally discovered.

Dr Harpel Singh Glyral told the court in horrific detail how he attempted to perform a preliminary test on the remains of Bettina.

"I found her lying on her abdomen face down," he told the

jury. "Her soles, calf muscles and palms were in an advanced state of decomposition. I lifted her head, which was very, very stiff. Her body was in a state of rigor mortis [and] was detached from the neck and faced down. Her spinal cord was also detached, that's how I saw the body."

A jury of seven men and five women returned a unanimous verdict against Murphy, finding him guilty of murder. Murphy sat motionless in court and continued to slowly chew gum while Justice Aindrias O'Caoimh handed down the mandatory life sentence.

It was only after the verdict had been returned that a startling revelation was made – this was not the first time Michael Murphy had killed. Murphy had served almost nine years of a 12-year sentence for the manslaughter of 64-year-old widow Catherine Carroll. He had strangled her to death in October 1983. Murphy also had a string of other convictions, including armed robbery and a six-month sentence for the assault of two girls outside a disco in Drogheda.

Speaking outside the court, Poeschel's father, Jorgen, thanked the Gardaí and the local community for bringing Murphy to justice. "It made a closure of a bad chapter for my family," he said.

Inspector Gerry O'Brien called the killing "an opportunistic crime" and said that it was "a terrible tragedy that a young girl like Bettina Poeschel came to this country to see the historic site of Newgrange and this happened".

Remarkably, given the weight of forensic and circumstantial evidence against him, Murphy appealed the conviction. This appeal was turned down on all counts in May 2005. One of the grounds on which Murphy had appealed his conviction was that it had never been established how Bettina Poeschel had died.

However, rejecting the appeal, Mr Justice Kearns said that the uncertainty over the method of death did not distract from the undisputable fact that Michael Murphy had murdered Bettina. He said that Bettina had been in perfect health prior to her disappearance. Kearns also said that there was no doubt that she had died either immediately after, or possibly during, sex.

"She was found in a state of undress in a location to which she could not have gone voluntarily and indeed there was the clearest of evidence that she could not even have been force-marched into the position of concealment where her body was later found," he said.

Kearns said that although it would never be known how Bettina had died, there was "no doubt" that Michael Murphy had murdered her.

Michael Murphy remains behind bars.

The killing of Bettina Poeschel stood out as a particularly heinous crime as she was a random victim. If Bettina had not been walking along that stretch of road on the morning of September 25, 2001, perhaps some other unfortunate woman would have encountered Michael Murphy. It will never be known for sure how Bettina died, although it is strongly suspected that she was strangled. While shootings and stabbings account for the majority of male homicide in Ireland, a higher proportion of women are killed from violent assaults. Strangulation alone accounts for one-third of all female killings.

It is a shocking truth that over 60% of women killed in Ireland have died literally at the hands of their killer.

Three

Drink, Drugs and Machismo

The ambulance lights were all that coloured the night sky. Aside from the flickering of red and white coming from the top of the parked emergency service vehicle, all was dark on the leafy surburban street.

Damien Devine stood passively, in shock at the scene unfolding around him. Just yards from where the Dublin youth was standing, paramedics were desperately trying to save the life of a young man. Nineteen-year-old Brian Mulvaney was still breathing, but his pulse was weak. He was unconscious and attempts to resuscitate him were failing.

It was Devine who had made the gruesome discovery. He had been walking home with two friends when they saw a man lying conscious on the ground, shortly after 2.30 am on March 11, 2000. They could tell instantly that he was in serious trouble. His face was cut and bruised and his shirt had been ripped from his body.

Devine and his two friends rolled Brian Mulvaney onto his side and called the emergency services from one of their mobile phones. As they waited for the ambulance to reach Templeogue, they stood helplessly as Brian's life slipped away.

Ten minutes later, the paramedics began work on Brian. Devine and his friends stood back, allowing the ambulance workers the space they needed.

As the situation deteriorated, Brian was placed on a stretcher and his unconscious body was removed into the ambulance, which sped off in the direction of Tallaght Hospital.

Still in shock, Devine was approached by two youths. He knew both Brian Willoughby and 15-year-old Stephen Aherne, but was not friendly with either. Twenty-one-year-old Willoughby, had a terrifying reputation for violence in the area. Devine, like many youths in the neighbourhood, was frightened of him.

Devine would later tell the court that as they left the scene, Aherne made a startling revelation. He turned to Devine and admitted that he and Willoughby had been part of the gang that had attacked Brian Mulvaney.

"He said "we done that", like he was worried," Devine would later tell the court.

Willoughby was stunned that his accomplice would admit to the assault. "Brian Willoughby said that if I said anything he would kick my head in and he called [Aherne] a fucking eejit," said Devine.

The three men went their separate ways. When they woke in the morning, they would all be greeted with the news that Brian Mulvaney was dead.

On the afternoon of March 6, 2000, five days before the fatal attack, Therese Willoughby had opened the front door of her home in the south Dublin suburb of Templeogue and been greeted by a sight she had long dreaded – her son's blood. A trail of blood had led her to Brian, who had slit his own wrists in an attempt to end his life.

Therese Willoughby had managed to get her son into the car and rushed him to nearby Tallaght Hospital. Here, she had pleaded with doctors to take her son into a psychiatric unit, insisting that he had become a danger to himself and to others. Despite it taking two security guards to restrain a hysterical Brian, her request had been refused. Doctors had said that there was no room for her son in the hospital. Therese Willoughby was distraught as she was sent home in the car with a son she had feared would soon kill either himself or somebody else.

Brian Willoughby's mental difficulties had begun at the age of four when his parents and teachers noticed a pattern of unusual behaviour. Even in a classroom of small children, Brian's giddiness stuck out. He was impulsive, clumsy and lacked concentration. By the age of seven he was becoming a major disruptive figure in the classroom.

"I'm wired backwards," he kept telling his mother, repeating to her a phrase he often heard from teachers.

Brian was 16 years old before the Willoughby family had finally received a diagnosis for his condition. Dr Michael Fitzgerald, a private psychiatrist hired by the family, concluded that Brian suffered from a severe form of Attention Deficit Disorder (ADD, also commonly known as AD/HD). The family finally had a medical term to explain their son's increasingly difficult behaviour, but it was of little use to them. Despite continued psychiatric help, Brian's condition worsened as the years went by.

ADD does not necessarily cause violent behaviour. In fact, experts warn that ADD sufferers are more likely to kill themselves than others, as they struggle with low attention rates and learning difficulties. However, in a small percentage of cases, this frustration results in aggression towards others. Brian Willoughby's condition was not helped by a motorbike accident in 1998 that put him on a life support machine for a week and left him in need of constant medication.

Even as a teenager, Willoughby's propensity for violence was all too clear. The year before the motorbike accident Willoughby had repeatedly stabbed William Brereton during a random assault in College Green in Dublin. Brereton lost the use of one of his eyes as a result. Shortly after, James McConnon was left needing 100 stitches after an unprovoked knife attack by Brian Willoughby on Baggot Street. A few months later, Willoughby was one of a gang who had attacked Stephen Quinn on a city-centre bus.

It was around this time that Therese Willoughby rang the *Irish Times* claiming that her son would kill somebody unless he received the necessary psychological care. That care never arrived.

Willoughby was out on bail awaiting sentencing for the assaults on Brereton, McConnon and Quinn on March 6, when he attempted to take his own life. Before sending him home from Tallaght Hospital later that day, doctors quadrupled his medication. Therese Willoughby would later recall how her son became zombified by the additional medication.

He took the increased medication that Tuesday and Wednesday but his mother reduced the dosage on Thursday so that he would be able to attend a psychiatric appointment.

Therese Willoughby does not know whether her son took his medication the following day, Friday March 10, 2000. What is known is that he attended a party in Templeogue that evening, at the home of Orla Carroll. There was a large crowd in the house and some of the party-goers were consuming either alcohol or ecstasy, or both.

Brian Mulvaney had been invited to the party by a friend. Party-goers said that Mulvaney was in good form. He was an extremely popular young man and he found it easy to talk to people and to make them feel comfortable. Aside from being a good student, he was also a talented sportsman. Basketball was his sport of choice and he had even represented Ireland at under-16 level. When he wasn't playing sports, Brian enjoyed playing the guitar.

The two young men did not know one another but, without knowing it, Mulvaney had angered Willoughby. The

David Brennan was found guilty but insane of the killing of his nephew, baby
Jack Everitt Brennan, in 2000.
(© *Collins Photo Agency*)

Patrick, Paula and David Everitt, grandparents and uncle of murdered baby Jack Everitt Brennan after David Brennan was found guilty but insane of the killing.
(© *Collins Photo Agency*)

Mikahla (4) and Abby (3) Grace died after being drowned by their mother, Sharon, who also took her own life.
(© *PJ Browne*)

Deirdre O'Sullivan was abducted by her father, Christopher, in 1999 when she was four years old. Two years later, he shot her in the head before taking his own life.

The search for 11-year-old Robert Holohan in January 2005 captivated Ireland. The school boy's body was found after eight days.

Engineering student Wayne O'Donoghue after his arrest for the killing of his neighbour, 11-year-old Robert Holohan.
(© Irish Independent)

Wayne O'Donoghue at the State's appeal against his "unduly lenient" sentence.
(© PA)

Left: Twenty-three-year-old Emer O'Loughlin's charred remains were found in April 2005. Her killer has not yet been caught.
(© *John Kelly*)

Below: Johnny O'Loughlin with a photograph of his murdered daughter, Emer. Gardaí believe her killer may have faked his own death.
(© *John Kelly*)

Left: Rachel O'Reilly on the day she was married to her husband Joe. He would later be questioned by Gardaí in relation to her murder but no charges were brought.

Below: Rachel O'Reilly's badly beaten body was discovered in her home in Naul, Co. Dublin, in October 2004.

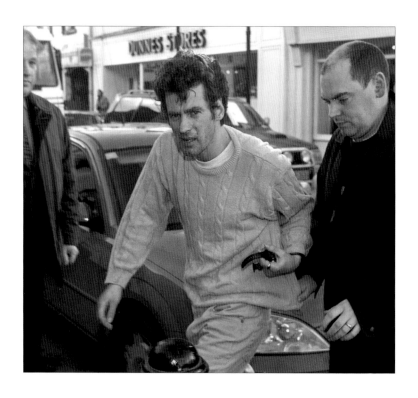

Kevin Bridgeman (centre) told Gardaí that he had killed his mother because she was "wrecking my head".
(© *Collins Photo Agency*)

Former brothel owner Marie Bridgeman was kicked to death by her own son, Kevin. She was under investigation by the Criminal Assets Bureau at the time of her death.
(© *Collins Photo Agency*)

The family of 65-year-old grandmother Joan Casey, shot dead in Tallaght in April 2004, leaving the court after 26-year-old Timothy Rattigan was convicted of her murder.
(© *Collins Photo Agency*)

Nineteen-year-old Brian Mulvaney was beaten to death in a savage attack led by Brian Willoughby outside a party in south Dublin, in March 2000.
(© *RTE*)

The investigation into the killing of Brian Murphy outside Anabel's Nightclub in south Dublin was perhaps the highest profile case this decade. Only one man was convicted for his manslaughter and this conviction was later overturned.
(© *Collins Photo Agency*)

popular young architecture student had consumed an ecstasy tablet and was dancing off the effects of the drug with a local girl by the name of Suzanne McVey. The two danced to the music unaware that Willoughby was standing just yards away, staring at them. He was infatuated with McVey and was overcome with jealousy of the stranger dancing with her.

As the night progressed, Willoughby got talking to Mulvaney. The pair chatted and agreed to walk to a nearby shop, in order to buy cigarette papers so that they could roll a cannabis joint.

At 1.30 am the two men left the party and began walking towards Templeogue Village. Mulvaney was a naturally relaxed man and would have had no reason to suspect that Willoughby wanted anything but to smoke a joint and return to the party. The effects of the ecstasy tablet he had consumed would have relaxed him further – the drug releasing serotonin into his brain and leaving him in a state of bliss.

While Mulvaney went to the shop to purchase the cigarette papers, a plan was forming in Willoughby's mind. He noticed two youths whom he knew standing near the shop and approached them.

Fifteen-year-old Stephen Aherne and 18-year-old Neal Barbour had both been drinking heavily and were intent on violence. The pair had attended a 21st birthday party in the nearby CYM Terenure social club and were heavily intoxicated. Despite his youth, Aherne had consumed up to ten pints of beer and a sambucca shot. Barbour had consumed up to seven pints of beer.

Once the bar at CYM Terenure had closed, the pair were offered a lift by car to Templeogue Village, which they accepted. Their orgy of violence was about to commence.

Matthew O'Dowd was walking through Templeogue on his own when he came across Barbour and Aherne. He had gone to a late-night take away but had left his friends there in order to go home. Barbour and Aherne crossed the road towards O'Dowd carrying empty pint glasses in their hands. They began to taunt O'Dowd, who attempted to ignore them and walk on. Aherne smashed the pint glass over O'Dowd's head, causing a laceration behind the ear. He then punched O'Dowd, who managed to fight back and run away from his attackers.

Barbour and Aherne had no desire to return to their homes, however, and 20 minutes later they were still in Templeogue Village. Three men emerged from a local pub and the two youths approached them. A scuffle broke out and Barbour held a pint glass to the face of one of the group, Karl Dunne. He threatened to smash the glass into Dunne's face unless they were given money. After another scuffle, the three men managed to escape the area.

It was precisely at this time that Brian Mulvaney and Brian Willoughby were walking into Templeogue Village. As Mulvaney went off to buy cigarette papers, Willoughby approached the two young thugs. Barbour would later testify that Willoughby claimed Mulvaney had called them "queers". He told the two that he wanted to "get" Mulvaney and asked for their help.

"Yer man [Mulvaney] was just standing there and Willers [Willoughby] said, 'he's a queer from Knocklyon' and will we get him. We agreed to get him," said Aherne.

The three youths walked towards Mulvaney, who offered to roll a joint before returning to the party.

"Willers said, 'Yeah, follow me, follow me'," said Aherne in his statement. "Halfway around the corner, Willers gave him a box and he [Mulvaney] ran away."

Willoughby had lured Mulvaney off the main road and had suddenly thrown a punch at him. Mulvaney was stunned but managed to run away. He ran around 100 yards away from his attackers, who continued to pursue him. It was Barbour who caught up with Mulvaney first.

"I caught up with him near the dirt track, I started to tussle with him," recalled Barbour. "I caught the back of his jumper; I grabbed this fellow and put him on the ground."

Mulvaney was now lying on the ground. Within minutes he would be dead.

"I was using my fists and my feet on this guy," Willoughby would later tell Gardaí. "He got away and we chased him over to the Watercourse. I caught up with him and I began to beat him again. I was using my fists and my feet. I was punching and kicking him. I was kicking and jumping on his head when he was on the ground. I kept kicking, kicking. I did not use any weapon; I just kept kicking him and jumping on him."

In a matter of seconds the assault had escalated to barbaric levels. Aherne found a stick and struck Mulvaney with it three times. Willoughby kicked his victim and was stamping on his head.

"I started to hit him with the stick, I hit him around three times," recalled Aherne.

Aherne told Gardaí that Willoughby was jumping up and down on Mulvaney's face. While he was doing this, Willoughby was laughing and shouting, "this is carnage, this is deadly."

"I kept dancing on his head while he was on the ground, kept kicking and jumping on his head for around two minutes," Willoughby would tell Gardaí.

Barbour realised the scale of the assault and fled the scene. "I took a few steps back," he would tell Gardaí. "Brian Willoughby was jumping and dancing on his head. I said, 'that's taking things a bit far'. I started to run."

The assault lasted just two minutes, but its ferocity would

kill Brian Mulvaney. The extent of his injuries was so horrific that his father would later have to identify his body by his feet and hands.

The three men involved in the assault all fled the scene. Incredibly, Willoughby and Aherne returned to Orla Carroll's party, their clothes covered in the blood of Brian Mulvaney. When questioned about the bloodstains, the pair told partygoers that they had been involved in a minor scuffle with a gang in Templeogue.

While Willoughby and Aherne were fabricating stories at the party, Brian Mulvaney was dying. They were still enjoying themselves at the party when Damien Devine and his friends stumbled across Brian's body.

Mulvaney was pronounced dead in Tallaght Hospital, the very hospital to which Therese Willoughby had pleaded in vain to have her son admitted just four days earlier.

A post-mortem examination showed that Brian had suffered serious injuries during the assault and had swallowed blood from the major cuts to his face. He died from asphyxiation caused by the inhalation of blood into the lungs. The then State Pathologist, Professor John Harbison, concluded that Mulvaney's cough reflex, which might have enabled him to cough up this blood, was suppressed due to concussion caused by multiple head injuries during the assault.

Brian Willoughby, Stephen Aherne and Neal Barbour were all charged with the murder of Brian Mulvaney. The State argued that the nature of the assault was enough to suggest that the three men had intended to kill or cause serious injury to the deceased. The prosecution team was confident that they could prove beyond doubt that the three men were guilty of murdering Mulvaney.

However, their attempts to bring Brian's killers to justice were dashed in February 2002.

Dr Bridin Brady, a senior chemist in the State Laboratory, told the court that the quantity of ecstasy consumed by Mulvaney on the night was potentially fatal. Dr Brady qualified her comments, however, by stating that many persons could take such a dosage without any significant ill-effects.

The decision to collapse the trial was a major set-back, but it did not allow Brian's killers to go unpunished for long. Thirteen months later, a re-trial was held. At the new hearing, Professor Harbison did not change his opinion that Mulvaney's death was as a direct result of the assault and was not related to the effects of ecstasy. Professor Busuttil, a Scottish pathologist hired by Stephen Aherne's defence, did not disagree with Professor Harbison, although he stated his belief that ecstasy may have been a contributory factor to the deceased's unconsciousness, which had suppressed his cough reflex.

Counsel for the defence also questioned Willoughby's mental state at the time of the assault. They claimed that their client was insane. Professor Michael Fitzgerald, who had treated the defendant for years, testified as to the level of ADD suffered by Willoughby. Therese Willoughby told the court of her son's mental difficulties, especially in the week leading up to the assault. However, the State called up its own psychiatrist, Dr Cleo van Velsen. The psychologist acknowledged Willoughby's mental condition but denied that this would have led to him not knowing what he was doing. Willoughby was disturbed, she said, but not insane.

Brian Willoughby was found guilty of the murder of Brian Mulvaney and sentenced to life imprisonment. Stephen Aherne was found not guilty of murder but guilty of manslaughter and sentenced to ten years. Neal Barbour was acquitted of all charges.

"Brian Willoughby is going to be where he belongs, he's

a danger," said Aoife Mulvaney, after her brother's killer was sentenced.

Brian's father, Larry Mulvaney, told reporters that the pain he and his family would feel would last forever, regardless of what sentences were handed down. However, in an emotional speech, he said that people who commit horrific crimes should be made to pay. "There has to be a line in the sand to show that, if you cross it, this is what's going to happen to you," he said. "If Stephen Aherne gets 50 or five years, for him it's finished. For us it's everlasting."

Annie Mulvaney, Brian's mother, described her son's killers as "evil" and accused the two men of being intent on causing violence and destruction.

"We feel Brian met two evils that night and that is why he is dead," she said. "He met Willoughby, who was out on bail, and he met Stephen Aherne. These are the kind of gurriers that at the weekend go out to enjoy themselves, drink plentifully and part of their enjoyment at the end of the night is to inflict pain on others. That is an evil in our society and we have to recognise it."

All three men received further custodial sentences for their roles in earlier assaults. Willoughby was sentenced to five years for the attack on William Brereton, the man who lost an eye after being stabbed by Willoughby on College Green.

Stephen Aherne was jailed for a further three years, to run concurrently with the ten-year sentence for manslaughter, for the assaults on Matthew O'Dowd and Karl Dunne earlier on the evening on which Brian Mulvaney was killed.

"A halt must be called to gratuitous violence in our society and a loud and clear message must go out from these courts that it will not be tolerated," said Mr Justice Barry White.

Referring to the quantity of alcohol consumed by Aherne

on the night of Mulvaney's death, Justice White was heavily critical of CYM Terenure for allowing a 15-year-old youth to consume ten pints and a shot of sambucca: "The holders of licences, publicans and their staff have a responsibility," he said. "I don't say this excuses your conduct but this matter should be on their conscience for the rest of their lives."

Neal Barbour was sentenced to 18 months' imprisonment for the assaults on O'Dowd and Dunne. Defending Barbour, Erwan Mill-Arden SC said his client was "older and wiser" and was now a "sober citizen" who did not drink too much when it was offered to him by others.

Mr Justice Carney demanded to know what counsel meant – "Was it poured down his throat?" he asked.

No, counsel accepted, adding that his client had been "happy to take it". However, Barbour had gone on to be named Student of the Year at business college and regretted his past.

"This court is repeatedly dealing with situations in which persons of previous good character and good families commit acts of extreme violence in circumstances in which they can scarcely remember," said Mr Justice Carney after imposing his sentence.

The closure the Mulvaney family hoped the jailing of Brian Willoughby would give them, however, was not guaranteed yet. Having read newspaper reports of the trial, a retired pathologist, Professor Dermot Hourihane, contacted Willoughby's solicitors. Professor Hourihane raised further questions over the role of ecstasy in Mulvaney's death. Hourihane claimed that blood in the lungs was a classic symptom of ecstasy poisoning. "The possibility of inhalation of blood from a cut lip seems fanciful and unconvincing to me," he said in a sworn affidavit to the court.

Willoughby's legal team appealed his conviction on the basis of this new evidence. A three-man judicial team

– comprising Mr Justice Nicholas Kearns, Mr Justice Eamon de Valera and Mr Justice Frank Clarke – rejected the appeal on several grounds, including the fact that Professor Hourihane did not have access to eyewitness statements.

"His report seems to us to have been compiled in something of an evidential vacuum, in that he lacked the critical accounts of lay-witnesses, including fire and ambulance crew, who saw Brian Mulvaney on that night," said Justice Kearns in his judgement. "To describe the deceased's facial injuries simply as a "cut lip" grossly understates the severe injuries described in detail by Professor Harbison. Professor Harbison's report refers to a "cut lip" but from his evidence we know that this was more than an ordinary cut lip – it was a deep and extensive laceration which was accompanied by other nasal and facial injuries."

The decision to reject Willoughby's appeal came just ten days before what should have been Brian Mulvaney's 24th birthday. For his parents and sister, it marked the end of the judicial process following their son's death.

"We have a sense of overwhelming relief," said Annie Mulvaney, Brian's mother. "It has been a very long five years since Brian's death and we are now so happy to close this chapter. We hope that we never have to come back to this place again."

The Willoughby family, however, were distraught at the court's dismissal of Professor Hourihane's opinion. "I know there is a lovely young man dead but our son was not in his right mind when this happened," said Therese Willoughby. "I can't understand the injustice of it."

The killer's mother would later tell Kathryn Holmquist of *The Irish Times* that the State was unwilling to deal with her son's mental condition. The murder of Brian Mulvaney was "waiting to happen," she said. Her son's condition was worsened on the night, she claimed, due to the consumption of alcohol, which combined with his medication had an overly powerful effect on him.

Therese Willoughby had attempted to offer condolences to Annie Mulvaney during the trial but had been rebuffed. "I wanted to shake hands and say I am terribly, terribly sorry for the grief and suffering you have gone through," she said. "Our son had problems that were not addressed. I want the Mulvaney family to know that we are so sorry and we pray for them and their son Brian every day. I would prefer it if Brian [Willoughby] was dead. I would rather be in Annie Mulvaney's position. At least she knows that her son is in safe hands in the afterlife. I will have to live with the fact that Brian is in prison untreated for his disorder and suffering for the rest of my life."

The comments did not go down well with Annie Mulvaney. "His mother is going on the airwaves saying that she did everything she could and that he had Attention Deficit Disorder. That is ridiculous," she said. "He is a vicious, evil person and, if he is ever let out, he will kill again."

* * * * *

Brian Mulvaney was another innocent victim of Ireland's growing culture of late-night violence. While one of his assailants had a history of violence, the presence of alcohol certainly had a major role to play in the assault that claimed his life. Willoughby's 15-year-old accomplice had consumed enough alcohol to make a grown man drunk. In Stephen Aherne's case, alcohol brought out a vicious, violent streak.

Ireland has the second-highest level of alcohol consumption in Europe, with the average Irish person drinking almost 14 litres of pure alcohol a year. That is over twice what Swedes drink, nearly twice what Americans drink, and five litres higher than the European average.

And it's getting worse – alcohol consumption has almost doubled over the last ten years.

The consumption of alcoholic drinks is worth €6 billion to the Irish economy each year. However, its benefits are matched by its costs. Each year, alcohol abuse and misuse costs the Irish health service well in excess of €2 billion. Alcohol's true cost to Irish society cannot be measured solely in monetary terms; the seemingly never-ending line of road deaths, suicides, serious assaults and violent marriages also have to be taken into account. And, increasingly, as a direct consequence of how much alcohol they have consumed, Irish people are resorting to violence and sometimes murder.

While, in the absence of toxicology reports into each killing, it is not possible to get fully accurate figures to gauge the role of alcohol in the violent deaths of men, it can be estimated that alcohol was a factor in at least 97 male killings in Ireland between 2000 and 2005. That figure, which could even be deemed conservative, accounts for over 40% of non-gangland-related male killings that have taken place in Ireland during this timeframe.

While there has been much media and political focus on the rise in murders connected to the illegal drugs trade, it appears that the trade of a legal drug – alcohol – has claimed 50% more lives than those taken by drug gangs.

On March 11, 2002, Charlie Maher and John Paul Ryan were drinking cans of cider on the grounds of a football pitch in Waterford City with a group of friends. They had started drinking early in the day and were in jovial form. Both men were originally from Clonmel in Co. Tipperary but were now living in Waterford City. Being 20 years of age, they were both old enough to drink in pubs, but it was a nice day and, besides, it was cheaper to drink cans.

Eventually, when night fell, the group moved from the football ground into a house, where they continued drinking. After a period of time, they got hungry and decided to walk down to the local fast food restaurant for some food.

"We decided to go down to the takeaway in The Glen to get something to eat," recalled Kenneth Wall, one of the group of friends. "We walked down having a laugh; I don't think John Paul had any money at the time."

Memories of the night are hazy. Wall said he wasn't sure who ordered food or what they ordered, but he did remember what happened when John Paul Ryan took a sausage out of Charlie Maher's bag of food without asking.

"John Paul took a sausage out of Charlie's bag," he said. "Charlie took it the wrong way...I seen a lot of digs thrown by people, they were fighting three or four times...we separated them and Charlie went to walk off."

Maher left the scene but his friend's actions had angered him. As he walked away, he violently punched the window of a nearby off-licence. Maher stormed off on his own towards his house in Grange Cohen, St Johns Park, all the time getting more furious.

Behind him, the rest of his friends, including Ryan, couldn't understand why Maher had lost his temper to such a degree over something as insignificant as a sausage. Ryan decided that he would go to Maher's house to try to calm the situation down.

"John Paul walked off in front of us to Charlie Maher – he said he wanted to go up and sort it out, because it was only over a sausage," said Wall. "He wanted to call it quits."

Maher's girlfriend, Ciara Gater was in the house by the time her boyfriend arrived home. She was lying down in bed when she heard Maher storm into the kitchen.

"He had blood on his face," she recalled. "He picked up two knives."

She asked her boyfriend whether there had been trouble.

"Nothing yet," he replied. "But there will be damage done tonight." He picked up two knives and walked out of the house, just as John Paul Ryan was arriving. Just behind him, Kenneth Wall and the other friends were approaching.

"I saw the two of them coming together," said Wall. "I thought they were going to make up but then all hell broke loose. I saw Charlie Maher hit John Paul first, the two of them started fighting and fell onto the ground."

What he heard next, he will never forget. As the pair lay on the ground fighting, Ciara Gater could be heard screaming at her boyfriend: "Drop the knife."

Wall ran towards his quarrelling friends. "Charlie was on top of John Paul," he recalled. "I ran over and stood on his wrist and took the knife out of his hand." He dragged Maher off Ryan and "threw him into his house".

It was too late.

Ryan had been stabbed twice, once in the thigh and once in the heart. He was lying on the ground "gasping for air". Attempts to resuscitate him at the scene failed. Ryan was dead – killed for the sake of a sausage.

When Gardaí arrived at the scene, Maher presented himself to them and told them, "put the handcuffs on me, I did it."

At the trial in May 2003, Garda Alan White said that the accused denied intending to kill his friend. "He said he used the small knife and was asking for John Paul," said Garda White. "He said he didn't mean what happened." The jury found Maher guilty of murder and Mr Justice Nicholas Kearns imposed the mandatory life sentence.

Eleven days after John Paul Ryan was stabbed to death outside Charlie Maher's home, James Murphy was stabbed to death following a row over alcohol in a bed-sit in Sligo. The 50-year-old alcoholic, who had resided in hostels and shelters, was drinking with Patrick McGrath (60), of Holborn Street, Sligo, whom he had previously befriended in a hostel in Wexford. McGrath was drinking wine when Murphy demanded some. "[We got into] a bit of a tussle and I must have stabbed him," said Murphy, who was found guilty of manslaughter and sentenced to six years' imprisonment.

Eighteen days after Murphy's death, Patrick Pepper was beaten to death in St Stephen's Green in Dublin's city centre. Pepper (40) had been drinking with Thomas Corway (24), with an address in Coolock, when a row developed. "I think I cracked him in the head, I just started hitting him in the head with my fists and kicking him," Corway told Gardaí. "When I knocked him out, I just kept kicking – I didn't think he was dead, I just thought he wasn't moving."

Pepper died from inhalation of blood, as a result of serious facial injuries consistent with someone stamping on his face. "Enormous force" had been used in the assault, the Judge heard, before sentencing Corway to six years with the final 18 months suspended.

Pepper had been dead four days when Peter Joyce was killed following a late-night row outside a GAA club in Portmarnock on April 13, 2002. Glen Carroll (23) was cleared of manslaughter but found guilty of assault and given a two-year sentence.

Two nights later on the other side of Dublin, John Murphy (27) was beaten to death with a pick-axe handle following a row that broke out in the Buda bar, across the road from Blanchardstown shopping centre. Murphy became involved in an altercation with Terence Keogh (37), of Pine Brook,

Blanchardstown. He accused Keogh of being a child-molester and, aided by his brother Mark, began to assault the 37-year-old.

Keogh, however, retrieved a pick-axe from his car before chasing John Murphy into the Sheepmore Grove housing estate, 600 yards away. He struck him with the pick-axe handle.

"The whole area was covered in blood," said Detective Sergeant Liam Kelly of Blanchardstown Garda Station.

Keogh, who had 36 previous convictions, including burglary, larceny and assault causing actual bodily harm, was sentenced to ten years for manslaughter. "I'm the victim here; I was attacked by ten of them. How can you sit there, you fucking liars? I can't believe this," he screamed at Murphy's family, as he was led from court.

Later that week, Peter Ward (49), died following a late night assault in a house in Park Avenue, Sandymount.

A little over a fortnight later, Thomas Maloney received a phone call from Gardaí informing him that his son, Thomas, was in a critical condition in hospital. He and his wife rushed from their home in Limerick to Dublin's Beaumont Hospital to be with their son following the assault. It was the second tragedy to hit the Maloney family. Their other son, Alan, had died following a hit-and-run incident in 1995, at the age of 11.

"[At 4.10 am] I went down to make a cup of tea and this thing came over me that there was something wrong," he would later say. "Next thing a call came in...We arrived [at Beaumont] and Thomas came out of theatre after they removed a clot from his brain. I was saying to myself, 'please God, not again'. I was looking into the next room in the hospital where Alan had previously died."

Thomas Maloney (26) died following an assault outside the Statoil station on Usher's Quay in Dublin city centre.

Maloney had travelled up to Dublin from his native Limerick on the morning of April 21, but had missed his return train. He had spent the day drinking, both on the train and in a bar at Heuston Station.

Maloney clashed with Francis Kenny, of Basin Street flats, and William McDonnell, of Mary Aikenhead House. Both men had also been drinking heavily and a row developed, during which Maloney was pinned to the ground and beaten severely. The Limerick man, from the Moyross area of the city, was put into a coma by the ferocity of the beating and later died.

McDonnell was sentenced to five years for the manslaughter of Maloney, while Kenny received a three-year sentence. Kenny had pleaded guilty to manslaughter, while McDonnell contested the charge.

The sentences angered the family of Thomas Maloney: "There was some evidence that our son provoked the trouble by arguing with McDonnell, but surely the violence used by McDonnell and Kenny was not only excessive but grotesque," Thomas Maloney Senior wrote in a letter to the DPP. "The lenient sentences seem to be an indication to any potentially violent criminal that they can use the most grossly excessive force in response to the slightest provocation."

The DPP appealed the sentences but the appeal was rejected.

Four days after the horrific assault on Thomas Maloney, Andrew Foley (54) was stabbed to death during a drunken incident at his flat in Nelson Street, Dublin 7. Foley had been drinking all day with Christina Williams (25), a Welsh woman who had only recently arrived in Ireland, in a pub in Dorset Street.

"She was vomiting outside," recalled Nicholas Maher, co-owner of The Meeting Pint bar. "She came back in and sat down. Mr. Foley bought her a drink and she said she'd bring him outside the back for a fuck for buying her that and she touched him on the leg."

The pair left the pub and returned to Foley's apartment. Here, she claims, he became aggressive when she refused to have sex with him.

"He grabbed me by the neck and I had my back to the worktop. I stabbed him in the eye first, he let me go then I stabbed him again, with force, probably from the drink," she told Gardaí.

Williams stabbed Foley 13 times with three different knives. She then boiled a kettle and poured boiling water over his body.

"The kettle was on the worktop," she said. "I boiled it. I filled it and waited and I chucked it over him when he was in the chair. I just got carried away."

Williams was sentenced to life imprisonment by Mr Justice Kevin O'Higgins. As she was found guilty, Williams turned to the jury and told them to "fuck off". Her sister had previously testified that the accused suffered alcoholism.

In total, eight people were killed in alcohol-fuelled disputes in the two-month period between March 11 and May 11, 2002 – one person a week. The fact that four people were killed in non-alcohol- related incidents during the same timeframe makes it one of the bloodiest two-month periods in the history of the Irish State.

The fact that this spate of violence occurred just weeks before a general election helped to turn late-night violence into a major political issue. The Government responded immediately by publishing the Criminal Justice (Public Order) Bill, which made it an offence to be intoxicated in a public place and allowed Gardaí to apply to the district courts to close any public house deemed to be at the centre of late-night violence. The legislation was criticised as being a knee-jerk reaction by civil liberties groups concerned at the wide-spread powers of arrest it gave to Gardaí.

Even as he announced the bill, however, the then Minister for Justice, John O'Donoghue, warned that it would take more than legislation to tackle the culture of alcohol abuse that had developed in Ireland: "Measures taken in the criminal justice area can help to curtail street violence, but they cannot by themselves be viewed as the only solution," he said. "State agencies cannot solve the problems associated with excessive drinking – parents, teachers, politicians, the drinks industry and the creative media must also play their part in helping to address the problem."

This echoed the comments that had been made just under two years previously when one of the most public cases of alcohol-related violence had occurred on August 31, 2000. Brian Murphy (18) died following an altercation outside Club Anabel, a disco frequented by youths from the South Dublin area. The fight erupted when Murphy attacked another youth, Andrew Frame, but Brian was soon greatly outnumbered. He was knocked to the ground as a crowd of up to a dozen young men assaulted him.

Frame was found by the court to have played no role in the fight. However, three of his friends – Sean Mackey, Desmond Ryan and Dermot Laide – were all subsequently found guilty of having played a role in the fight that killed Brian Murphy. Laide was the only one to be convicted of manslaughter. However, this conviction was sensationally overturned when the State Pathologist, Professor Marie Cassidy, judged that the level of beating inflicted on Murphy was not severe enough to kill him. Cassidy claimed that drink played a major role in Brian Murphy's death.

Murphy's death and the subsequent trial of four men accused of having taken part in that fight, turned into a media

circus. The age and perceived wealth of the people involved
– all had recently completed their Leaving Certificates in
Dublin's exclusive Blackrock College and lived in some of
the capital's most sought-after addresses – led to a media
fascination with the Brian Murphy case.

Somewhat bizarrely, it was rarely mentioned that another
youth, David Langan (19), had died in similar circumstances
the previous week just a mile from the site of Murphy's death.
Langan, from Castleknock, died after he was twice struck in
the head by Fergal Cagney.

The row broke out after Langan had pushed Ronan
McGrath, Cagney's cousin, outside a night-club on Camden
Street. All of the men involved had been drinking over the
course of the night. The then State Pathologist, Professor John
Harbison was later to state that Langan's blood alcohol level
could have been as high as 210 mg per 100ml, compared to
the legal limit for driving, which is 80.

McGrath and Cagney followed Langan and his friends
to Portobello, where the two blows were struck. Langan fell
to the ground and, realising the seriousness of the situation,
McGrath and Cagney immediately attempted to resuscitate
him.

"At the moment he [Langan] fell the other four guys
seemed to be stunned, I got the impression they were stunned
by what happened, that [they] were frozen for a second or
two," said Colm Burgess, a local resident who had witnessed
the altercation. "I remember the guy who [had been] trying
to calm things down ran over to the guy on the road and
he seemed to be trying to lift him up and I remember him
shouting to the others to give him a hand and I think two of
the others came over and they lifted his body up and lifted it
back onto the pavement and placed him in a sitting position
on the pavement, propped up against that low wall between
the pavement and the canal."

Langan had fallen heavily to the ground and was unconscious. McGrath and Cagney were now panicking, as they desperately called the emergency services.

"The guy who had been doing all the shouting had walked up a little bit towards Portobello Bridge and he seemed to be talking on a mobile phone so I presumed he was phoning an ambulance," recalled Burgess. "After a few moments he stopped talking on the phone and walked back towards the main group and I remember being aware that he seemed to be very upset because I remember one of the other five seemed to hug him as if he was trying to comfort him. He possibly might have been crying but I am not sure."

David Langan was in a coma for five days before he died. Ronan McGrath and Fergal Cagney were both sentenced to 15 months' imprisonment for their roles in his death.

However, it was to be the alcohol-fuelled row that claimed Murphy's life one week later that would capture the headlines, and ultimately act as a watershed in terms of the public's reaction to late-night violence outside pubs and nightclubs.

As details emerged of the hours in the run-up to Murphy's death and the quantities of alcohol consumed by students in Anabel's that night, calls for government action intensified. Although much of the media coverage of the case was over-the-top, the public were genuinely shocked by the culture of drinking that young Irish people had immersed themselves in. Witnesses at the trial of the four men accused of taking part in the altercation testified to the extent of alcohol consumption that night. Michael McFadden, who was working behind the bar on the night in question, told the court that people had been drinking shots of spirits from early on. Famously, one witness described himself as being "tipsy", after consuming five cans and four pints of lager, a naggin of vodka and two bottles of Smirnoff Ice.

Public debate surrounding the death of Brian Murphy and the culture of binge drinking that had ultimately led to his killing culminated in the enactment of the Intoxicating Liquor Act, which was first introduced in bill form in June 2003. The Act outlawed the practise of "happy hours" – where pubs offer reduced-priced drinks during specified hours – and cut-price drink promotions.

The legislation was broadly welcomed, even by the Licensed Vintners' Association, whose Chief Executive, Donal O'Keefe, commented that "the social responsibility thing has moved up the agenda".

Like his predecessor John O'Donoghue, however, Minister for Justice Michael McDowell warned that legislation could only go so far:

"When we look at the factors that have contributed to the increase in alcohol consumption – societal and demographic changes; changing lifestyles and expectations; more disposable income, especially among young people; a lessening of parental control on young people – we realise that the problem of alcohol-related harm is multi-dimensional and that simplistic solutions will not work," he said. "The State has an important role to play in addressing the problems associated with alcohol-related harm, but it must be combined with action at other levels: local community action; action within the family, where values and parental example are crucial; and finally at individual level where self-esteem and self-respect are all important."

But still the killings have continued. In the 30 months following the publication of the Intoxicating Liquor Act, over 40 people died in violent incidents involving the consumption of alcohol.

No society will ever be homicide-free – people will always kill for revenge, out of greed and passion. However, in virtually every case involving alcohol, aggression is heightened to a point far disproportionate to the dispute. In many cases, the perpetrator cannot even remember killing the victim.

The tendency for young men to react violently when under the influence of alcohol has led to life being lost over the most minor of disputes. Brian Gorey and Sean Lundon, for example, were friends. Yet, one of them would end up killing the other after a boozy night out in Dublin in April, 2001.

The two men were both working on board the L.E. *Eithne*, one of the Defence Force's flagship vessels. The ship docked in Dublin on Friday April 21, 2001 and the crew were given the weekend off in order to relax.

Twenty-one-year-old Brian Gorey, originally from Castletroy View, Limerick, loved his job on board the vessel. He was looking forward to a weekend relaxing with the rest of the crew in the numerous pubs near to where the L.E. *Eithne* was docked at Sir John Rogerson's Quay.

The crew hit the town on Saturday night, venturing into the nearby Busker's night-club. As would be expected on a Saturday night in Dublin, there was a large crowd in the club. The lads spent the night drinking and dancing before returning back to the ship at around 3.30 am.

Spirits were still high, however, and the crew had no intention of ending the evening. Instead they decided to continue the party on board the vessel. In the recreation room, Brian Gorey soon fell asleep, leaving his crewmates to continue the night without him. As the hours went by, the crowd fell off, as one by one the sailors went to bed. By 5 am, Gorey was alone in the recreation room with Sean Lundon, a young ship's mechanic from James Connolly Park in Tipperary town.

Twenty minutes later, the alarm bell was raised. The other crewmen rushed onto the deck of the ship only to see a man struggling in the water. He was screaming and flapping his arms. A buoy was thrown into the water but it was too late – Brian Gorey drifted under the water and lost consciousness. He was dead before his body could be recovered.

At first it appeared as though it may have been an accidental fall. Within minutes, however, it became clear that Brian Gorey had not been the victim of an accidental slip. There was blood on the deck, and the blood formed a trail that led directly to the recreation room. The trail also led directly to Sean Lundon, whose clothes were splattered with the dead man's blood.

Nobody could explain what happened in the recreation room that caused Sean Lundon to viciously assault Brian Gorey before throwing him overboard. The two men had not had any sort of dispute and had both been in good form all night. A number of young sailors testified at the trial that there had been no ill feeling between Lundon and Gorey prior to the incident.

A post-mortem examination showed that Gorey had been on the receiving end of a significant beating before he was thrown overboard. However, despite the intensity of the assault, he was alive when he hit the water. Lundon used both an ashtray and a brush handle during the course of the assault, breaking the latter over his victim's head. He later told Gardaí that after he carried Gorey to the deck: "he was struggling, slapping out at me. I pushed him back hard into the chest and he went over the rail." Lundon's defence team, led by Brendan Grehan SC, argued that he had never intended his crewmate to go overboard.

Sentencing Sean Lundon to five years for the manslaughter of Brian Gorey, Mr Justice Paul Carney said that it was "frightening" that such gratuitous violence was now set off by drink alone. "It is frightening that it [drinking alcohol] is going to lead to this without the involvement of cannabis," he said.

The amount of alcohol consumed by Lundon on the night of the assault – between eight and ten pints – was a major factor in what transpired. Sean Lundon had savagely beaten Brian Gorey and propelled him overboard "for a reason that is not clear and probably never will be," said Mr Justice Carney.

Speaking outside the courthouse, Gorey's father, Michael, said that the amount of alcohol consumed on the night of April 22, 2001 should not have affected the severity of the sentence imposed on the man who killed his son. Lundon had apologised to Michael Gorey for his actions that night, but the apology "meant nothing".

Despite showing remorse for his actions on that alcohol-fuelled night, Lundon should have faced a stiffer sentence, he said. "At the end of the day, if taking a life is only worth five years, there's going to be a lot more killings in the country," said the distraught father.

* * * * *

Michael Gorey was right – the killings have continued.

"Alcohol abuse is rampant in Ireland and getting worse," says Dr Conor Farren, consultant psychiatrist at St Patrick's Hospital, Dublin. "Irish people consume vast quantities of alcohol, above and beyond what is normal in Europe. Alcohol consumption has increased by a staggering 40% in the ten years to 2003. This is unprecedented in Irish history, runs counter to the overall European trend and is unique in the world. Essentially, we went from a nation of normal drinkers to alcohol abusers in this ten-year period."

Not only did Ireland experience a dramatic growth in alcohol consumption during the ten-year period to 2003, but the gap between what Irish people drink and what the rest of Europe drinks widened: ten EU countries experienced a drop in consumption rates over this period, with a further three showing only marginal rises.

According to Dr Farren, the results of recent alcohol abuse in Ireland are not just being seen in the rising murder rate, but are also evident in the rise in suicide and road deaths too. He says that it is no coincidence that the Irish suicide rate has risen by 44% during the same time frame as the almost identical rise in alcohol consumption.

The role of alcohol in Irish deaths as a whole is alarming – not only are 40% of killings influenced by drink, it is believed that one-third of all drivers killed on Irish roads have been drinking, while over 90% of male suicide victims have alcohol in their system.

It is now estimated that 5% of the Irish population is alcohol dependent, while a further 7% are alcohol abusive. This means that there are 200,000 alcoholics in Ireland, with a further 280,000 people who are alcohol abusive.

Experts say that the correlation between a rise in alcohol consumption and suicide is not coincidental. It is also no coincidence that murder rates amongst young men have risen dramatically over this same time period. Results show that 9% of alcoholics are under the age of 25, while alcoholism is three to four times more common in men than in women. A simple look back over the list of young men who have lost their lives violently over recent years, shows that alcohol abuse is fuelling the killing on Irish streets.

Father Neal Carlin, director of the White Oaks Centre in Donegal, cites figures which show that alcohol consumption in Ireland has tripled over the last 30 years. This has lead to a situation where Ireland now leads the European table in terms of binge drinking amongst 15- and 16-year-olds. Fr Carlin says that it will take a massive shift in culture to halt the situation whereby it is acceptable for 200,000 Irish people to suffer from an illness such as alcoholism. The issue must also be tackled at a political level – "Is there a political will to face the reality that the Celtic Tiger has the mechanism to bring itself down as the Roman Empire did?" he asks.

The massive rise in alcohol consumption is due to many factors, none more so than the rise in disposable income over the past ten years. Dr Farren also blames drinks companies for targeting young people and the Government for failing to emphasise the massive health risk posed by alcohol.

"Teenagers see hundreds of advertisements for alcohol but not one suggesting that alcohol is bad," he says. "Drinks companies have campaigns telling people to drink sensibly but the message given is to drink anyway. It is not suggested that drink is bad because it will kill the liver. No drinks company would put up a poster of George Best with the statement, 'Drink kills you'. The advertising suggests that people should drink sensibly because if they do not, they will not attract beautiful women or they will look the fool, but the message is to drink anyway. If we are dependent on the drinks industry to provide health education, we are in a sorry state. Would we want Marlboro and Players to make our tobacco laws and provide our tobacco education? I do not think so."

Donegal TD Cecilia Keaveney has lobbied hard to have alcohol included in the National Drugs Strategy, a policy document which until now has dealt solely with illegal drugs, such as heroin and cocaine. According to Keaveney, the policy was formed at a time when heroin was devastating predominantly working-class communities in Dublin. Now, she says, there is a need to recognise that there is a new drug devastating Irish life – alcohol.

The issue of what will be included in the renewed National Drugs Strategy will not be resolved until late in 2007. The Minister for State with responsibility for the Drugs Strategy, Noel Ahern, however, told the *Sunday Tribune* that alcohol policy will more than likely remain within the remit of the Department of Health and will not feature on the Strategy.

That news delighted Seamus O'Donoghue, President of the Vintners' Federation of Ireland (VFI), who just weeks previously had told the Committee for Arts, Sports, Tourism, Rural and Gaeltacht Affairs – which has been discussing the matter – that "there is no justification, necessity, requirement or expectation that alcohol should be included in a National Drugs Strategy".

Dismissing the figures concerning alcohol consumption over the last ten years, O'Donoghue insisted that, "the problems associated with alcohol in society in Ireland are a consequence of abuse by a small minority of those who consume it regularly".

O'Donoghue told the committee: "the murders, gunfire, gunfights, stabbings and the fear of violence visited on society by the drugs gangs and barons are almost unique to that sector and are certainly alien and unrelated to any legitimate business. The turf wars in which these criminal elements engage and the deaths inflicted on so many young men and women in recent months must never be elevated or given the legitimacy of comparison with what constitutes normal life. To link such activities with any other legal or legitimate enterprise would be a betrayal. We can conceive of no reason that the question of alcohol should be considered in the context of a strategy that deals with the abuse and use of drugs."

Linking alcohol abuse to the use of illegal drugs may be a "betrayal" but not to link them might, perhaps, be to betray the 97 men who have died as an result of alcohol use over the past number of years.

Four

Southern Blood

January 15, 2005: Garda Eamon Lord was in his patrol vehicle on Dublin's Parnell Square when he saw the car speeding straight towards him. Quickly putting his car into reverse, Lord managed to swerve out of danger, just seconds before the oncoming navy Volkswagen raced past his window. He escaped a collision by less than one foot.

The Volkswagen had raced through a red light at the top of O'Connell Street and had continued up Parnell Square North at high speed. It was 3.45 am and the last of Dublin's late-night revellers were still on the streets. As Garda Lord chased the vehicle, at speeds of up to 80 mph, up North Fredrick Street and Denmark Street, the Volkswagen almost caused several accidents. Breaking a set of lights at the corner of Mountjoy Square West, the car forced two pedestrians to jump from the street onto the footpath in order to avoid certain death.

Turning onto Mountjoy Square West, the car broke another set of red lights before the driver lost control. The car skidded across two lanes of traffic and onto the footpath, where it smashed into a tree. Several cars had to swerve to avoid the Volkswagen as it plunged recklessly towards the tree. Not only had pedestrians and other drivers avoided injury, miraculously the three occupants of the Volkswagen also managed to emerge from the wreckage with no major injuries.

As Garda Lord arrested the male driver and two female passengers, it seemed like little more than a case of joy-riding, albeit one that almost had fatal consequences. Garda Lord could not have known it yet, but he had just arrested one of Ireland's most infamous hoods.

The driver of the navy Volkswagen, Liam Keane, was a young man with a reputation: a violent thug who, just two years earlier, had walked free from one of Ireland's highest-profile murder trials. Keane had been drinking heavily on the night in question and later pleaded guilty to reckless endangerment, driving without insurance and driving over the legal alcohol limit. In January 2006, precisely one year after the incident, he was jailed for 18 months.

For Liam Keane, the sentence was little more than a notch on the CV of one of Ireland's most infamous young hoodlums. At the age of just 20, Keane had built himself a national reputation. His guilty plea, in January 2006, led to his 25th criminal conviction. That Keane had more criminal convictions than he had years of age spoke volumes for his lack of respect for law and order, but it also spoke volumes about his reckless and careless lifestyle.

The 24 previous offences of which Keane had been found guilty, all related to public order and road traffic laws. In January 2004, exactly one year before he drunkenly raced the Volkswagen through Dublin city centre, Keane was jailed for four months after threatening the personal safety of another man on the steps of Limerick District Court. Keane shouted a number of serious threats at the man before running away from Gardaí. They later found the youth and charged him with threatening, abusive or insulting behaviour.

Defending Keane in Dublin Circuit Criminal Court in January 2006, Sean Gillane BL conceded that his client's driving was "unjustifiable and clearly very dangerous" but said that his client was under the influence of alcohol at the time. Keane's abuse of alcohol, said Gillane, was "central to every previous conviction" recorded against him.

The image put forward in court of Keane as a young man with an alcohol problem who was unable to stay out of trouble with the Gardaí was very different to the image Keane himself likes to put forward. Since having been thrust into the national spotlight in 2003, Keane had begun to think of himself as a hardman; somebody to be feared and respected in equal measure. Others were not quite so sure. According to informed sources in Limerick, Keane was increasingly being viewed by serious criminals in the city as a renegade; a loose cannon whose maverick actions were attracting far too much media, political and Garda attention.

As a young boy, Keane had watched as his father, Christy Keane, built a criminal empire from nothing. Starting from scratch, Christy Keane rose to become the undisputed godfather of Limerick crime, overseeing drug distribution networks as well as prostitution and racketeering. The younger Keane was born into a violent world, one where unpaid debts were met with savage beatings and where death or incarceration were always around the corner. As the criminal gang which Christy Keane headed grew in stature, so too did the focus on them. However, Christy and his criminal peers insisted on keeping a low profile – the less ripples you cause, the less chance of a wave coming crashing around you.

In October 2003, Liam Keane was to bring unwanted attention upon the family. Two years earlier, Eric Leamy, a 19-year-old from St Mary's estate, the working-class area of the city that had become a personal fiefdom for Christy Keane's gang, was stabbed to death after a row with local youths. Eyewitnesses told Gardaí that Liam Keane had plunged the knife into Leamy, causing the wound which left him to slowly die just 100 yards from his own home. Gardaí charged Keane with murder and were satisfied that they had an open-and-shut case.

When the trial came to court, however, each eyewitness would dramatically retract his statement. In total, seven local youths who had originally implicated Keane in the killing of Eric Leamy on the night of August 28, 2001 were suddenly unable to recall the events of that night.

David Murphy was first to be called to the witness box. Wearing a tracksuit and runners, Murphy told Mr Justice Paul Carney, "I'm answering no questions". Next up was James Price, followed by Paul Campbell. Neither could remember anything of the night.

"Put the knife down and I'll fight you," was what Leamy had said to Keane, according to Amanda McNamara in her original statement. In court she said that she was too drunk and stoned to recall who it was that had produced a six-inch blade and brutally plunged it into the body of Eric Leamy, causing blood to splatter all over the street. Stephen Blackhall could not remember anything either, nor could Tony McMillen.

Finally, it was left to Roy Behan, Leamy's best friend. He had given Gardaí a detailed statement of how he had seen Liam Keane strike Eric Leamy in the face with a nail-studded plank, before pulling out a knife and stabbing him to death. Behan had told Gardaí that Leamy was unarmed when Keane produced the weapon and threatened to stab him. When it came to court, however, Behan, who had helped carry Eric Leamy's coffin, could remember nothing about the incident.

The State had no option but to enter a *nolle prosequi* (no prosecution). Justice Carney was stunned and said that he had never before encountered the likes of what happened in the trial.

Liam Keane walked free from court with his constitutional presumption of innocence intact.

As he left the court, the baby-faced Keane remained behind his mother, who brushed aside media queries. "Leave him alone, leave him alone," she told the flock of reporters looking for answers.

Outside the courtroom, Keane gave a two-fingered sign to waiting photographers, an image that would be splashed across the front pages of the next day's newspapers.

As a snapshot of criminal life in Ireland, the image could not have been more apt – a young man suspected of a brutal and senseless killing walking free from court and giving the two fingers to the nation. It was an image that would turn Liam Keane from a small-time thug into a national figure, and was fast defining the city of Limerick, which was buckling under the weight of growing criminality.

The parents of Eric Leamy were devastated. Speaking exclusively to the *Sunday Tribune*, Geraldine Leamy told of her heartbreak at seeing the killing of her youngest son go unpunished. "He was a wonderful son," she said. "He wasn't a druggie. He wasn't mixed up in anything bad, feuds or anything. He was the kindest boy you could ever meet. I shouldn't have let him out that night. If I'd have told him to go off to bed early, he would have stayed in."

The family home, just 100 yards from the spot on which Eric died, and a further 50 yards from the home of Liam Keane's aunt and cousins, was turned into a shrine to the murdered youth. Two dozen images of Eric Leamy adorned the walls of the sitting room and his belongings remained untouched even two years after his death. "I couldn't part with anything of my boy's," said Geraldine Leamy. "His room upstairs hasn't been touched."

But living so close to the spot where their son was brutally murdered, and also so close to the family of the youth accused of the killing, became too much to bear for the Leamys. They applied to Limerick City Council to be relocated away from St Mary's estate, where they had lived for so long. Too many memories; too many unanswered questions.

Gangland activity in Limerick had just become a national issue 11 months before the dramatic collapse of Keane's murder trial. The murder of one of the city's leading criminal figures – Liam Keane's uncle, Kieran – had first brought the glare of the national media to the city.

The Limerick gangs had for years operated under the radar of the national press and enjoyed a position of relative anonymity, but the collapse of the Liam Keane trial, brought huge national attention to the city. The leading members of Limerick's criminal fraternities were turned into celebrities by the publicity generated by the Liam Keane trial. In the city itself, people in pubs talked about the criminals as though they were personal acquaintances – children on the street offered directions to their homes. It was a situation the leaders of the gangs were unhappy about. As one city source put it at the time, "Liam thinks he is the top dog in the city now, he thinks he is untouchable, but members of the gangs were not happy with the publicity the Leamy affair brought onto them and they weren't shy in telling Liam that."

In the years that have passed since the collapse of Liam Keane's murder trial, the gangland situation in Limerick has changed hugely. Gone are the days when members of Christy Keane's gang were the undisputed kings of the city, free to strut around St Mary's Estate as if it were their own personal kingdom.

The City has since been carved up by several local criminal gangs, all of whom now possess a deadly arsenal of weapons. Whereas the Christy Keane gang used to run the city on its own, there are now several gangs operating in Limerick.

Between 2000 and 2005, the feud between two criminal

families in Limerick cost the lives of five people. That is, of course, not the sum total of misery inflicted by gangs in Limerick. The murder of nightclub bouncer Brian Fitzgerald, for example, was not a product of the feud, although it was most certainly a product of the gangs that rule the city with such ruthlessness. Fitzgerald's second cousin, 23-year-old Robert Fitzgerald, was also shot dead by local criminals after he exchanged words with a well-known gang member at a party in May 2003. Likewise, the murder of David Nunan, a member of a separate drugs gang was gang related but any connection with the infamous feud between the Keane and Ryan families was ruled out.

Out of 32 killings to have taken place in Limerick between 2000 and 2005, 9% of killings in the State, five were related to the feud and six had connections with other gangland activity. That means that 14% of killings were directly related to the feud, but a total of 34% of killings were related to gangland. While Limerick has received a national label as the gangland capital of Ireland, those figures are only marginally higher than Dublin, where 32% of all killings between 2000 and 2005 were gangland related.

However, for a period in 2003 the feud between the Keane and the Ryan gangs placed the national media glare firmly on Limerick, a city that had been for many years trying to combat its unfortunate reputation as the most violent in Ireland. The feud increased Limerick's notoriety – no longer was it simply "Stab City," it was now a place where guns were cheap and life was cheaper.

The cause of the feud has often been put down to a schoolyard fight between two teenage girls. Samantha Ryan and Natalie Keane had known each other for many years. Their fathers, John and Christy respectively, had for over a decade been members of the largest Irish criminal gang outside Dublin. The gang was the brainchild of Christy

Keane, a career criminal born and bred in an area of Limerick called St Mary's Park but known locally as Island Field.

When Samantha and Natalie had a falling out one day, it came to blows. Adopting somewhat unusual parenting techniques, the two fathers agreed that the best way to resolve the situation was for their daughters to take part in a pre-arranged fight. After half an hour the bout was won by Samantha Ryan, who had managed to bite a segment of her opponent's ear off.

While it may have made a great story to blame a schoolyard fight for a bloody criminal feud, the truth was always more complex. The schoolyard fight between Samantha Ryan and Natalie Keane was a product of the feud, not the other way around. This feud was not about children disagreeing, it was about something far more dangerous – money, ego and power.

Born in 1960, Christy Keane grew up as a petty criminal. By the time he was in his early 20s he had a string of convictions for offences such as larceny. By the time he was moving into his 30s, however, Keane was eyeing up more serious business. Together with his younger brother Kieran, he went about establishing the largest drugs distribution network on the western seaboard, as well as operating prostitution and protection rackets.

Eddie Ryan grew up in Kileely, just across the Shannon from where the Keane brothers lived. Ryan was wild from his youth and by the time he was 18 he was in jail for the manslaughter of a man whom he had stabbed to death outside a cinema in the city centre. He was only released from that sentence when he ended up back behind bars, this time for receiving the proceeds of an armed robbery.

While Eddie Ryan was behind bars, the Keanes had gone about building their network. They established links with gangs in Dublin and Liverpool, shipping large quantities of narcotics into Ireland from Britain and selling them across the two countries. As the years went by, renegade Republicans also proved to be useful in arming the gang, providing a range of high-calibre weapons at very low prices.

When Ryan was released from prison, he went straight to work for the Keanes, becoming the most feared enforcer in Limerick. If you owed the Keanes money, Eddie Ryan paid you a visit; if you stepped in any way out of line with the Keanes, Eddie Ryan paid you a visit. Nobody wanted a visit from Eddie Ryan, a man renowned for his willingness to use extreme violence, to the point of murder, in order to solve disputes.

It wasn't long before Ryan began to consider himself undervalued by his criminal partners. By the late 1990s Ryan was growing increasingly frustrated and was beginning to set up his own drugs network. It is, however, an industry that is notoriously reluctant to tolerate competition.

In the midst of these growing tensions, it was a minor disagreement over damage to a car that would bring things into focus. Eddie Ryan's brother John fell out with the Collopy family over claims that one of Jack Collopy's sons had damaged the car of John Ryan's brother-in-law. Collopy denied all knowledge and as a result ended up on a life support machine after John Ryan stabbed him. Collopy survived but had to be re-taught how to walk.

There the dispute would have ended had it not been for the closeness between the Collopys and the Keanes. While Eddie Ryan sided with his brother, the Keanes began increasingly to take the side of Jack Collopy. The Ryans and Keanes were now on a collision course.

In October 2000, just months after defeating Natalie Keane in a fight, Samantha Ryan slashed the face of Christy Keane's sister-in-law with a Stanley knife. It was a step too far and the Keanes decided to take action, firing gunshots through the window of John Ryan's house later that evening. John immediately contacted Eddie who suggested that they go to Christy Keane's home for an explanation. Sensing that the situation might escalate, however, they went armed. As the two Ryan brothers approached the Keane house, their car was fired on by a gunman who had been waiting for them. The Ryans sped away, even managing to fire back a few shots along the way.

The relationship between the Ryans and Keanes was now officially over. All that mattered now was who would be killed first.

That particular race was almost "won" by Christy Keane the following month. On November 10, the Godfather of Limerick crime was sitting in a parked car outside Ignatius Rice College on Shelbourne Avenue waiting for his daughter, when Eddie Ryan walked up to the vehicle and attempted to shoot his former partner at point blank range. Thankfully for Christy Keane, the gun jammed and he managed to speed away, cheating death by the narrowest of margins.

Eddie Ryan travelled to Northern Ireland that weekend but returned home to Limerick two days later to attend the funeral of his brother-in-law. Perhaps it was a sign of the confidence Ryan had built up over a decade as Limerick's most feared hardman that he would return to the city two days after attempting to shoot dead his former partner-in-crime. But now that his relationship with Keane was dead in the water, Eddie Ryan was no longer untouchable. That weekend, he was to pay the ultimate price.

When word came back to the Keanes that their target was back in town, Kieran Keane wasted no time in assembling a hit squad to kill him. It was a hit squad that Keane would lead – he wanted the pleasure of killing Eddie Ryan himself. Keane and his gang burst into the Moose Bar in the centre of Limerick on November 12 and shot Ryan 11 times, also seriously wounding several other drinkers. Eddie Ryan, former enforcer to the Keane family, was dead, struck down in a hail of bullets fired by his former associate.

The feud led to a serious escalation in violence in Limerick, with countless gun attacks and assaults taking place throughout the city over the next two years. Remarkably, however, the feud remained bloodless throughout 2001 and 2002. The Ryans had lost their figurehead. They had to sit back and watch as Kieran Keane – the man they knew had fired the shots that had killed Eddie Ryan – strutted around Limerick, further expanding his criminal empire.

Christy Keane was arrested in August 2001 after being found in possession of €240,000 worth of cannabis. While he maintained a strong influence on the family business from behind bars, the day-to-day running of the gang was left in the hands of Kieran.

That is when the Ryans took deadly revenge. In January 2003 they executed a ruthless and elaborate plot to lure Kieran Keane into a trap.

When Kieran Keane and Owen Treacy pulled up outside the home of Anthony McCarthy they never suspected a double-cross. The two men were there to discuss the kidnapping of Eddie Ryan Junior and his brother Kieran Ryan, both sons of the murdered Eddie Ryan.

With Eddie Ryan Senior out of the way, the kidnap and presumed murder of his two sons was thought to be the final blow against the criminal family. So certain were Gardaí that the two youths had been murdered that they were already searching local woods for their bodies.

It didn't take long after stepping into the house in Fairgreen for Keane and Treacy to realise what had happened. McCarthy, known in criminal circles as "Noddy", pointed a gun at the two men and ordered them to sit down. His accomplice, Desmond Dundon, placed hoods over their heads and taped their hands behind their backs. The two men knew their fate was sealed – it was only a matter of time before they would be driven to a remote location and murdered.

Two more men emerged from the kitchen of the house wearing balaclavas. One of these was David "Frog Eyes" Stanners. The men ordered their prisoners to make a phonecall to two other men, brothers Philip and Kieran Collopy. Just as Keane and Treacy had been lured into a trap, the plan was to also lure the Collopys to their death.

Keane and Treacy refused to make the call. They knew that they would be killed and refused to lure two of their associates to a similar fate. For an hour the two men were "interrogated" by their captors. Like the infamous scene in *Reservoir Dogs*, Kieran Keane almost had his ear sliced off as he sat in the chair, receiving six knife wounds to his left ear.

Eventually, the men were ordered into the boot of a silver Micra parked outside the house. Noddy McCarthy drove the car to another house, where the pair were transferred into a waiting Hiace van. This time Stanners drove, with McCarthy sitting in the passenger seat.

Keane and Treacy knew that this was it. They knew that when the van stopped, they would be taken outside and shot dead. After driving for 35 minutes, the van stopped and David Stanners pulled Kieran Keane to the ground. Stanners took a gun off Christopher "Smokie" Costelloe and shot his victim once in the back of the head.

Treacy heard the gunshot and knew he was next. But as Stanners approached, the gun jammed. Wasting no time, Costelloe lunged at Treacy with a knife, stabbing him in the neck. Stanners took the knife off Costelloe and continued the assault. Treacy was stabbed a total of 17 times in the head and body. As Stanners stabbed him, he told his victim, "This is the last face you are going to see." It was Noddy

McCarthy who called a stop to the attack, telling Stanners that his victim was already dead and that they should hurry up and leave.

The men left the scene at Drombana, confident that they had just pulled off the most spectacular coup in the history of Limerick crime. Since the jailing of his brother Christy, Kieran Keane had been the top dog in the city's notorious underworld. The killing of Keane, together with that of his nephew Owen Treacy, would be a massive strike against the Keane family criminal empire and would pave the way for criminals aligned with the McCarthy-Dundon family to take over the city's lucrative crime scene.

Six hours after the assassination of Kieran Keane, the 'kidnapped' Eddie Ryan Junior and Kieran Ryan presented themselves at Midland Garda Station, completely unscathed. They returned to their home in Killely and proceeded to throw a party in front of the national media. Wearing matching white and red Reebok hoodies, the brothers posed with their mother Mary for the cameras while friends drank beer and celebrated.

But Treacy wasn't dead. Somehow he had survived 17 stab wounds, including one that sliced his throat and several that penetrated his stomach and chest. Unbelievably, Treacy managed to walk to a nearby house and raise the alarm. The McCarthy-Dundon gang had managed to kill the biggest figure in Limerick crime, but their failure to finish off his nephew would cost them dearly.

Desmond Dundon (20), of Hyde Road, David Stanners (31), of Pineview Gardens, James McCarthy (24), of Delmege Park, Christopher Costelloe (20), of Moylish Avenue and Anthony McCarthy (21), of Fairgreen were all arrested and charged with the murder of Kieran Keane, the attempted murder of Owen Treacy and the false imprisonment of both men.

The trial of the five men was one of the most dramatic in the history of the State. It was originally scheduled to take place in Limerick but had to be moved to Dublin after the court failed to empanel a jury. In a relatively small city, it proved impossible to find a jury willing to sit and potentially sentence five hardened criminals to life sentences in jail.

Mr Justice Paul Carney was due to hear the case in Limerick and was later critical of the allegedly over-the-top security put in place during jury selection. In a scripted speech Carney was due to deliver to the Law Students Debating Society of Ireland in February 2004, Carney claimed that security measures put in place had the affect of making potential jurors too nervous to sit during the case. "I am advised by the county registrar that the area around the courthouse was cordoned off. A Garda boat and water unit were on and under the river, a Garda helicopter was in the air, sniffer dogs were on the ground and snipers were on the roof and the jury panel were searched with metal detectors," he wrote. Carney pulled out of the student address after Chief Justice Ronan Keane objected to the contents of his speech, it was later reported.

The case was transferred to Dublin, where a jury was successfully empanelled. From the onset, it was declared a one-witness trial, with the prosecution's entire case resting on Owen Treacy. There were fears that criminals in Limerick would attempt to assassinate Treacy before the case could be heard, and he was placed under constant surveillance, as well as wearing a bullet-proof vest even when inside the courtroom. This remarkable situation was referred to in the speech Carney had been due to deliver to The Law Students Debating Society:

"[The case] was entirely dependent on the evidence of one witness who was being, and still is, perfectly openly threatened with death, who bore body armour in court as evidenced by the dull thud whenever he beat his breast and who was minded in court by two armed guards, wearing radio sets on their faces, as they inferentially told us, to keep in communication with each other within the courtroom if shooting or whatever broke out," wrote Justice Carney in the abandoned speech.

Indeed, the reliance of the State on one witness was reminiscent of another courtroom drama that had preceded the remarkable events of January 29 that saw Kieran Keane executed.

Hours before the two Ryan brothers were "kidnapped," Kieran Ryan had walked free from court in dramatic fashion. The young hood was on trial for the March 2002 stabbing of Liam Keane, son of crime boss Christy. The pair had clashed on the street and Ryan had stabbed his rival in the back. Keane's stabbing was not fatal but it was hugely symbolic of events that would follow – the hatred of two fathers being played out by their sons.

It appeared to be an open-and-shut case against Ryan. When Liam Keane took to the stand in court he identified his attacker as being one Kieran Ryan. However, when asked whether Kieran Ryan was in the courtroom that day, Keane stunned the prosecution by declaring "no". Despite his attacker sitting just feet from him, Keane had refused to identify him. The case collapsed and Ryan walked free. Hours later, he was reported missing. However, unlike Liam Keane, Owen Treacy co-operated fully with Gardaí and agreed to testify as the sole witness to the horrific events of January 29.

At the trial, which began in November 2003, Treacy recounted the events which led to the killing of his uncle and the horrific assault on himself.

Treacy told the jury that the gang had intended to murder himself, his uncle and the two Collopy brothers that night.

"What these men had in their heads was to kill the four of us on January 29," he said. "The four of us were going to be killed. If me or my Uncle Kieran made that call [to the Collopys], there was going to be four killed."

Treacy identified Desmond Dundon has the man who had taped his hands together and identified David Stanners as the man who had pulled the trigger to kill Kieran Keane before launching a savage knife attack against himself. "I witnessed that man shoot my uncle Kieran in the head."

Asked how he could be certain that the man wearing a balaclava was David Stanners, Treacy replied that he identified him by his eyes and his voice. "He's a man I know all my life," he said in a chilling reminder of how close the two gangs had once been.

"Not a scintilla of doubt about it?" counsel asked.

"No doubt whatsoever, My Lord. I could identify David 'Frog Eyes' Stanners."

"Wearing a balaclava?"

"That's right, My Lord."

Counsel asked Treacy how he had managed to untie his own hands from the tape in order to stand up and go to seek help after the attackers had left. His actions were similar to those of Houdini, it was put to him.

"My Lord, if you want to call me Houdini, you can. I was just a bit luckier than Kieran on January 29 – that's the way I put it," he replied.

The 31 day trial was headline news throughout the country and took place amidst security usually reserved only for trials involving paramilitaries. Armed Gardaí from the Emergency Response Unit formed a barrier between the five accused, their supporters and Owen Treacy. Everybody who attended the trial was forced to walk through metal detectors before entering the courtroom, amidst fears that Treacy would be assassinated before being able to take to the stand. There were occasional outbursts from supporters of the five men. On one occasion, as the jury was hearing about the victim, one of the accused shouted: "He sold drugs and killed people. He killed Eddie Ryan."

John Dundon (22), from Mayorstone Court, brother of one of the accused, was arrested and sentenced to four-and-a-half years in the middle of the hearing, for threatening to kill Owen Treacy. During Treacy's eight-day cross-examination, Dundon had approached Donna Treacy, the witness's wife, and told her, "I swear on my baby's life, when this is all over I'm going to kill Owen Treacy."

He wasn't the only one making threats over Treacy. Back in Limerick graffiti began appearing on street corners: "Owen Treacy – dead man walking." The threats did not deter Treacy, however, and his evidence was enough to persuade the jury of seven women and five men to convict all five men.

Justice Paul Carney sentenced all five men to life imprisonment and refused permission to appeal. As they were being led away from the court, Anthony "Noddy" McCarthy issued a chilling warning to the Keane family – "For every action there is a reaction – remember that."

Two out of the four Ryan and Keane brothers were already dead. The third, John Ryan, would follow six months later. Ryan was gunned down in a revenge attack while he laid down a patio at a house in Thomondgate. The shooting left the Ryans without a leader and gave further power to a third gang – the Dundon-McCarthy's – who had aligned themselves with the Ryans but who were now taking over the city's crime scene themselves. With Eddie Ryan, John Ryan and Kieran Keane all now dead, and with Christy Keane behind bars, a vacuum had been created and was being exploited to the full by the Dundon-McCarthy faction.

The killing of John Ryan resulted in some black Limerick humour. Shortly after his vicious killing, a joke went around the city which suggested that there were in fact two great unfinished masterpieces in the art world: Michelangelo's Madonna and John Ryan's patio.

2003 wasn't over yet, however, and there was still time for one more feud victim. On October 20, Michael Campbell-McNamara (23), a hardened criminal aligned with the Keane faction, was abducted and brought to an area close to the Southhill estate. His hands and feet were bound and he was shot in the head. Campbell-McNamara, who had only recently been released from prison, was also stabbed a number of times – his killers did not want to make the same mistake as they had with Owen Treacy.

The killing of Campbell-McNamara led to the Mayor of Limerick, Councillor Dick Sadlier, issuing a plea for the gangs to end the spiral of violence. "It seems to me that this type of barbarity is now becoming almost commonplace and we have to cry halt," said Sadlier. "I want to say to those involved, there are only two eventual outcomes. One is obviously death and the graveyard. The other is a very long prison sentence."

* * * * *

Today, the feud is far from over, although ironically it did much of the Gardaí's work for them. Of the two Keane brothers and two Ryan brothers who originally headed up the gangs, only one – Christy Keane – remains alive. The one remaining gang leader is currently behind bars, along with almost 50 other people with strong associations to the feuding families.

The power vacuum in the city has led to several younger thugs jostling for control of the drugs trade. Several female criminals have also stepped into the breach and assumed control of aspects of the gangs business over recent years.

Indeed, according to local sources, it was the female members of the Keane and Ryan families who caused the heightening of tensions – "some of the men that have been killed would be alive today if it wasn't for the women behind them," said one source.

The Limerick gangs have been weakened through death and incarceration. However, the situation remains highly volatile and has been worsened by the meddling of dissident Republican gangs who have supplied the Limerick gangs with weapons. Dissident Republicans have supplied many guns into the Limerick area using contacts in Eastern Europe. British gangs, mainly based in Liverpool, have also supplied weapons to the area, as have their counterparts in Dublin. Weapons are often supplied as a "thank you" along with major drug shipments.

In 2005, for example, over 30 firearms were recovered, including submachine guns, sawn-off shotguns, pistols and rifles. Whereas the gangs used to use old weapons that had a habit of jamming at crucial moments, they are now heavily armed with high-powered guns.

The activities of the Limerick gangs have also sparked interest from the Criminal Assets Bureau (CAB), who in late 2003 won the right to seize the home of Brian Collopy in the village of Fedmore. Collopy was a close associate of Kieran Keane and the CAB asserted that the then 31-year-old was the beneficiary of proceeds of the illegal drugs trade.

The Bureau has been investigating key gangland figures in the city since mid-2002 but has been frustrated by the suspected concealment and diversion of criminal funds. While the drugs trade in the area is worth millions of euro, senior figures in the city's drugs trade live in modest estates and deliberately show little sign of affluence. According to informed local sources, the gangs are now using the property market to shield their money from the CAB's watchful eye.

The gangs offer interest-free loans of up to €50,000 to local people wishing to purchase homes.

Speaking to the *Sunday Tribune*, Chief Superintendent Felix McKenna, former head of the CAB, said that there are incidents in the city of people on the dole with massive property portfolios, all of which has been gathered using the money of criminal relatives.

Criminals in the city have also moved millions of euro into off-shore accounts, with one gang leader thought to have invested an astonishing €9 million in the financial services industry in Dubai. The huge sums of money involved show the level of drugs distribution in the city and the surrounding counties, all of which are believed to be under the control of crime gangs in Limerick. Indeed it is believed that crime gangs in Limerick, Cork and Dublin control almost the entire drugs scene in Ireland. Several of these gangs – most notably the Keane gang and a drug gang operating in north-west Dublin – are believed to have close links.

Operation Anvil, which was established to track the movements of criminal figures in Dublin, was expanded to cover Limerick. In July 2006 it made one of its most important breakthroughs when an estimated €1 million worth of heroin and cocaine was recovered. More shocking than the quantity of drugs, however, was the sophistication of the weapons recovered during that seizure. Recovered in the July 2006 raid were seven high-powered handguns, which included two machine pistols, six stun guns, 1,000 rounds of ammunition and a number of silencers. When Gardaí displayed the weapons to the media, they were justifiably proud of their policing efforts. However, the message from the criminals was equally clear – over the space of just a handful of years, the Limerick gangs had developed international links that enabled them to get their hands on this lethal weaponry.

The gangs have also been greatly aided by a seemingly

never-ending line of youths willing to carry out the donkey work for the larger criminal bosses, even if such "donkey work" involves murder or serious violence. While the gangs operated for years in a relatively anonymous fashion, their recent celebrity status has led to countless youths in Limerick wishing to emulate them, forgetting that in the drugs business only a tiny percentage of players make it to the top. The vast majority living lives of poverty that are often cut short by death or incarceration.

The younger members of the main families have proven unable to take over the family businesses successfully, however, and power has shifted to a criminal based on the north side of the city who has taken over the gang once led by the Keanes. Tensions between the gangs on the ground are still simmering. In November 2005, 18-year-old Darren Coughlan, a relative of the Keane family, was killed in an incident related to the feud. Coughlan himself was not involved in criminality and had no role in the city's gangland feud. However, he was taunted by members of a criminal gang over his family links to the Keanes and unwisely chose to respond. Three men chased Coughlan and savagely beat him to death.

Coughlan's death was a sign that not only those directly involved in the feud were affected by it. Merely by living in certain areas of Limerick, you were automatically endangered by the dispute. The rising murder rate related to criminality, coupled with the easy access to high-power guns, was affecting the entire culture of the city. Even if gangland deaths were falling, the murder rate was spiraling out of control. Over the course of 2005 there were over 70 shooting incidents in the city, although not all were related to the feud.

Limerick's reputation has caused no end of frustration amongst the city's business and tourism chiefs, who have attempted to counter the stereotype. They point to the hive of economic activity that has transformed the city centre into a modern and extremely pleasant urban centre. However, figures compiled for this book prove beyond any doubt that Limerick is the murder capital of Ireland. In 2000, four people were killed in the city; in 2001, the figure rose to nine; five people were killed the next year; eight people were killed in 2003; 2004 saw four homicides in Limerick; while in 2005 the figure was reduced to a low of two. With 32 killings between January 2000 and December 2005, Limerick has a murder to population ratio of 1:5,478, making it officially the most dangerous county in Ireland. Only Dublin has seen more people killed, although a population over six times the size of Limerick's ensures that Dublin has a lower per capita rate of killing. The gravity of Limerick's problem can be seen by comparing its homicide rate to that of Munster neighbour Cork. Even though Cork has a population almost three times that of Limerick, it recorded ten less killings over the same period.

The county's killing ratio is also well above that of like-sized counties. For example, a person is three times more likely to be killed in Limerick than in Kildare; almost four times more likely than in nearby Galway; and a remarkable 13 times more likely to be killed in Limerick than in Donegal. For all the city's leaders claims that Limerick has been unfairly tarnished with a violent reputation, the facts speak for themselves.

Even more startling than the city's high homicide rate is the level of killing amongst Limerick's youth. Of the 32 homicide victims, 16 – exactly 50% – were under the age of 25. That young people are killed in Limerick in numbers far greater than any other Irish county indicates the culture of violence that exists in many parts of the city.

Five homicide victims were between the ages of 26 and

35, while 11 of those killed were between the ages of 36 and 50. Interestingly, nobody over the age of 50 has been killed in Limerick since the start of the decade.

The murder rate is almost entirely dominated by men, with just three women having been killed in the city between 2000 and 2005 – Jennifer Donnan, who was strangled by her son Damien in 2000; Geraldine Kissane, who was shot dead by Mark Simms, a former boyfriend, in 2001; and Gráinne Dillon, a trainee hotel manager who was shot dead by co-worker Paulo Nascimento during a bungled robbery in January 2002. Just one child was killed in Limerick during that timeframe – four-year-old Katelyn Ryan, who died following an arson attack in April 2003.

A further six young people were shot to death, which highlights how criminal gangs in the city with high-powered weapons have contributed towards the statistics.

In line with the City's nickname of "Stab City," almost half of the young people killed in Limerick died as a result of stab wounds, often inflicted during late-night disputes. The many arguments that lead to fatal stabbings in Limerick is a telling indication of the pathetic price placed on human life in certain quarters of the city. It also indicates the willingness of a generation of youths to resort to extreme violence in order to solve minor disputes. Knives are increasingly being used in Limerick to solve arguments, and their use is not limited to men in their late teens and early 20s. Seven people between the ages of 26 and 50 have been stabbed to death in Limerick during the last six years. This compares with six victims of fatal gun attacks, two victims of assault and one – Jennifer Donnan – who died as a result of strangulation.

Forty-two-year-old Patrick Crawford died after he was stabbed 13 times in a savage assault by two men, Stuart Maloney, from Moyross, and Patrick Desmond, from St

Mary's Park. The attack was a brutal example of the cowardly nature of many fatal knife attacks – two armed men accosting and killing an unarmed man.

Crawford's son, Ger Crawford, had exchanged words with Desmond and his nephew Stuart Maloney, earlier in the day of June 2, 2002. Later that evening, the two men arrived outside the Crawford home in the Moyross area of the city, a district where assault, stabbings and shootings have become an almost nightly occurrence. Patrick Crawford, who had been drinking earlier in the evening, went outside to confront the men. He would not have known that the men were both armed, nor could he have imagined their willingness to use their weapons to such devastating effect.

One of the weapons carried by the men on that fateful night was a makeshift hedge trimmer – a four foot pole with a steel spike attached. The men also carried a knife. When Crawford confronted them, they set about using these weapons with brutal force, stabbing the father-of-two 13 times. The wound that killed Patrick Crawford was a stab wound to the right side of the chest, which punctured the right lung and caused extensive bleeding. This wound obstructed his breathing, causing him to collapse to the ground, while the assault continued.

Maloney later admitted to his aunt that he had been involved in "giving the man a beating". The entire attack was captured on the CCTV cameras which had been installed into the area in an attempt to combat serious crime. Desmond and Maloney were both found guilty of the murder of Patrick Crawford and sentenced to life imprisonment.

Disputes which lead to fatal knife assaults are often over the most trivial matters. On February 21, 2004, Charlie Craig was stabbed to death by a neighbour for refusing to drive to a local fast food restaurant. The 39-year-old father-of-four was stabbed five times. His attacker used such force that the knife broke inside Craig's body. The jury in the trial against 17-year-old David McInerney, charged with Craig's murder, would be shown horrific photographs of the broken knife protruding from the dead body of Charlie Craig.

In the early hours of February 21, McInerney asked Craig to drive him down to the local fast food restaurant to get some food. Craig refused and a furious row erupted. McInerney's mother attempted to resolve the situation by locking her son into the family home. However, McInerney was seething with his neighbour and made his way to the kitchen, where he picked up a knife. He then escaped out of the house through a bedroom window.

He caught up with Craig, produced the knife and proceeded to stab the man five times. Charlie Craig collapsed to the ground, bleeding profusely, and died. McInerney stood over the body clutching the broken handle of a knife, the blade of which remained inside his victim's body.

Craig's murder came just ten days after his sister, 34-year-old Sarah Craig, had received a four-year jail sentence for the manslaughter of 21-year-old Brian Hanley, who was killed after being stabbed following a dispute outside a pub in the city. Hanley, who was on bail at the time in connection with a massive seizure of ecstasy tablets in the city, was stabbed to death after being chased by a group of up to 12 people after he left the pub.

At the trial of David McInerney for the murder of Charlie Craig, defending counsel Brendan Nix said his client "wants the court and the Craig family to know how much he regrets the great wrong he did and the great suffering that he has caused...David McInerney doesn't know what came over him that night. He thinks about Charlie Craig every day and he wishes he could turn the clock back".

Anne Doyle, a sister of the victim, said that the family was "still very sad and lonely after suffering our great loss".

McInerney was found guilty of murder after a jury delivered a majority 10-2 verdict. He was sentenced to life imprisonment.

* * * * *

Much of the violence in Limerick is restricted to a small number of housing estates, with up to ten of the 32 killings which took place between 2000 and 2005 traceable in someway back to the St Mary's Park and Moyross areas. In fact, the concentration of violence into a relatively small area has led to the bizarre situation whereby the majority of Limerick's population follows newspaper reports of murders and killings almost as though they were referring to a separate city. There are huge areas of the city where the armed Garda patrols and nightly drive-by shootings are totally alien.

Local politicians have claimed that the continued deprivation of certain areas of the city led to the fostering of criminality and violence in those communities. Councillor John Gilligan claims that the Garda force in troublesome areas has continually been scaled back, even as the situation in those estates has deteriorated. Gilligan claims that Gardaí were taken away from trouble spots and relocated to other, less crime ravaged areas of the city. According to Gilligan, "they [the Gardaí] basically fucked off."

Despite these claims, local Gardaí have been successful in apprehending local criminals and have seized many weapons and explosives destined for use amongst the city's underclass.

Regardless of their success against the criminal gangs, however, Limerick city remains awash with criminality, and is the centre of drugs distribution on the west coast of Ireland. Even though constant feuding and personal disputes have weakened criminal gangs in the city, recent years have shown that there is always a constant supply of young hoods willing to fill the vacuum left by the death or incarceration of their elders. Furthermore, the total disregard for law and for the people of the City shown by the criminal gangs, has led to a culture of violence amongst Limerick's young generation, particularly on a handful of housing estates.

Local business and tourism chiefs may have fought the city's tag of "Stab City" for years, but the facts clearly show that Limerick remains the most dangerous city in Ireland.

Five

Strangers in a Strange Land

The evening of July 20, 2001 was warm and sunny. Children all across Dublin that day were enjoying the outdoor freedom of their summer holidays. It was no different for one group of local kids playing near Binn's Bridge on the Royal Canal that evening. Some were emulating their heroes on the Dublin Gaelic football team, others Premiership heroes, until a simple distraction brought them away from their game. One of the children spotted an unusual object floating on the surface of the canal.

It seemed to be some sort of case. Whatever its contents, the odd container was almost bursting at the seams. The children's attention was transfixed by the idea of the potential treasure that lay inside the mysterious floating box. They pulled the tightly packed container over to the edge of the canal, before using a sharp-ended stick to squeeze open the lid. Their eyes were suddenly met with a horrifying sight. Crammed into the case was a discoloured, bloated and battered human corpse.

The 'Body in the Suitcase' murder perplexed Gardaí from the start. The male corpse was so badly mangled and damaged that it was impossible to tell at first sight how the man in the case had met his death. Binn's Bridge was sealed off and the grotesque remains were removed to the City Morgue in Marino where a post-mortem was carried out. A subsequent autopsy carried out by the then State Pathologist,

Professor John Harbison, showed that the cause of death was a fracture to the skull and laceration of the brain from a blow to the left side of the head.

But while Gardaí now knew how the dead man met his death, they had not got a single clue about his identity. The victim's facial features had suffered extensive damage as a result of a severe beating and corrosion caused by unnatural swelling, after spending several days in the water. At best, detectives could tell that the dead man was of foreign origin.

After checking numerous databases of missing persons, Gardaí found no match for the body they had taken from the canal. It was then that Gardaí took an unprecedented step in a bid to establish the murdered man's identity. If his killer, or killers, were foreign then it was possible that they might try to flee the country once it became public that the body had been recovered from its watery grave. Knowing that speed was imperative, the Garda Public Relations Office (GPRO) forwarded photographs of the dead man's facial image to national newspapers for publication. It was a brave step, and it yielded just what was hoped for.

The victim was identified as Adrian Bestea, a 21-year-old Romanian asylum-seeker who had been living in Dublin City. Garda detectives from the National Bureau of Criminal Investigations (NBCI) quickly compiled the patchwork of connections in the dead man's life in Ireland. It didn't take long for detectives to learn that Adrian Bestea had a girlfriend, Marina Sourovtzeva. And it emerged that she, too, was missing.

The couple had come to Ireland for completely different reasons. Marina wanted to learn English fluently in the hope that she could work as an interpreter in her native Russia. Adrian wanted to find work in Ireland so he could make money and perhaps someday return to his homeland with sufficient funds to start a small business and buy a house. Both had come to Ireland with hopes that they could find work in Dublin's booming black economy. The pair first met at a hostel on Dublin's Charlemont Street in October 1999, having been placed there by the Department of Justice when they had separately applied for asylum. Marina was the mother of a young daughter from a previous relationship. Her child had remained in the loving care of her family in Russia while Marina sought to find a better future in Ireland. Adrian Bestea was single and carefree. He was just a 19-year-old youth when he and Marina became lovers. She was ten years older than her new boyfriend. After leaving the hostel in mid-2000, they applied individually for rent allowance while their separate applications for asylum were being processed and later they both rented private accommodation in the centre of Dublin City so they could be close to each other..Marina and Adrian's relationship had started off well. She was deeply affectionate and believed that he loved her. But Adrian Bestea's mood was prone to dramatic shifts. His temperament could waver between delightfully charming and irrationally jealous. When he became agitated, he could be possessive and violent. And his violence was directed against his girlfriend. Over a 12-month period he beat Marina regularly, sometimes hitting her so hard that she had barely the strength to stand.

After less than two years as lovers, Marina desperately wanted to end her relationship with Bestea but she feared what the young Romanian man might do if she reported him to the Gardaí. She also had a deep-rooted suspicion of officialdom, fearing that if she went to the Irish authorities, it might have an adverse effect on her application for asylum in Ireland.

It was after one violent beating, on July 8, 2001, at Marina's flat on Strand Road, Sandymount, that she decided that she could take no more. She ran from her house in fear.

Less than an hour later, weeping and inconsolable, Marina met two female Russian friends in Synnott's pub on South King's Street. That meeting would prove a bloody watershed in her life.

Marina's female friends advised her that they knew of some 'Russian' men who could protect her from her vicious boyfriend, but that it would cost her. She arranged to meet three men, who were known to her female friends, later that day on O'Connell Street. She had never met them before. Together, Marina and the men got a taxi back to the flat. Marina would later insist that she told the men that she just wanted Bestea evicted and gone from her life. However, she had no doubt that her one-time lover would be severely beaten as part of the arrangement. She quietly brought the men into her small flat. There, they found their target. Marina was soon to have her wish of having her violent boyfriend out of her life, but things did not go the way she had wanted. The men began immediately to beat Adrian Bestea, who was startled at the unexpected arrival of the big, burly trio. The men threw Adrian Bestea on top of Marina's bed and punched and assaulted him for 15 minutes before they dragged him across the floor and put him sitting in an armchair. Marina's former boyfriend sat almost completely limp in the seat. He had already been battered so much that he did not have the energy to raise his arms in defence. The men beat him continuously for four more hours. They took the occasional break to drink vodka as the dark evening turned to night-time.

As the night gave way to the early hours of the following morning, a discussion started up between the three men about what they should do with their victim, after they had finished beating him up. One of the men suggested that they should kill the badly injured and bleeding Romanian. Feeling the situation growing more desperate and out of her control, Marina shouted 'No'. She tried to call a taxi, hoping Bestea could be taken to the safety of a friend's home. But the men had taken command of the brutal proceedings. The bed sheets, walls and furniture of her tiny home were now covered with splatters of Bestea's blood. His face was swollen and growing discoloured from the constant punches to his head. His eyes were almost hidden by the swelling around the sockets. During a brief break in the savage attack, one of the men asked Marina to go out to a nearby shop and buy him some cigarettes. When she returned to the flat one man was holding a wheel brace in his hand. Adrian Bestea lay dead on the floor. Marina found herself the unwitting accomplice to a brutal killing. She lay awake that night certain that she would spend the rest of her life in prison.

She had just two choices, she believed: go to the Gardaí and confess everything; or try and obliterate all traces of her ex-lover's murder. The following morning, Marina bought a suitcase. Adrian Bestea's corpse was stuffed inside. Once the container was packed and tightly closed, she and two of the men carried the grim cargo on a bus to Drumcondra. They dumped it off Binn's Bridge and into the murky depths of the Royal Canal.

The planned disposal of the bloody remains was as ill-judged as had been the attack. The suitcase swelled with pockets of air that brought it back to the surface of the water, until, just over a week later, the body was discovered.

When Marina learned that the unidentified remains of a murdered man had been discovered in the Royal Canal, she knew her days of freedom were numbered. It was just a matter of time before police would find out the victim's name. Once they discovered that, she was certain that they would learn that she had suffered violently at the dead man's hands. She alone had the strongest motive for causing Adrian Bestea harm. She was convinced that it could only be a matter of time before detectives discovered that she had hired a group of men to exact retribution on her violent partner.

Over the following days, Marina scrubbed the walls of her flat until her fingers were sore. But so much of Bestea's blood had been spilled it was likely that Garda forensic experts would have little difficulty in finding the clues to reveal the crime scene. Marina fled to Britain. But after forwarding her details to the London Metropolitan Police, Gardaí tracked the frightened woman down to a flat in Kensington two months later.

Marina had enough of running. She gave detectives a detailed statement of how Bestea had met his bloody death. She pleaded guilty at Dublin District Court to false imprisonment and assault causing harm to Bestea. The revelations that she, too, had been a victim of violence was enough to make an already fascinated public enthralled with the tragic case. But Adrian Bestea's mother had a starkly different image of her dead son than the one of an abusive young thug who regularly beat up his partner whenever the mood came upon him.

She travelled to Ireland to help the Gardaí to encourage people to come forward with information during the initial stages of the intense murder investigation. The middle-aged Romanian woman said the killing had sapped her will to live. "I have taken drugs – sedatives…you could cut me and I wouldn't feel it. I still don't believe it is my child. He was my only child and now I have no motivation for life, no motivation to keep living."

She said her son had lived happily in Ireland since 1999. "He was satisfied there. He phoned home twice a week," she said. His last phone call to his mother was on July 3, 2001, just over a week before his body was found. "He was happy and had no problems. He told me he was going to get married to his Russian girlfriend," Marianna Moraru told reporters. The dead man's mother said she had no feelings toward her son's killer. "I do not hate them. I am not the one who has to judge them. God will judge them," she said.

Moraru said that her son had been fascinated with Ireland since he was in his teens. The young man had obtained a Schengen visa, which legally entitled him to live and work in a number of continental European countries. However, he chose to go to Ireland where the visa was not valid. At the time of his death he had been appealing against a Department-of-Justice decision not to grant him refugee status.

"In Timisoara [his home region in Romania] he had everything he wanted – an apartment, a car – but he wanted to fulfill himself, so he travelled to Ireland," his mother explained. She said that her son was a popular young man among his friends and acquaintances in his homeland but he wanted to travel and see new parts of the world like many of his peers. "All his friends had the same idea to emigrate," his mother said.

Judge Yvonne Murphy accepted that Marina Sourovtzeva had never intended to see her former lover beaten to death. "The accused felt powerless to stop the situation getting out of control and I am fully satisfied it was never her intention to have Mr Bestea killed," the Judge said in court. Sourovtzeva received a three-year sentence for falsely imprisoning and assaulting her former lover.

At her trial, Gardaí said that the man who had struck Bestea fatally with the wheel brace had fled the jurisdiction. Their intelligence had led them to believe that the chief suspect had crossed the border into an Eastern European country three days after the killing. Two of the three men who had come to the flat to administer the beating, Ukranian nationals Igore Derjhack (30) and Dmytro Semenyuk (24), were apprehended by Gardaí and were convicted of falsely imprisoning and assaulting the Romanian man.

The brutality of Adrian Bestea's death shocked the Irish public from the moment that Gardaí splashed his bloated image on the front of national newspapers. But Bestea is just a small statistic in a disturbing new trend in Irish homicides. An analysis of all murders and manslaughters of foreign nationals in Ireland since 2000 shows that the most common category of victims is men of Central or Eastern-European origin, who are fatally stabbed or beaten to death. And among the violent deaths, one country stands out above all. In what may be a conservative estimate, more than 30 Lithuanian nationals living in Ireland have been victims of near-fatal knife attacks in violent rows, from 2004 to the end of 2005 alone.

On May 11, 2003, 25-year-old Valerij Makarov and his wife returned to their rented Lucan home after a trip to Dublin Zoo with their two young children. When the Lithuanian family got home, they saw that a cement block had been smashed through the windscreen of their car.

Earlier that day, Valerij's mobile phone had rung several times. When he answered the first call, another Lithuanian man demanded money that he claimed was owed to him. The tone of the call worried Valerij, who decided not to answer the subsequent calls to his mobile. The other man had threatened him on the phone and, as the calls from the same number kept ringing, Valerij believed that his family was in danger.

Valerij had been paid €500 by a fellow Lithuanian national, whom he did not know too well, some weeks earlier. The money was in payment for 'selling' his former job to the other man, as is the custom among sections of the Lithuanian immigrant community when working abroad. The job that Valerij had sold to the other man was a labouring job on a construction site. But the man who paid Valerij the

€500 was not happy with the terms of the deal. He didn't like the job and now he wanted Valerij to pay €50 back. Valerij did not want to pay any of the money back but he believed that the man might send some friends to his family's Dublin home to collect the money. That evening, at around 6 pm, on the suggestion of her husband, Valerij's wife went out in a desperate search to find somewhere else for the couple and their children to stay that night. Valerij stayed in the house with their three young children, the youngest just an infant. Valerij's sister-in-law was also in the house.

At 10 pm, Valerij was sitting in the kitchen when a loud bang erupted from the front hallway. His sister-in-law stepped into the hall to find a man whom she had never seen before rushing past her.

Valerij grabbed a knife as the man, 30-year-old fellow-national Tomas Lukosevicius, charged towards him. A struggle followed, in which the kitchen floor became covered in blood. Valerij Makarov's sister-in-law screamed for help.

Injured and bleeding from the wounds that Valerij had inflicted on him, Lukosevicius retreated. Outside the house were two other Lithuanian men who had travelled to Lucan with their friend that evening. Seeing the fight erupt, the two other men entered the Makarov house.

Valerij Makarov swung the knife widely, roaring at the three men to get out of his house. Blood splashed on the hallway walls. Valerij chased the men as they ran out the front door and onto the street. Valerij slashed one of the trio, Aldevinias Gudavicius, across the stomach. Meanwhile, Tomas Lukosevicius collapsed and died from his wounds. In the subsequent post-mortem, the State Pathologist, Professor Marie Cassidy, identified nine knife wounds on Lukosevicius's body.

Dr Cassidy's expert analysis indicated the bloody nature

of the struggle. "Although there were nine stab wounds in total, five had caused severe damage to the internal organs," Dr Cassidy said. The pathologist said the victim had received four stab wounds to the chest, three to his arms and two to his legs. The most severe stab wound had gone "in through the ribcage, across the lung and in and out of the heart," and that this wound measured 9.5 centimetres in depth. Three ribs had been cut across, the liver and heart had been stabbed, both lungs had collapsed and that the chest cavities had two litres, or five pints, of blood in blood clots, which was a "substantial loss of blood".

"The cause of death was due to blood loss and damage to internal organs as a result of these stab wounds," Dr Cassidy told the court.

The severity of the injuries indicated that Mr Lukosevicius had collapsed "fairly quickly," she concluded in her report. "Given that there were several stab wounds to the lungs and one to the heart, I would expect that within minutes there would be no chance of him surviving." Judging from the depth of the wounds in the arms, Dr Cassidy said these "were not typical defence injuries, they just seem to be stab wounds caused to that part of the body in a struggle".

At Makarov's trial in December 2004, the court was told that the fatal row had been over a disputed sum of just €50. Presiding Judge Barry White said the jury had concluded that Makarov was acting in self-defence. However, "sight cannot be lost" that the force used was, "disproportionate and excessive vis à vis the threat offered by the deceased." Judge White said he also had to take into consideration when sentencing, Makarov's family circumstances. "I must have regard to your previous good character and that you are obviously a devoted and dedicated family man," said the Judge. Nonetheless, the Judge said he did not want this sentence to create a precedence of "going soft" on fatal stabbings. Valerij Makarov was sentenced to ten years, with eight years suspended. He had been found not guilty of murder but guilty of manslaughter, in relation to the killing of Lukosevicius. The dead man had been in Ireland for less than one year. Both he, and the man who had killed him, had come to Ireland to find gainful work and financial independence, away from their unemployment-ridden homeland.

Tomas Lukosevicius's death is far from unique in terms of 21st century Irish homicide, particularly in the Lithuanian community. The startling statistics speak for themselves. Lithuanian adult males are more than twice as likely to be violently killed while living and working in Ireland as they are to be murdered in their homeland. The annual murder rate in Lithuania, per capita, is 1.13 per 10,000 people. Among the Lithuanian community in Ireland, that rate has reached double that figure – over 2.5 per 10,000. Gardaí who spoke to the authors in relation to this violence have identified a near-consistent and growing trend. Many of the knife attacks occur after a drink-fuelled day, or days, spent in a residential house in the company of 'friends'. A row erupts and an assault occurs. The victims are almost always young males who have poor English language skills and who have consumed an excessive amount of alcohol.

Amazingly, four times more Lithuanians have been violently killed in Ireland over the three years from 2003 to 2005, than citizens from any other foreign country of origin.

Looking at the homicides of foreign nationals in Ireland over the six years from the start of 2000, people from 21 separate non-Irish countries were victims of murder or manslaughter. In total, 34 foreign nationals were victims of homicide in Ireland from 2000 to the end of 2005. Remarkably, this accounts for 10% of all homicide victims in the State over that period.

In fact, Lithuanian victims, all of whom have been male, account for half of all foreign nationals killed in the State over the two years of 2004 and 2005. And there is little sign that that trend is in decline. There is a remarkable consistency to the manner in which many of these young Lithuanian men met their deaths. Thirty-six-year-old Grazudas Strelciunas was found beaten to death in a ditch near Dunboyne, Co. Meath, on June 20, 2004. He had been beaten and kicked to death in his Clonsilla home and dumped at the entrance to a field on the Dunboyne-to-Confey road. His injuries were so severe that identification proved difficult at first. He had been in Ireland for only a few weeks prior to his killing.

Some months later, Lithuanian national Andrius Zakarauska was stabbed to death at St Joseph's Villas on Dublin's northside, shortly after midnight on November 20, 2004. A 22-year-old compatriot was later arrested in Mullingar in relation to the incident.

In 2005, four further Lithuanian men were violently killed. Twenty-one-year-old Mindaugas Janavicius staggered through the streets of Clones in Co. Monaghan on a sunny Sunday morning in the last week of July 2005. His stomach was covered in bloody wounds. He stumbled and fell as he tried to rush past alarmed Mass-goers at the local Saint Tiernach's Church at 9 am, before collapsing and dying.

Detectives from the National Bureau of Criminal Investigation (NBCI) focussed their attention on the guests at an all-night house party in Clones that Janavicius had attended the previous evening with other Lithuanian nationals. Gardaí had been called to the party following complaints from neighbours. A number of men at the party had consumed a lot of alcohol. Around 7 am, a row broke out and Janavicius fled in an Audi car. A group of foreign men followed in two cars. His car was intercepted and he was dragged from the vehicle. A knife was plunged deep into his chest.

Gardaí have expressed concern that the rising murder rates among Lithuanian men may represent a broader problem. Young males from poorer regions of Eastern Europe and former Soviet States are travelling to Ireland to work but end up failing to integrate. Many of the young men have poor English language competency and their only outlet for social interaction is through excessive alcohol consumption with other young males from their homeland. Anecdotal evidence indicates that the level of alcohol consumed often leads to violence and knife play. Indeed, 44% of all foreign nationals killed in Ireland since the start of the decade are from Central/Eastern Europe or former Soviet States, which include Georgia, Moldova, Croatia and Slovakia. All except one of these victims was killed from 2003 onwards, perhaps in parallel with the increased number of Eastern European workers coming into the booming construction sector.

Whether the surge in numbers of Eastern European men killed since 2003 will continue, only time will tell. It appeared in the early years of the new Millennium that Ireland was also facing an insurmountable surge in the number of young Chinese citizens violently killed. However, the number of Chinese nationals slain here peaked in 2002 and has, in fact, declined since that year.

Department of Justice documents obtained by the authors go some way to explain why. According to a confidential briefing document prepared by the Department of Justice's Nationality and Immigration service (INIS), dated May 2006, thousands of Chinese students entered the State in the early 2000s using high-quality illicit documents and fraudulent bank records. These students came from two, predominantly rural, Chinese provinces in particular, which the Department identified as "high risk" for illegal immigration.

The document cited "endemic" fraud and corruption by many Chinese students and visa agents in procuring student visas to get into Ireland. In addition, Chinese criminals who were manipulating the visa system saw Ireland as a "soft touch", the INIS document stated. Irish officials also noted that a significant number of the Chinese students coming here over the period did not fit the profile of persons seeking to learn English as a professional tool, being several years older than secondary-school-leaving age and not being third-level college students or graduates. A significant number of Chinese people arriving in Ireland under the terms of student visas at the time were seeking to simply work here. Their plan was to repatriate money back to their homeland by working in the black economy.

From mid-2002 onwards, the Department sent special agents to Beijing to study all documentation and records submitted at source. Under the conditions of the visa application system, prospective Chinese students had to submit a bank certificate to show that they had sufficient savings to live in Ireland without having to work full-time. But the agents found that the use of falsified financial records was widespread. Over the following 48 months, the Department's scrutiny of all applications significantly reduced the number of students coming to Ireland using illegally acquired papers.

The State was eager to ensure that genuine Chinese students who travel to study in Ireland would have the financial security to allow them to survive without being sucked into working in the black economy. These apparently simple measures dramatically altered the profile of young Chinese citizens coming to Ireland from 2003 onwards. In comparison to the large number of Chinese traveling here in the early years of the decade, from impoverished and crime-ridden areas of their homeland, the typical Chinese student now studying in Ireland is increasingly middle-class, financially viable and well-educated – a category that typically sees less exposure to violent crime.

However, if the disproportionately high number of Chinese nationals killed in the six years since 2000 stands out, then so, too, does the brutality of some of these cases. When Gardaí were called to investigate the remains of two people found dead after a fire at an apartment at Blackhall Square off Dublin's North King Street, in the third week of March 2001, they uncovered a macabre crime. It seemed at first that the two young Chinese students had become tragically caught up in a residential fire, but in fact, this was a double murder scene. The two teenagers, Liu Quing and her 19-year-old boyfriend Feng Yue, had been murdered. Their bodies had then been burned to conceal the killing that had taken place. A team of 40 Garda detectives from local and specialist units was assigned to trace everyone and anyone who knew or had contact with the couple. That seemed a difficult proposition, as Gardaí had to try to obtain information from a community, some of who may have overstayed their visas and would be naturally reluctant to come under the spotlight of the police.

Gardaí were perplexed at first as to why anyone would target the teens. The young couple's Chinese friends gave heartfelt testimonies that the two were model young people. Both had come to Ireland to learn English. Both worked hard to support their studies in Dublin. Feng Yue was a student at the Centre for English Studies in Dame Street. He also worked part-time at a southside pub. His 19-year-old girlfriend was also a student and worked in a Chinese restaurant in Malahide. What was clear from the start was that the killer, or killers, went to painstaking efforts to destroy the crime scene. The couple had been found in their bedroom, but they had clearly been carried there in a bid to give the impression that the fire had caught them unawares as they slept. The perpetrator also clearly hoped that vital forensic evidence would be destroyed in the flames.

As is common among Chinese families, neither Feng Yue nor his girlfriend had any brothers or sisters. In one brutal act, their killer had wiped out a generation of two separate families.

The pain and anguish suffered was apparent in an interview given by Liu Quing's mother to the then Asia Correspondent for the *Irish Times*, Miriam Donoghue, six months after the murders. Song Xiumei told how her daughter arrived in Ireland to take up a place at the Swan Training Centre in Grafton Street in March 2000. Her boyfriend followed her two months later and enrolled in the Centre for English Studies on Dame Street. They loved Dublin and were happy, the girl's mother said. Both Liu Quing and Feng Yue had excelled at their studies. They had never once given their families any cause to worry. The teenage girl's father had died of a heart attack when she was just three years old. Her mother, a tax official, reared the girl single-handedly. "She was my whole life. We were very happy," the distraught woman said. Mother and daughter had lived in Jiamusi City in Heilongjiang Province in north-east China, until Liu Quing had moved to the larger city of Shenyang to attend senior middle school. There she had lived with her aunt and uncle who were like parents to the girl. "She was bright and intelligent and everyone loved her. She was very popular and had lots of friends," her uncle said

It was at this school that Liu Quing met Feng Yue, the son of divorced parents who lived with his mother in Shenyang. His father was the president of a petroleum company. The family was wealthy, even by Western standards. The teenage couple planned to go to Europe to improve their grasp of the English language before they started their university degrees in China. Quing was interested in doing law; Yue was undecided about what he wanted to do with his life after school.

Quing organised her English language training in Ireland through the Heng Ge Lai agency. The fee to the agency to look after the complicated procedure from start to finish, including getting the student visa, was £800.The college fee was £2,000 and had to be paid up front. Bank statements had to be produced proving there was enough money to sustain Quing in Dublin, a pre-requisite insisted upon by Irish immigration authorities. The girl's mother emptied her life savings. She borrowed money from several family members to raise $15,000 for her daughter.

For Yue, the prospect of travelling to Ireland and seeing somewhere new and foreign was an adventure. His family had none of the financial burdens that were shouldered by Quing's mother. Feng Yue was able to produce a bank statement with $30,000 to prove he had the means to sustain himself in Ireland and to pay fees. But it was the young man's easy access to money that would ultimately attract the attention of a calculating and vicious killer.

Feng Yue left for Ireland in February 2000. But a few months later, in June 2000, he returned to China to visit his sick grandmother. During that visit to his homeland, his father gave him another $30,000. When the son returned to China for a second visit in late January 2001, he told his father that he still had $5,000 of the $30,000 left in his bank account.

But 27-year-old Yu Jie, a fellow national who knew the young couple socially, believed that if Feng's wealthy father had given him $30,000 after his first trip home in 2000, then he would be returning once again with lots of money in early 2001. Yu Jie was first questioned by investigating detectives as one of the few people from the Chinese student community who knew both the victims. In fact, he formally identified the bodies of the dead couple and gave a lengthy witness statement, over four days, at the Bridewell Garda station. But, when detectives asked when he had last seen them, he made no reference to having called on his friends in the days leading up to the fire.

Yu Jie was not aware that a roommate at his Finglas home had identified him from CCTV images taken at the couple's apartment block. These images showed him entering and leaving the apartment building at different times between 2 pm on March 12, during the following day, and up to 12.56 am on March 14. Jie was now the chief suspect in the couple's murder. He was arrested and questioned in the presence of a third Assistant Commissioner of the Chinese police, Zijhin Zou, who had been drafted in to assist Gardaí as a translator.

Under questioning by Garda detectives, Yu Jie quickly changed his version of events. He admitted that it was him on the CCTV footage and also on more security footage taken at the USIT office on Aston Quay at around noon on March 13. But he claimed he had returned to the apartment at 12.56 am on March 14 because he was worried about his friends. A fire explosion had occurred when he got to the front door of the apartment block on March 14 and he had run away in fear. Yu Jie's appearance on the USIT footage, wearing the same clothes as in the Blackhall Square footage, however, contradicted his movements at crucial times when he claimed he was elsewhere. Gardaí carefully dissected his initial statements and his newly revised version of events. His comments were exposed as a fabrication. The CCTV footage put him at the scene at all the crucial times, and Yu Jie was charged with two counts of murder.

The prosecution case was that Yu Jie acted alone and that he was motivated by robbery. Lawyers for the State argued that he was aware that the last time Feng Yue had gone to

China in June 2000, he had returned with some $30,000 in cash. Yu Jie believed Feng would have a similar amount on his return from China just weeks before the murder.

At his trial in the Central Criminal Court, Jie pleaded not guilty to the charge of having murdered his two friends. Mystery still remains over how he overcame the physically superior 19-year-old Feng Yue. The then Deputy State Pathologist Professor Marie Cassidy told the court that, in her expert opinion, the diminutive killer had probably strangled six-feet-tall Feng Yue from behind, while the young victim was seated on the living-room settee. There were marks on both of Yue's wrists that suggested he had been restrained with force. A piece of pink cotton cord produced in evidence could have been the ligature used, she told the trial. Dr Cassidy said the couple had been dead at least 20 hours before the discovery of their bodies by fire officers, shortly after 1 am, on March 14. Forensic examiners found partially evaporated petrol on the remains of the couple.

Yu Jie strangled Feng on the afternoon of March 12, the prosecution insisted, then left the apartment before returning later to wait for Feng's girlfriend. When she came home, he strangled her too. He then dragged the bodies to the couple's bedroom and laid them on a double bed. He returned the next day and again in the early hours of March 14, when he doused their bodies with petrol and set fire to them. He then cycled to the house he rented in Finglas. One of his roommates would later tell the court that on returning home to the Finglas home, Yu Jie seemed "the same as usual".

It had been a brutal death for the happy young couple. Both had come to Ireland with great hopes for the future. On Quing's bedroom in her uncle's apartment in Shenyang, she had kept an atlas on the wall. "She wanted to see the world and we bought her this map," he told *The Irish Times* in an interview prior to the trial. "As big as the world is, she wanted to go to Ireland to learn English. She heard so many nice things about your country."

On April 13, 2004, a jury convicted Yu Jie of the double murder, for which he would later receive two life sentences. After the verdict Yu Jie remained impassive. He showed no sign of remorse.

Of the 34 foreign nationals killed violently in the last six years, less than one quarter of the victims were women.

Twenty-five-year-old Paiche was the privileged daughter of the Malawian Chief Justice, Leonard Unyolo, the highest-ranking legal officer in the African State. The attractive young woman had left college in London where she was studying business administration and moved to Ireland after becoming involved with Nigerian businessman, Chika Onyemaechi. He was six years her senior, and her family did not approve of the match. But Paiche loved him and the couple decided to make a fresh beginning in Ireland, where friends of Chika's from his homeland had settled.

The couple got married at Waterford registry office just over one year after coming to Ireland in 2001. Paiche and Chika planned to raise a family and to build a prosperous life for themselves. As Paiche gave birth to their first child, Anthony, a few months after arriving in Waterford, the couple were eligible to remain in Ireland as parents of an Irish-born baby. Paiche Onyemaechi had much to look forward to.

But soon, Paiche's marriage began to flounder. She and her husband began to grow apart amid claims of domestic violence. Paiche complained to Gardaí that she was a victim of physical abuse at the hands of her husband. Paiche and Chika became estranged and she found a new partner, an African man who lived in Dublin.

It was four years after her arrival in Ireland, that Paiche was found brutally murdered. So grotesque was the nature of her killing that her head had been severed from her body and her remains were wrapped in plastic bin bags. Paiche Onyemaechi's corpse was dumped at the edge of the River Pil near Piltown, Co. Kilkenny, later to be discovered by two local women out for an evening stroll.

Gardaí investigating the murder are convinced that crucial information in relation to Paiche Onyemaechi's death may lie in her personal relationships. Soon after her murder detectives learned that there was considerable conflict among a small number of men because of Paiche's estrangement from her husband. Gardaí have reason to suspect that Chika Onyemaechi was attacked by a man, or men, who were connected to the dead woman's new partner. However, there is nothing to suggest that Paiche's new boyfriend was in any way directly connected to these events.

The Garda investigation into the young woman's murder examined the possibility that this attack may have sparked off a series of events that resulted in the vicious killing of the woman. They have not discounted the possibility that the killing was carried out by more than one person. However, despite the involvement of a large team of detectives from several Garda units, including the National Bureau of Criminal Investigation, the Garda National Immigration Unit and officers from the local area in Kilkenny and Waterford, Gardaí have been hampered in their work by the lack of physical evidence available from either the scene where the body was found or the body itself, due to the state of decomposition of the remains.

Within days of the woman's body being discovered dumped at the side of the river, investigating Garda officers moved the focus of the investigation to Waterford. The dead woman had lived there, with decreasing frequency, with her husband and two children. Her two boys were aged just three-and-a-half and 18 months at the time that their mother's life was taken away.

For operational reasons that apply in a sensitive investigation, Gardaí have not to date released the details of forensic tests carried out on the couple's house at St Herblain Park, in Waterford City.

In a bizarre step which suggests the grotesque nature of the woman's murder and the gruesome steps which the killer would have undertaken to dispose of the body, members of the Garda forensic unit also carried out tests on a public pathway near the couple's house. Residents had told Gardaí that a large black refuse bag had been left on the footpath opposite the house. Passers-by had noticed that the refuse bag had emitted a stench similar to rotten meat. The bag had been left on the path for some time before being moved in the days preceding the discovery of Paiche's body.

Paiche Onyemaechi was not well-known to her neighbours in the respectable Waterford estate. Residents who spoke openly to the media in the days that followed the launch of the murder probe said that other Africans visited the couple's house often but that the family did not mix socially outside the city's small African community.

Her grieving and visibly shaken father, Leonard Unyolo, attended his daughter's funeral service in Waterford City, along with her brothers and sisters. Chika Onyemaechi failed to attend the service. In an impassioned plea at the service, which was held at St Patrick's Presbyterian Church in the city, the chief celebrant, Reverend John Parkin, urged anyone who knew where Chika was to contact the church or Gardaí. But to date his whereabouts are unknown.

The story of Paiche Onyemaechi's brutal death, like the vast majority of homicides, gradually diminished from public view over time. But there was one further brief flurry that reignited public interest in the case about a year after the murder. In circumstances similar to the 'Body in the Bag' case four years earlier, a Garda sub-aquatic team pulled the dismembered remains of a body from the Royal Canal on March 30, 2005. The remains were wrapped in refuse bags, and had been discovered by a man walking along Ballybough Road. The victim's torso, arms and legs were found, but, despite extensive searches of the canal, the head was not recovered. Such was the level of damage done to the body, Gardaí could not initially identify the gender of the victim. When they eventually determined that the dead person was an adult male, they faced the laborious undertaking of identifying the man from a series of databases. Among these was the registry of all foreign nationals who have entered the State to seek asylum and refugee status.

It emerged in the days after the man's body was found that one of the avenues being probed was that the dead man was Chika Onyemaechi – the missing husband of Paiche. Gardaí confirmed that one of the theories they were working on was that Chika Onyemaechi had met a fate similar to his wife and his dead body was decapitated and dumped. A request was made by detectives from the Garda National Immigration Bureau (GNIB) to the office of the Refugee Commissioner to compare samples from the dead man with the records of Chika Onyemaechi. But the records didn't match.

The body found in the canal was later identified as that of 38-year-old Kenyan man, Farah Swaleh Noor, who was also known by the name Sheilila Salim. The dead man had been in Ireland since 1996, and was living in the North Circular Road area. To date, the whereabouts of Chika Onyemaechi remain unknown.

Like Paiche Onyemaechi, 23-year-old Lindita Kukaj had also come to Ireland to seek a better life. The pretty young Albanian woman had travelled over from her native country in the spring of 2000 and settled in Sligo Town. Her easy-going manner and industriousness were quickly rewarded with gainful employment. Lindita sent home as much money as she could from the three separate jobs that she worked around the town. The money that she could send home was an invaluable support to her family, especially her elderly mother, who remained living in impoverished Albania.

Lindita quickly grew to love the town. In letters and phone calls to her loved ones back home, she told them that she was so happy that she hoped to settle in Sligo permanently and build a life there. Lindita lived a good life in the town. The young woman was likeable and popular in equal measure and she quickly made many friends both within and outside the immigrant community in Sligo. Life could not have been better.

On February 21, 2003, Linda, as she was known to her Irish friends, received a visit from a 26-year-old fellow national who had travelled over six months before to live in Dublin.

Eduart Kulici had been living in Bonham Street in Dublin since his arrival in Ireland. Linda did not know him personally, only through the tenuous connection that he had formerly dated the sister of her brother-in-law. However, when Eduart Kulici contacted Linda to say that he was coming to Sligo to meet with her and bring news from home, the young woman eagerly looked forward to the meeting. Linda was hopeful that he would bring news of her friends and relations.

Eduart Kulici was accompanied on his trip to Sligo by a man he had met just weeks beforehand. The man was a Kosovar in his 20s who had introduced himself as Bashkim Osaj, although he was known to others by several aliases. The young woman did not know of Osaj at all before she met him along with Kulici, but she politely welcomed the Kosovar as her visitor's friend.

On the night of February 21, Linda brought her two visitors to Toffs nightclub in Sligo Town, where she worked as a waitress. She wanted the men to relax and enjoy their time and to socialise and have a few drinks in her adopted home. Disputed versions later emerged as to what happened that evening and in the early hours of February 22, but there was little doubt that Linda and Eduart Kulici started to argue as the evening progressed.

It was not in Linda's nature to be argumentative. She was known among her workmates and friends to be an outgoing and pleasant young woman, who was good company. Precisely what occurred between Linda and Eduart Kulici early on that evening remains a mystery. But what happened later is certain. By the following morning Linda would be dead.

Friends of the young Albanian woman would later tell Gardaí that she had been visibly upset in the nightclub before she was killed. There were conflicting accounts as to why Linda Kukaj was crying. One friend said she was crying because she missed her home, but another witness said it was because of "boyfriend trouble". The friends who saw Linda crying in Toffs said she had been with two men, but they did not know the identities of the strangers, as nobody had seen either of them in the town previously.

What happened when the three got home to Linda Kukaj's flat in Wolfe Tone Street remains partly clouded in mystery. But the account given by Bashim Osaj was to prove crucial to the Garda case.

Osaj told Gardaí that when they got home from the club he had made a bed for himself in the sitting-room of the young woman's flat, where he slept until the morning. He said that Eduart Kulici and Linda Kukaj both went into the young woman's bedroom and spent the night there. In the morning, Bashim Osaj woke Eduart up. Osaj later told Gardaí that, moments after waking him from his sleep, Eduart Kulici calmly confessed that he had just killed the young woman in her bedroom. Shocked at the revelation, Osaj asked his companion why he has done it. Kulici laughed and said: "the fucking bitch was annoying me all night."

Osaj would later tell Gardaí that he immediately feared for his own safety. He believed that if Eduart Kulici could so callously take the pretty young woman's life then he would hardly hesitate to kill again. Osaj told Gardaí that he thought about running from the house to alert Gardaí to the woman's murder, but he thought it was too risky to try to escape the Albanian man's attention. Instead, he agreed to drive Kulici back to Dublin later that afternoon.

Eduart Kulici was charged with the murder of Linda Kukaj. The attractive young woman's death was as brutal as it was unexpected. It would later emerge in the Central Criminal Court that she had been strangled with considerable force. The pattern of a necklace that Linda was wearing on the night was imprinted on her throat, counsel for the prosecution, Mr John O'Kelly SC, told the jury. Eduart Kulici pleaded not guilty to Linda's murder. The State's chief prosecution witness was his Kosovar friend Bashkim Osaj. Osaj said that he had known the Albanian man for only five or six weeks before the murder but he agreed to drive Eduart Kulici to Sligo to see Linda. He told the jury that when the two men met the young woman in Sligo she was relaxed and happy to talk to Kulici about her mother and sister back in Albania.

Osaj told the court that the Albanian man strangled Kukaj in her bedroom as he slept in the sitting-room of her flat after the three of them attended the night club earlier that night. He admitted that he did not call Gardaí immediately but that he did finally manage to raise the alarm when he and the accused man called in to a petrol station in Carrick-on-Shannon, as they returned to Dublin after the murder.

The State faced considerable difficulty in making a successful prosecution against Eduart Kulici, because, as it transpired, their chief witness was not what he seemed. Osaj admitted, under scrutiny by defence counsel, that he had obtained and used false documentation to get into Ireland after having been deported from Germany. It also emerged that in July 2004 he had stolen a shotgun from a farmhouse in Co. Tipperary. After Osaj stole the shotgun, he then sawed off both barrels, almost certainly for the purpose of using the weapon in an armed robbery. He had also procured 50 rounds of ammunition. Interestingly, he told the court that the ammunition he illegally procured was a packet of bullets. Bullets are not used in shotguns but are used in handguns, rifles and machine guns, suggesting that Osaj may have had access to other, more lethal, types of firearm.

Osaj gave a detailed, and at times bizarrely honest, account to the court of his criminal dealings. He said he always used gloves when committing crimes. He told Gardaí that he gambled and that he owed €9,000. The defence team would also refer in court to the Kosovar witness's conviction for robbery, in the Dublin Circuit Criminal Court in July 2002. He had been charged with false imprisonment in connection with the crime, during which an employee of the City West Hotel was tied up. Osaj also had a history of domestic abuse complaints against him. Some months prior to the murder trial, Gardaí were called to Osaj's home in Ballymun after being called by his wife during a serious dispute. Early in the cross-examination by Peter Finlay SC, defending counsel for Eduart Kulici, Osaj bizarrely told the judge that he needed to leave the courtroom urgently "for my personal security". Mr Justice Carney was having none of it. The Judge ordered him to answer the questions and warned him not to discuss the case with anyone. "If my instructions are disobeyed I have unlimited powers of fines and imprisonment," Carney said.

It also emerged in court that the State's chief witness had attempted to make contact with the accused man while Eduart

Kulici was being held in Cloverhill Prison pending his trial. Osaj told the court that he had tried to visit Kulici in prison but the Albanian man had, "refused my visit". However, in spite of his dubious credentials, Osaj was able to pinpoint the approximate time when both Eduart Kulici and Linda Kukaj began to row, although he could not shed any light on what had happened between them specifically that had soured the connection. He said that the young woman was in a happy mood until just before they went to Toff's nightclub, at about 1 am on February 22. Several witnesses told the court that Linda had been in a distressed state in the club later that night, though there were disputed versions given to explain why. Counsel for Eduart Kulici accused Garda Kenneth Gallagher of colouring his evidence to suggest that the dead woman had been having a dispute that night with the accused man. Garda Gallagher, who at the time of the murder had been a doorman in the Equinox nightclub in Sligo where Linda also worked, but who had been socialising in Toffs that night, said he had found her "bawling crying" in the club on the night of February 21, 2003. Gallagher said it was his impression that she was having boyfriend trouble. It seemed to Gallagher that Linda's distress was to do with some boy who was visiting, although Garda Gallagher had not met the two men who were with Linda that night.

Another friend of Linda Kukaj's, Mary Norton, gave a different opinion of the source of the Albanian woman's distress. She also worked in the Equinox nightclub with Linda, but on the night of the murder, had met her in Toffs nightclub with two foreign-looking men. Towards the end of the night Linda had been upset and was crying. Norton told the court that she got the impression that Linda was upset because she missed her family at home in Albania.

But the court heard other evidence that suggested that

the young woman had indeed been having a row with the Albanian man that night. After leaving the nightclub, the three foreigners were driven home to Linda's flat in the town by local taxi driver Donal O'Brien. Whatever Eduart Kulici had said or done to the young woman in the nightclub, a bitter row ensued between the two on the journey home from the club, the taxi driver later testified in court.

Linda Kukaj's family members – her mother and sister – sat and listened through an interpreter as the State made its case against Eduart Kulici. Also through an interpreter, the dead woman's sister, Shrepsa Hyseni, told the court she first met the man accused of killing her sister in August 2002 as the boyfriend of her sister-in-law. The dead woman's mother, Nexhmije Plorishti, also addressed the court. She told how she had travelled over to Ireland to identify her murdered daughter's remains at the morgue at Sligo General Hospital. She could not bear to see her daughter's corpse, so the victim's sister formally identified Linda's body. Linda's sister said that while the family had been reared as Muslims, Linda had converted to Catholicism at the age of ten. Asked whether this had caused a problem in the family, she said that it had not.

Pathologist Dr Declan Gilsenan told the jury of seven men and five women that Lindita 'Linda' Kukaj had died of asphyxia due to manual strangulation.

Despite the serious questions over the reliability of the chief witness, the jury returned a verdict of guilty against the 26-year-old Albanian man. The victim's mother and sister broke down and wept in court as the jury delivered the verdict, after four hours and 13 minutes of deliberation.

Following the unanimous verdict, the mother and sister of 23-year-old Lindita Kukaj recalled how much she loved Ireland. The Kukaj family pleaded with the judge to impose the maximum sentence on Eduart Kulici. Linda's mother told the Central Criminal Court that she feared that he would kill again when released from jail.

Lindita Kukaj's heavily pregnant sister again addressed the court through an interpreter. She said: "She worked day and night just to support us." She said her sister had come to Ireland to make a better life and had loved her new home. "She thought that her life would go on here, not that it would end here."

Linda had welcomed Eduart Kulici to her Sligo home "like a brother," Shrepsa said. Lindita's mother said her daughter had come to Sligo so that she could help her family at home. Linda had found great happiness here and had hoped one day to put down roots in the town. "This man prevented her every happiness and desire," she added.

Speaking after the verdict, Sligo Garda inspector James Kearins, who headed the successful murder investigation, said he was very pleased with the outcome, "although I know it will not bring Lindita back".

Justice Paul Carney imposed the mandatory sentence of life in prison on Eduart Kulici.

Six

The Mean Streets

Armed Gardaí stood pensively outside the bedroom door. The officers wore metal-plated body armour. Their weapons were readied at their sides. The Gardaí braced themselves for something to erupt at any moment, even a hail of bullets from behind the closed door. Inside the room was one of the most volatile and ruthless young criminals in the capital's underworld. Surprise was of the essence.

The officers burst in the bedroom door with lightning speed. They found Declan Curran lying in bed. But to their astonishment Gardaí saw that he, too, was prepared for something. As he lay under the sheets he was wearing a bullet-proof jacket. Curran was expecting trouble that cold and wet November morning, but not necessarily from the Gardaí. Aged just 23 at the time of his arrest in late 2003, Curran had already carved out a formidable reputation in Dublin's gangland. He was known by detectives, and even by many ordinary people in the estates of Finglas and across west Dublin as an armed robber. He was also a violently unstable cocaine addict and a killer with a deep hatred of Gardaí. Curran was a man with many enemies.

Known to his friends as "Deckie", Curran and his cohorts ruled their own personal fiefdom around his native Cardiffsbridge Avenue in Finglas, with frightening efficiency. Since he was 16 years old, Gardaí suspected that Declan Curran would either die in bloodshed or make his mark on the capital city's homicide statistics. The latter theory they got absolutely correct. That November morning, Gardaí had come to arrest Deckie Curran for murder.

Thirty-three-year-old Willie O'Regan made the mistake of dating Curran's ex-girlfriend, Christine Mahon. The younger man was bitterly jealous. Curran challenged O'Regan to a fist-fight when the pair locked horns in Finglas in late May 2003, and the younger man lost. Without a gun in his hand, Curran wasn't much of a fighter. But he would strike back.

Revenge was swift. On the evening of June 10, 2003, just a fortnight after the row, two men pulled up on a motorbike outside a three-storey, red-brick house on New Cabra Road. The duo parked just outside the low, white-plastered wall of the house, beside a nearby bus stop. The front door to the house, which was divided into flats, was at the first floor level, up a flight of grey stone steps. The two men looked up at a window to the immediate right of the front door. The light was on. Willie O'Regan was at home. The two gunmen waited outside the house. After a few minutes, a resident arrived at the main front door. The pair raced up the steps, pulling balaclavas over their heads. They pushed a gun into the innocent resident's face and ordered him to keep quiet and to lie on the floor of the inside lobby. The door into O'Regan's flat was directly to the right of the hallway.

Willie O'Regan was sitting down in his small living-room watching television when the door of his flat burst in. One of the two men who walked into the flat carried a handgun. He aimed at Willie O'Regan at point-blank range and opened fire. Five gunshots erupted in a space of seconds. One of the high-velocity bullets amputated Willie O'Regan's right hand at the wrist. Two other rounds struck him through the head.

Gardaí knew within hours of the fatal shooting that Declan Curran was their chief suspect. Building up a strong enough case to see the young killer charged would not be an easy assignment, but after five months, having obtained a series of statements from Curran's ex-girlfriend, they were certain they had got their man. The armed unit deployed to Curran's home at Cardiffsbridge Avenue arrested him and charged him with the murder of Willie O'Regan.

Curran's murder trial was held at the Central Criminal Court in June 2004. The basis of the prosecution's case was a series of statements that 23-year-old Christine Mahon had given them when questioned about the murder of O'Regan. Senior Gardaí were certain that Declan Curran would be sent to prison for a long time. He was facing a mandatory life sentence if the State could make its case. But it did not take long before the trial erupted into confusion. Mahon – the State's chief witness – was declared a hostile witness after she retracted some of her statements and denied the veracity of others. The jury heard that Mahon had been under round-the-clock Garda protection since the Gardaí had arrested Curran for the murder of O'Regan.

Christine Mahon agreed with prosecuting counsel, Paul O'Higgins SC, that she had given signed statements while under questioning by Gardaí. She accepted that these statements had implicated Declan Curran in Willie O'Regan's killing. But sitting in court, over six months later, Christine Mahon had changed her tune. She now said she had "made them up" because she was annoyed with Deckie Curran.

Paul O'Higgins suggested to Mahon that what she had told the Gardaí was in fact completely true. He put it to her that she was retracting her statements out of fear that Declan Curran would kill her too. The prosecution read out the four statements that Christine Mahon made between June 17 and October 17, 2003. In one of them, Christine Mahon told Gardaí that three days before Willie O'Regan was murdered, Curran had shown her some bullets, telling her that Willie O'Regan's "name was on them. He took them out of his pocket. They were small gold bullets," her statement read. But in court Christine Mahon said her statements to detectives were "all lies". She was annoyed at the accused because, she said, "Deckie was using me." She claimed that she had made it all up.

In another portion of her statement that was read before the jury, Mahon allegedly told Gardaí that she knew that she was providing Curran with an alibi around the time of the killing. She said that he had asked her to cover for him: "I knew Deckie was going to shoot Willie O'Regan but I didn't think he was going to kill him," the statement read.

"Did you say that?" prosecuting lawyer Paul O'Higgins asked her.

"No," she replied.

In a further unusual and unexpected incident, the State's counsel put it to Christine Mahon that at one stage during a brief adjournment in the criminal proceedings she passed her brother and said, "I'm doing it right, aren't I?" Mahon denied that she said this and insisted that she and her brother just went outside for a cigarette.

"The reason you're giving your evidence the way that you are is you've been told you'd better not swear up to what you told the Gardaí truthfully," O'Higgins pressed her.

"That's not true," the witness replied.

"Haven't you had a bad time since you told the Gardaí? You've been terrified ever since by the fact that you said it," counsel asked her. He suggested that Curran, or associates of the accused, had threatened her that if she gave evidence against him, "the same would happen to her".

Christine Mahon had received Garda protection in the months leading up to Curran's murder trial, but she had slipped away from a Garda unit deployed to keep watch over her and left the jurisdiction, travelling to the UK. While there, two armed men broke into the place where she was staying.

Christine Mahon denied that the armed men had threatened her not to give evidence against Curran. Nonetheless, when the case came before the Central Criminal Court she withdrew her allegations against her former boyfriend.

The State's case against the ruthless young criminal had been dealt an irrevocable blow. Christine Mahon had been the chief witness for the prosecution and her statements formed the foundation of the State's bid to see Deckie Curran convicted of murder. On the third day of the trial, on June 28, 2004, the case collapsed dramatically. The director of public prosecution (DPP) entered a *nolle prosequi,* allowing Curran to be set free, with the proviso that the State could bring the case back to court if further information emerged.

Senior Gardaí were bitterly disappointed about the way the case against Curran had disintegrated. They had been confident that Christine Mahon's evidence would see one of the most feared young criminals in the Dublin area locked away behind bars, for a long time. Such a result would have come as a major relief to the local community in Finglas. But months of painstaking investigation had been ruined when Christine Mahon withdrew her statements in court. Deckie Curran would walk free, but sooner or later, his past would catch up with him.

Curran was known to Gardaí in Finglas and Blanchardstown from an early age. At just 16 years old he was a regular cocaine user. By age 18 he was a chronic addict. His actions were made even more volatile by his use of steroids, amphetamines and ecstasy, as well as cocaine. He was arrested over a dozen times in his late teens for vehicle theft, assault and damage to property.

One retired senior Garda recalls his time in the force in the late 1990s when Curran was a teenager: "He was tough as iron and very determined. There was a strong feeling that he [Deckie Curran] was going to be more difficult to handle than most of his contemporaries by the time he got older and more established." The senior officer's analysis would prove correct.

But at 19 years old, Deckie Curran was dealt a blow that would stall his criminal exploits. He came into dispute with a well-known family of criminals in the west Dublin area. The dispute became bitter. A gunman ambushed Curran outside his home, and when the unarmed Curran tried to escape, the assassin shot him in the back. Curran lost a kidney in the attack and doctors later told him that he would have to wear a colostomy bag for the rest of his life. By then, Deckie Curran was already known to be a member of one of the toughest gangs of armed robbers emerging in west Dublin. The group rivalled the likes of the "Westies" in ruthlessness, even if they had not established the same market share of the capital's drug trade as the Blanchardstown gang led by Shane Coates and brothers Stephen and Bernard Sugg.

As Curran approached his early 20s, his cocaine habit continued to spiral. He began taking steroids that swelled his physique. He underwent bouts of uneven health, suffering dramatic mood swings in which he often turned on close associates.

At the age of 21, Curran went on a bender that would see him ram a stolen car into the side of a Garda squad car. He was heavily under the influence of drink and drugs. Before Gardaí nabbed him in Ashbourne in Co. Meath, he was doing 100 mph on the wrong side of the road. He would later receive a three-year sentence for the offence, but was back on the streets in less than half that time.

Experienced Gardaí say that Deckie Curran's graduation from teenage drug user to murderer was not by any means unique in the capital's underworld. Curran was just one soldier among a veritable army of young gangsters who rose to prominence at a time when the availability of illegal guns surged beyond all previous levels.

It was this access to weapons – mostly sawn-off shotguns at first but increasingly semi-automatic and automatic pistols with lethal 9mm rounds – which allowed Deckie Curran and his criminal crew to carry out shootings and armed raids on banks and credit unions. It also allowed them to spread their influence by giving guns to youths as young as 15. They enforced their own bailiwick in west Finglas, terrorising the local community and guaranteeing its silence about any of their transgressions.

In addition to the O'Regan killing, Gardaí have connected Curran to at least two other murders. On October 9, 2003, the body of father-of-three Peter Sheridan (27) was found dumped at Scribblestown Lane in Finglas. The dead man had been hooded and shot in the head. Information since given to investigating Gardaí suggests that Curran feared that Sheridan was about to inform on his criminal activities. Nobody has ever been charged in relation to Peter Sheridan's assassination.

Two months earlier, the remains of Victor Murphy of Deanstown Green, Finglas, were found at Dunsink Lane. Wounds to the lower body indicated to investigating Gardaí that the victim had been travelling in a car when a gun went off accidentally. Garda intelligence suggests that Murphy believed he was on his way to "do a job" along with Curran but something had gone wrong. Nobody has ever been charged in relation to Murphy's death. Gardaí have not ruled out the possibility that Curran planned to murder Murphy at a remote location but in a scramble to grab the weapon inside the car, the gun went off. Victor Murphy had been a friend of Deckie Curran's older brother, who had died in a car accident 15 years before. But Curran had little regard for sentiment.

Just how much weaponry Deckie Curran had access to would become clear to Gardaí. Six months after the collapse of the State's case against Curran for O'Regan's murder, Gardaí made a find in the course of probing a series of robberies on cash-in-transit vans. Detectives recovered a high-powered machine gun, handguns, a sawn-off shotgun and an assortment of ammunition. They found the stash of weaponry at a house in Clonee, Co. Meath. Investigating officers believed that the firepower belonged to Curran and his associates.

It was almost inevitable that Deckie Curran would ultimately become a victim of the drugs culture in which he was immersed. Twelve months after his arrest for the murder of Willie O'Regan, Curran was one of two men who made a daring attempt to rob a branch of the TSB bank at Sutton Cross in Dublin, in mid-afternoon on Thursday November 11, 2004. Curran left the bank holding a handgun but he did not plan on the intervention of a brave female Garda who was out on patrol. Spotting the raid in progress, she drew her baton as Deckie Curran was making his escape with the other gang member. She slammed the baton down on Curran's arm and held him down until assistance arrived. Curran was arrested for robbery and remanded to Cloverhill Prison.

The 24-year-old was placed in a cell with two men, both of whom were relations. Four days after his arrest, on the morning of Sunday November 14, 2004, the two men attended morning Mass at the prison chapel. When they returned to the cell, they found Deckie Curran's dead body – poisoned though self-administered drug use.

A subsequent pathology examination would show just how much drugs, and especially painkillers, that Curran had pumped into his body. Traces of Diazepam and Temazepam were found in his blood, along with Codeine. Most likely taken as a single recreational 'cocktail', the combined effects of all three substances proved lethal.

The violence after Declan Curran's death perhaps best illustrates the volatile and internecine disputes that are a feature of the capital city's criminal underbelly. Less than 24 hours after Curran's death in Cloverhill, Deckie Curran's associates targeted the Finglas family home of murder victim Willie O'Regan. Two shots were fired at the property but there were no injuries. In another attack on the home of a relative of a family in dispute with Curran, a man was seriously wounded. He was rushed to hospital for emergency treatment. Two teenagers, the youngest one just 15 years old, were among several people later arrested and questioned in relation to the gun attacks on the homes of Curran's former enemies.

Events took a bizarre turn just days after Declan Curran's death. Gardaí were told that a gang in Finglas intended to steal the fallen criminal's body as it lay in church before being interred at Glasnevin Cemetery. The gang planned to dump the corpse at Dunsink Lane, just as Victor Murphy's body had been dumped, allegedly by Curran, 18 months before. Gardaí mounted extra security in proximity to the church, to avert the macabre theft.

Just a week later, one of Curran's closest allies and partners in crime would be the victim of a gun attack. Twenty-three-year-old Paul Cunningham lived at his mother's home at Dromheath Avenue in Mulhuddart. In the early hours of November 21, 2004, he was in bed with his partner when two gunmen quietly made their entrance at the rear of the house. The raiders made their way up the stairs, kicked in Cunningham's bedroom door and fired off two cartridges of lethal pellets from a sawn-off shotgun, striking their target with both. The young couple's 18-month-old baby son was also sleeping in the room at the time. It was only sheer luck that neither the child nor his mother was peppered with gunshot.

Paul Cunningham was rushed by ambulance to James Connolly Memorial Hospital in Blanchardstown but his injuries, inflicted at near-point-blank range, proved fatal.

Cunningham's family story is blighted with misfortune and misadventure. He was the third sibling in a family of eight to have died violently. In 1995, his then-16-year-old brother Gary was one of three boys killed at Ratoath in Co. Meath, when the stolen car they were in went out of control, hit a tree and burst into flames. Another brother was stabbed to death in 2000. Paul Cunningham had over a dozen previous convictions. He was facing firearms offences at the time of his death. He was also facing sentencing for receiving stolen vehicles. Cunningham had also been closely connected to members of the Westies.

Detectives believed that Cunningham was, in fact, the second raider in the robbery at the TSB in Sutton Cross, Dublin, in which Declan Curran was apprehended. He was also believed to have been involved in a series of other armed raids. Detectives probing Cunningham's killing could not rule out the strong likelihood that his murder was a revenge shooting linked to the attacks on Curran's former enemies in the days following his death.

Deckie Curran and Paul Cunningham were both participants in, but ultimately victims of, the drug-gang culture in which they were involved. Neither man was in any way a major beneficiary of the drugs industry. In their short lives they had accumulated almost nothing in the way of personal wealth or even moderately valuable assets. Their stories illustrate the worst of the underworld culture, where life is cheap and killers are often unstable drug addicts, with easy access to guns.

Can the series of murders connected to Declan Curran's circle of associates and rivals be properly called 'gangland' assassinations? That is one of the major questions facing any analysis of so-called gang-related homicide data. Willie O'Regan's murder, for example, raises an important point made by some senior Gardaí about the categorisation of so-called gangland murders. O'Regan was not a major criminal figure. There was nothing in the row between himself and Deckie Curran that would be found in Sicilian Mafiosi disputes. There was no mislaid cash for drugs. There had been no encroachment on one gang's criminal territory. The killing was not related to organised crime. Willie O'Regan merely picked a row with the wrong person. But homicides among the criminal underworld do not exist in a vacuum. The connection between rising gun-related homicides and the growing drugs market is compelling. And the consumption and supply of illegal substances in Ireland has spiralled in recent years.

In the last ten years, seizures valued at over €1 billion have been made by the Gardaí and the Customs National Drug Team. The value and scale of these seizures is dramatic: cocaine worth €537 million, cannabis to the value of €512 million, heroin worth €34 million and ecstasy valued at €6 million. But these figures only hint at the amount of drugs getting past the authorities. The international norm is that about 10% of illegal drugs are detected by policing authorities. Applying this ratio to the Irish case means that drugs with a street value above €10 billion have arrived in Ireland over the last ten years.

Not all of these drugs are destined for local consumption, as Ireland is recognised as a transit point in the delivery of large quantities of drugs to Britain. However, it is at the point of transit that many people who are minor players in the Irish drug scene are involved, attempting to bring the lucrative cargo into the State despite the watchful eye of both Customs and Gardaí. The United Nations World Drug Report 2005 places Ireland in joint third place, out of 30 European countries, for cocaine use and in joint sixth place for ecstasy use.

Data suggests that consumption of illegal drugs is a problem facing all sectors of Irish society. One recent survey indicated that 37% of Irish 15 to 16-year-olds had used cannabis, three times the average of teenagers in the same age range in other EU countries. Some 54% of 15 to 16-year-olds in Ireland also said it was either 'very easy' or 'fairly easy' to buy ecstasy.

However, it is the increase, in very recent years, in the amount of drugs entering the State that suggests the value of the drugs trade has skyrocketed. Of the €1 billion drugs market in 2005, cocaine, in particular, now accounts for the largest growth area, with the amount of the drug seized in 2005 – over €20 million in value – representing a 33% rise on the 2004 figure, and extraordinarily, a 500% increase on seizures of the same substance in 2002. Cocaine-users in Ireland – a group that is as varied as young professionals to middle-aged blue-collar workers – are now consuming approximately €180 million worth of the drug per year. While cocaine accounts for the largest growth area in both supply and demand, cannabis remains the most popular drug of choice. Cannabis accounts for an estimated €700 million of the annual €1 billion Irish drugs market. Heroin, the drug which paved the way for the formation of many of the major Irish gangs which dominated the criminal underworld up to the mid-1990s, shows little change over recent years, with the value of the illicit market at around €60 million on average annually. All of these figures add up to one thing. There is now more drug money than ever before in the hands of Irish organised criminals. And there are more cash incentives than ever before to murder those who get in the way of the gang's share of the illicit profits.

As volatile and as dangerous as the Dublin underworld has become, it is quite benign compared to the Spanish crime scene, which is populated by Moroccan drug dealers, Eastern European and Russian Mafiosi and South American drug cartel gangsters. Many of Dublin's criminals, who have been involved in drugs and gun murders on Ireland's streets, have close associations with continental European gangs. These gangs are among the most violent in the world. Both Spain and Holland are major centres for the organisation of international drug-smuggling operations. The modern generation of Irish criminals now own large property and investment portfolios in Spain and have adopted the ruthless tactics used by Russian, Lithuanian and other mafia outfits who have long been major players in the Mediterranean.

It was to Spain that the leaders of the infamous 'Westies' gang, Shane Coates and Stephen Sugg, fled in 2003, after a series of close encounters with Gardaí and criminal enemies. Thirty-three year-old Coates and his compatriot Sugg, 28, had been friends since their teens in the working-class Corduff estate in Dublin's north-west and had stolen cars together, leading to numerous convictions. In the late 1990s, they saw a vacuum in the hash and heroin trade north of the city and moved in with brutal effectiveness. For over four years Coates and the Sugg brothers conducted their affairs with relative impunity. Despite several parallel investigations, Gardaí struggled to break the grip of fear the gang held over the drug pushers and debtors that they terrorised. At times, Gardaí constructed seemingly watertight cases that for various reasons fell apart, largely because the only people who could finger the gang lived in absolute fear of their wrath.

The secret to the Westies' success lay in the level of fear they instilled both in those who worked for them and in their enemies. The Westies' gang encouraged brutality among its network of pushers. Junkies and dealers who owed as little as €10 were severely beaten. One mother-of-four was tortured by having her breasts burned with cigarette butts, in front of her children. Another, junkie Derek "Smiley" McGuinness, from Corduff Park in Blanchardstown, owed the gang €200. He was set upon by two other pushers who, along with Stephen Sugg, smashed all his teeth, slashed him across the face and beat him with an iron bar in a public park. McGuinness gave a statement to Gardaí identifying Sugg.

Forty-three-year-old rival heroin dealer Pascal Boland had dealt with tough men such as the notorious PJ Judge, a particularly violent drug dealer who was ultimately assassinated. Boland decided to push in on the Westies' turf by bringing drugs into the west Dublin area and using some of the Westies' own distributors to move the illicit cargo on the street. A Westies' pusher who helped Boland was severely beaten and told to pass a mobile phone number to Boland. When Boland rang the number he was told to get off the Westies' patch or he was dead. Boland told the gang leader to "fuck off…you're nobodies". Within weeks, a gunman fired 11 bullets into Boland's body.

It was the Westies' first big mistake. It prompted Gardaí in Blanchardstown to mount a special investigation into the gang's activities. Increased surveillance and intelligence-gathering generated new leads for the Gardaí. Coates was no fool and he proved elusive. Neither he nor senior gang members dealt directly with their merchandise and seemed almost untouchable. But Gardaí got a boost from an unexpected source when, in October 1999, Westies henchmen shot 18-year-old Blanchardstown local Paul Dempsey in his bed, disconnecting his right calf muscle from his leg with one shot. His offence? The teen was so bold as to date Sugg's 16-year-old sister, Frances, without her elder brother's permission. Dempsey's brother Robert was a friend of Sugg's but he was beaten with an iron bar in the brutal attack. Dempsey and his brother agreed to give evidence in court.

Evidence from both Dempsey and McGuinness could put the senior gang members away for a long time. Hopes were also high that stronger prosecutions might emerge once the pair were off the street. Coates spent 14 months on remand. But by October 2000 the cases against the pair were in shreds. Nobody could forget that to mess with the Westies was to invite a painful death. Neither Dempsey nor McGuinness would give evidence in court.

Between the end of 2000 and late 2002 the gang brazenly stamped their authority on their west-Dublin territory. Three small-time drug pushers were tortured and shot over bad debts. Gardaí believe a large number of people who fell foul of the gang were beaten and tortured with knives, vice grips and iron bars. But the ultimate fate of Stephen Sugg and Shane Coates shows that even the most deadly of criminals in Dublin's underworld live short lives. Stephen Sugg panicked after an attempt on his life in mid-2003 and fled to Alicante. He was joined there by Coates three months later, after he was injured in a shootout with members of the Garda Emergency Response Unit (ERU) at a safe house in Cavan. Gardaí initially believed the pair had established some loose connections to a number of expatriate Irish criminals in Costa Blanca.

The final strike against the Westies' Dublin Empire occurred in their absence. Stephen Sugg's brother Bernard was the gang's chief enforcer. He remained at home after the duo fled to Spain. While he remained in Dublin, the crime bosses effectively kept a presence in the capital and nobody was likely to forget that the gang hadn't gone away completely. Whether Bernard Sugg planned to follow his brother to Spain is not known. On August 17, 2003, Bernard Sugg sat inside the door of the Brookwood Inn in Corduff in Blanchardstown. It was a familiar haunt of his and of other gang members. A gunman walked in to the pub and shot Sugg several times in the chest. The Westies' claim to north-west Dublin's lucrative drugs turf was dealt a final, irrevocable blow.

The chief suspects in the shooting dead of Bernard Sugg were two brothers who had been closely connected to the Westies gang. Andrew 'Madser' Glennon and his brother Mark had known the Westies' leaders since they, too, were in their teens. The brothers had been a vital part of the gang in the early 2000s but a dispute between the brothers and the gang's leaders led to bad blood. When Coates and Stephen Sugg fled to Spain, the Glennon brothers decided it was prudent to remove the gang's enforcer for good.

Their control over the Westies' former stomping ground in Corduff was short lived, however. On April 30, 2005, Andrew Glennon was gunned down at his Clonee home by another rival west-Dublin outfit. Less than five months later, on September 7, 2005, his brother Mark was shot dead in Blanchardstown

For over two-and-a-half years, Shane Coates and Stephen Sugg went off the radar completely. They went missing while in Spain, amid rumours that they had become involved in the Alicante drugs scene. A further twist in the plot emerged when it was revealed that Shane Coates may have received €50,000 from a Dublin drug boss to pass onto an associate in Spain who was living with the daughter of jailed drug-dealer John Gilligan. The associate has since died, and there have been allegations that this money may not have been passed on, leading to further potential friction in the criminal underworld.

When they ruled their lucrative drugs empire, the

Westies operated with chilling ruthlessness, often employing needlessly gratuitous violence against their adversaries. In Alicante and Costa Blanca, it seems, Coates and Sugg were muscle without power. The epilogue in the Westies story occurred in July 2006, when the two men's disintegrated remains were found under a slab of concrete in Alicante.

The growing fraternity of Irish gang expats living in Spain and Holland includes some of the most notorious names in the Dublin drugs scene of recent years. Amongst these is George 'The Penguin' Mitchell, 51, who allegedly continues to run his hash business from Holland. He was a suspected member of the £30 million Beit art robbery gang led by Martin Cahill in the 1980s.

Gardaí believe that a small core of these expatriate criminals remain the chief beneficiaries of the Irish drugs market. In the early 1990s, the growth of these individuals seemed almost unstoppable. They struck terror into their own gang members. This passed on to members of the public, who feared retribution if they contacted Gardaí. It took the tragic and brutal murder of journalist Veronica Guerin, on June 26, 1996, to see the establishment in Ireland of one of the world's most effective tools in fighting crime bosses. The Criminal Assets Bureau (CAB) was set up by the Government in the aftermath of Guerin's murder to target the drugs gang led by crime boss John Gilligan. The special unit was set up as a statutory agency under the Criminal Assets Bureau Act 1996, passed into law on October 15 of that year.

The Bureau's success in tracing and seizing the assets of crime lords in its first decade of operation has been remarkable. The mechanism the Bureau has used under that legislation has seen the CAB squeeze over €90 million from the pockets of organised criminals since its inception.

Former CAB bureau chief, Felix McKenna, has been one of the first senior officers in the force to link massive cocaine use among young men in the criminal underworld to an increase in gangland homicide. McKenna's credentials in law enforcement add much weight to this thesis on the rising gun homicides on Dublin's streets. The County Monaghan native has been instrumental in most of the State's major anti-crime probes in the past two decades. A member of the Garda 'Tango Squad' that targeted Martin 'The General' Cahill in the 1990s, McKenna is also a former head of the Garda Bureau of Fraud Investigation.

In a *Sunday Tribune* interview to mark the Bureau's 10th anniversary in 2006, McKenna stated that that there is now a consensus among top Gardaí that the surge in gun homicides is closely connected to the rise in drug use: "They attribute it to the use of cocaine by these people, the shooters…I've asked my counterpart in the drugs squad, and other senior officers, what is driving these fellas to do these killings and they've said its cocaine."

Victims of gun murders are disproportionately young men with a minor involvement in drugs, often as users themselves. But senior Gardaí argue that it is inaccurate to describe many of these murders as "gangland" killings. There is ample evidence to suggest that in many of these cases the murdered men are, in fact, victims of what could be more accurately described as 'gun culture'.

Indeed, one senior Garda has strongly disputed the recurring use of the term "gangland" to categorise many of these murders. In an interview with *Irish Times* journalist Conor Lally in May 2006, Chief Superintendent Peter Maguire said that labelling these murders with one simplistic catch-all phrase is nonsense. Chief Superintendent Maguire is the senior officer in the Dublin Metropolitan Region (DMR) North division – the Garda section that experiences a higher number of homicide investigations than any other, either in the capital or indeed nationwide.

Crucially, Chief Superintendent Maguire says that there are more illegal guns than ever in circulation on Dublin's streets. The experienced Garda said that the use of the term "gangland" suggests that the rule of law and the safeguards attached to it did not apply in disadvantaged communities in Dublin city. "It diminishes and marginalises the victims and those who are left behind grieving," he said.

The senior Garda insists that many of the murders were simply criminals with guns, rather than "big-time criminals or big-time gangsters". He said that very significant progress had been made in major investigations into murders and other serious crimes.

Nonetheless, the investigation of armed gangs takes up valuable Garda time and resources. Garda Commissioner Noel Conroy made just that admission in April 2006, when he said that gun crime now requires so many resources to contain it, that detection rates for other crimes have suffered. In a note of warning to Garda chiefs in provincial towns across Ireland, he said that the drugs trade was no longer confined to cities. The same can be said for gun-related homicides, even though public support for Garda probes into shootings is hampered by understandable fear.

"We are doing extremely well in terms of detecting the trafficking of drugs. But when you come down to the whole area of shooting individuals, of course the help and co-operation coming from the people involved is, you could say, nil," Conroy said.

But where are the young gunmen getting their weapons? Some indication as to where the deadly firearms are being sourced was contained in the 2005 *European Union Organised Crime Report* (EUOCR), prepared under the auspices of the European police network, Europol. The report indicated that senior Gardaí were aware that automatic weapons from Eastern Europe, particularly from places such as Bulgaria, have made their way into Ireland in significant quantities. An incalculable number of firearms have also entered the State along with shipments of drugs from Continental Europe, Gardaí believe. It still remains almost impossible to state clearly what proportion of so-called gangland killings are indeed connected, in any tangible way, to drug wars between different criminal groups. Is Ireland in the grip of a major surge in gangland-style gun murders? An analysis conducted for this book of all the homicides involving firearms since 2000 – excluding six killings that involved the use of a legally held firearm – shows that 64 people were fatally shot in cold blood. Effectively, almost one in five homicides (just over 19%) in the state is a gangland-style fatal shooting. On average, ten people a year have been killed in gangland-style assassinations since the new Millennium began.

But while there is grave public concern over gangland murders, it is important to note that this figure is far below the annual number of fatal stabbings and deaths that have resulted from alcohol-induced rows involving young men.

Only twice since this decade began – in both 2005 and 2003 – has the number of gangland-style murders gone over the average number of ten a year. In 2000, there were six gun murders which could be described as gangland killings. The following year five people were shot dead in similar attacks. In 2002, eight people were assassinated. The figures went off the chart in 2003: a 12-month period in which 19 people were murdered in gangland-style hits. Likewise, in 2005, the number of young men killed in such gun attacks was dramatically out of sync with the average, with 20 shot dead during that year. The middle year between these two peaks – 2004 – recorded just six fatal shootings, however, that could accurately be described as being gangland murders.

This raises a significant question in relation to such murders. Do the high numbers of gangland-style assassinations recorded in 2003 and 2005 represent an upward spiral in the rate of these attacks that is likely to continue? If this is so then why was the number shot dead in 2004 so dramatically lower? Alternatively, is it possible that the two years in which high numbers of gangland-style killings occurred, are, in fact, an aberration within a longer timeframe? If so, is it likely that these types of homicides will stabilise at an average of around ten or less per year? Gangland murders are still such a new phenomenon that only the passage of time will provide answers to these questions.

There is one aspect to gangland style homicides, however, in which there is a remarkable consistency. The profile of the people who have been killed, in such gun murders since the decade began, is remarkably uniform.

The vast majority of these killings have occurred in the Dublin area. In fact, 73% of all victims of gangland-style murders were killed in the capital. A further 5% of victims were young Dublin men who were shot dead in a bordering county. Among these was 22-year-old Owen McCarthy. He was taken from near his Clondalkin home and brought to Allaneka Bridge in the Wicklow Gap on November 4, 2005 and shot in the head. Dubliner Andrew 'Madser' Glennon, The Westies' rival, and member of a notorious Blanchardstown-based criminal gang was shot dead at his home in Clonee in Co. Meath on April 30, 2005. The average age of these young male victims is between 31 and 32 years old.

There is one other astonishing pattern among gangland-style murders: of the 64 gun murders from 2000 to the end of 2005, only one was female.

Grandmother and daily mass-goer Joan Casey was clearly no gangster, but her murder in April 2004 was arguably a watershed. Sixty-five-year-old Casey was a Eucharistic Minister at her local Saint Dominic's Roman Catholic Church in Tallaght, an area in which she had lived most of her life.

She was regarded warmly by neighbours, as a popular and kind member of the community who would help anyone who was in need of assistance. The day she was killed she had, only hours earlier, been working at the local Church, organising flowers for the decoration of the altar.

Casey was sleeping in the bedroom of her home at Avonbeg Park on April 3, 2006 when a young man entered the house with a shotgun at 6 am. He crept in and peered through a bedroom door. Believing that he saw his intended target move, he opened fire.

Gardaí later recovered a bag that was discarded in nearby bushes, inside which was a dismantled double-barrelled shotgun, three spent cartridges and two live rounds. A fingerprint analysis of the weapon matched the left hand finger mark of 26-year-old local man Timothy Rattigan, from Saint Dominic's Terrace in Tallaght. Timothy Rattigan was charged with the Joan Casey's murder but denied he was the killer when brought to trial in the Central Criminal Court in June 2006.

Rattigan's sister had once been married to the murdered woman's son, Gerard, the likely target of Rattigan's attack. The couple were estranged from each other for some time before April 2004.

Rattigan had two previous convictions, though both were for minor offences. Presiding Judge Paul Carney nonetheless felt compelled to note that Rattigan was a man who clearly knew where, or from whom, to obtain a gun. The court heard that there was no clear motive for the killing. It was proposed by prosecuting counsel that a feeling of bad blood may have led Rattigan to target his former brother-in-law. The jury convicted Rattigan of Joan Casey's murder. The Casey family saw justice done for their mother's murder but did not get an answer to explain why the shooting had occurred.

The dead woman's daughter, Martina, described her

mother as the best mum in the world. "She was the most kind, loving, caring, gentle and amazing lady, but no matter what I say, it is not going to make a difference," Martina told the media after the verdict.

As the court was being cleared, associates of Timothy Rattigan were heard to say to members of the dead woman's family: "At least we have someone to visit tomorrow; we won't be visiting a headstone."

The murder of the elderly lady caused public revulsion. Whilst many victims may be tainted by their association with criminals, there was no doubt in the public mind that Tallaght pensioner Joan Casey was an utterly innocent victim of the capital's gun culture.

Joan Casey's tragic murder is even more interesting in the context of the findings of a public opinion poll in relation to gangland crime. That poll, conducted by IMS for the *Sunday Tribune* in mid-2005, showed that the public is greatly concerned about gangland crime, but their sympathy does not extend to victims who were criminals or who were part of that gangster culture themselves. A significant majority of respondents to the poll said that they "did not care" if gang members killed other criminals, so long as "innocent people" were not injured or killed in the process.

Whatever the public attitude is to homicides among the criminal fraternity, it is nonetheless a priority of Gardaí to detect and bring prosecutions in such cases. However, research shows that there is a comparatively low success rate in bringing assassins to justice. For instance, Gangland assassins operating in Ireland are five times more likely to escape detection than their counterparts in the notorious gang-ridden city of Los Angeles.

Organised criminals who carry out murders here have a risk of conviction of less than 20%. This compares dramatically with the successful prosecution and jailing of over 90% of hitmen who carry out similar murders in LA. Data from the Irish Department of Justice on 66 murders involving firearms that were carried out here over a six-year period from 1998 shows that over 80% remained unsolved. However, less than 6% of gang-related assassinations carried out in LA remain unsolved.

United Nations' data shows that, compared to police forces internationally, Gardaí achieve a comparatively high level of success in the investigation of homicides. Figures from the UN Office on Drugs and Crime show that the level of convictions achieved in the European Union is approximately one for every two homicides – or in 50% of all killings. In the United States, there is roughly one conviction achieved for every eight homicides – roughly 12%. As the research conducted for this book shows, the Gardaí achieve a success rate of over 60% in the investigation of homicides leading to criminal convictions in court.

The different approaches adopted at political and law enforcement level between the two countries explains why Irish gang murder has a comparatively low conviction rate, compared to the US. Much of the high conviction rates in relation to gangland murders in Los Angeles is attributed to the use of witness protection programmes which allow criminals to give evidence against other senior gang members in exchange for protection, according to the Los Angeles County District Attorney's Office. Such a mechanism has only occasionally been used to combat Irish gang crime. With the exception of the US, few jurisdictions favour the prospect of paying large sums of tax-payers' money to relocate dangerous criminals to a new life abroad, even if their evidence in a court of law could send some of their criminal colleagues to jail.

Even if a conviction is secured, there is striking anecdotal evidence from Gardaí and members of the Irish Prison

Service to suggest that a handful of dangerous convicts are directing their gangs from behind bars. The activities of three gangs in particular can be traced back, to a large extent, to the control of around half a dozen crime bosses currently behind bars. It is believed the gangs are collectively responsible for at least a dozen gangland murders in recent years, as well as the theft of several million euro in bank heists, ATM and cash-in-transit robberies. These gangs are heavily involved in the heroin and cannabis trade in particular. Senior Gardaí believe that increased measures are desperately needed to curtail the activities of a small core of senior gang members who are effectively ordering retaliatory shootings, planning robberies and making drug deals, from their cells.

It is understood that one of the most powerful new figures to emerge in the criminal underworld is a 25-year-old Northside Dublin man, who is presently imprisoned in Portlaoise Prison on armed robbery charges. He is believed to be heavily involved at a senior level in a new gang that has taken the place of the once-powerful Westies and is regarded as particularly dangerous.

This jailed gang leader was a close friend and criminal associate of Declan Curran. He is believed to be linked to a series of shootings that culminated in the death of Paul Cunningham at his mother's Mulhuddart home in November 2004. The crime boss ordered the retaliatory shooting of a long-term rival of Curran's, who was believed to have been celebrating his death. Paul Cunningham was a close ally of both Curran's and the jailed gang leader. The series of gun attacks that the crime boss ordered later resulted in Cunningham being shot dead in retaliation.

This jailed criminal has become increasingly well connected to other powerful crime figures outside his local patch, Gardaí believe. It is understood that he has become close to the Limerick crime boss Christy Keane, who is serving a ten-year term at Portlaoise, for possession of drugs. Keane is believed to be active in the running of his gang from behind bars, although there is evidence to suggest that he no longer takes a leading role in the outfit. A large number of Christy Keane's gang were present at Paul Cunningham's funeral in west Dublin, which Gardaí believe was an ominous sign of an alliance between the two groups.

It is also believed that the jailed Dublin crime leader ordered the killing of a major crime figure in Limerick in mid-2006 – sparking fears that an inter-city war could erupt as a consequence. However, Gardaí intercepted the murderous assassin and criminal court proceedings by the State are imminent in the investigation. A man is currently awaiting trial and cannot be named.

Another major criminal presently behind bars is leading a third gang in south Dublin. The man is serving a lengthy sentence and amazingly he runs his outfit's operations via mobile phones in his cell. This raises major questions about security at the prison where he is serving his sentence. Contact between top crime bosses and their criminal colleagues on the outside relies largely on access to mobile phones and pagers. They acquire the phones by supplying drugs to fellow inmates or, if that does not work, it is believed, simple physical coercion is used. There are indications that the Irish Prison Service is considering introducing equipment that may be able to block mobile phone signals from specific wings, although no formal announcement of this has been made.

The jailed Dublin criminal is involved in a bitter dispute with another gang. A major row developed between the young men over the loss of a shipment of drugs that was intercepted by Gardaí. Two distinct gangs emerged from this conflict. One group was led by 19-year-old criminal Declan Gavin. The other gang was led by Joseph Rattigan, who was just 16 years old, at the time when his gang became established in the distribution of cocaine in the south-Dublin area. Despite claims that both gangs were closely connected to Martin 'The Viper' Foley, the former associate of the infamous Martin 'The General' Cahill, Foley has consistently denied this link.

On March 3, 2000, Gardaí raided the Holiday Inn Hotel on Pearse Street and seized a shipment of cocaine. A gang member was attempting to 'cut' the substance so it could be diluted and spread out to more dealers. Declan Gavin was suspected by the rival gang of informing Gardaí about the cache of illicit drugs. Gavin was attacked outside the Crumlin Shopping Centre on the evening of August 25, 2001. He was fatally stabbed.

Gavin was the first to be killed in the conflict between the rival gangs, but he would not be the last. Just over six months later, on March 17, 2002, the now-jailed gang leader was attacked at his home and shot a number of times. He suffered major blood loss and lost his spleen as a result of the attack, but he survived.

Four months later, on July 16, 2002, Joseph Rattigan was shot dead. Rattigan had just turned 18. His murder would prove to have a major significance in the intractability of the feud. Rattigan was a very close friend and associate of the wounded man, who would later lead the gang from behind bars to carry out even more bloodshed in revenge. Rattigan's former lieutenant effectively succeeded the dead man as gang leader in 2002 but he was jailed in early 2004 for a total of ten years for drugs and firearms offences. He was found in possession of €40,000 worth of drugs by a Garda patrol. Gardaí have absolutely no doubt that the jailed gang leader is very dangerous. During a chase in which he was pursued by Gardaí, he fired off a series of rounds from a loaded shotgun at a patrol car. He later received six years for this separate offence, in addition to the drugs offences.

A series of shooting incidents followed in which members of both gangs were targeted by armed attacks. On March 9, 2005, John Roche (24), a major drug dealer and key member of the imprisoned south Dublin criminal's gang, was shot dead outside his apartment in Kilmainham. Before the end of the year his elder brother would also be murdered as part of the bloody feud.

The gang led by the jailed criminal struck back with a hail of bullets. On November 13, 2005, rival gang members Darren Geoghegan (26) and Gavin Byrne (30) were lured to a quiet location at Firhouse in South Dublin. Both men were shot dead at point blank range. Gardaí had regarded Darren Geoghegan as the prime suspect in the murder of John Roche eight months earlier. Two days later, in an attack that was covered widely in the media, partly due to the fact that the shooting occurred in a well-off middle-class area of Dublin, one of the jailed gang leader's most senior associates was murdered in retaliation for the double killings. Noel Roche (27), the elder brother of drug dealer John Roche, was killed as he drove his car through Clontarf on his way home from a music concert, on November 15, 2005.

These four connected murders, in just one year, did much to publicise the perceived increase in gangland homicide. To have such a high number of killings, linked to any single criminal dispute over a 12-month period, is, however, atypical of most gangland feuds.There are few experts who can provide a clear analysis of such a new phenomenon. Nobody could have expected that at the start of the decade, over 60 young men would be murdered in six years, in gangland-style gun murders. There is no doubt that a massive growth in the use of cocaine has gripped Ireland since the decade began. But perhaps it is overly simplistic to believe that there is a direct connection between the competition among criminal gangs for illicit drug profits and the growing numbers of young Dublin men shot dead every year. It may be that the high number of assassinations has more to do with the surge in available guns and the reportedly high levels of cocaine being consumed by minor criminals. However, the Irish public's main concern is whether the apparent rise in fatal shootings is part of an upward trend, set to rise dramatically in the years ahead.

Dr Ian O'Donnell, Director of the Institute of Criminology at University College Dublin, is perhaps the best informed and most reasoned of commentators on the subject of gangland-style homicides. O'Donnell insists that the rate of lethal violence in Dublin is not out of line with other European capital cities. But the number of violent deaths in the capital has increased dramatically at a time when the trend in many other capitals is going downward. Urban areas have seen a significant increase in killings related to so-called gangland activities, often drug related, O'Donnell has commented. It is only natural, that such a new phenomenon as seemingly constant gangland-style gun murders, would arouse much public concern and fear.

O'Donnell notes that there is no evidence of a relentless upward trend in crime, although the homicide problem has worsened. He has consistently argued for greater funding for research into all aspects of homicide. A frightened Irish public, that is convinced society is in the grip of an endless escalation in gang murders, may sanction its Government to introduce draconian laws that the public may ultimately regret.

Seven

The Tools of Death

It was the day, said parish priest Monsignor Gerard McSorley, that the town of Ballybay changed forever. Not only had the small rural town in Co. Monaghan lost one of its own in horrific circumstances, but the perpetrator was also local – a young man who had never before been in trouble. "We are not an innocent community anymore and we somehow have to deal with that," said Mgr McSorley.

The murder of Sister Philomena Lyons is arguably the most shocking killing of all to have taken place in Ireland in recent years. The 68-year-old nun, who had dedicated her life to educating successive generations in the small Co. Monaghan town, was subjected to a shocking sexual assault before having her life choked away, with her own scarf.

Ironically, the day that was to be Sister Philomena's last, had been one she had been looking forward to. December 15, 2001 was to be the beginning of her Christmas holidays, which she intended spending with relatives in Dublin.

The elderly member of the order of the Daughters of Our Lady of the Sacred Heart rose early for breakfast at the convent that morning. She was in high spirits and eagerly anticipating her impending trip. She planned on getting the 8.30 am bus for the two-hour drive to the city.

Sister Philomena departed from the convent at 8.10 am, accompanied to the gates by the head nun, Sister Aloysius. The pair had known each other for years, since Sister Philomena had came to Ballybay to teach in the local national school. Born Christina Lyons in Rahan, Mallow, County

Cork in 1932, Sister Philomena had spent the last 35 years in Ballybay, having entered her order at the age of 18. She trained as a primary school teacher in Carysfort Training College, Blackrock, Co. Dublin. She spent a number of years teaching in New Jersey before returning to her native Ireland, where she spent her remaining years in St Brigid's National School in Ballybay. Although she had retired in 1999, Sister Philomena remained actively involved in a local nursing home near the convent, continuing to serve the community as best she could.

As she walked down the convent avenue to get her bus, Sister Philomena carried two small suitcases and a plastic bag. Near the gate she realised that she had forgotten to bring her mobile-phone charger and returned to her room to fetch it, leaving Sister Aloysius to mind her bags. When she got back, she insisted that her colleague return indoors and not to bother waiting with her as the morning was icy cold.

Sister Philomena was a short and frail-looking woman but stronger and more robust than her age suggested; she was just eight days short of her 69th birthday. The cold morning air was all pervasive and she swung her arms and paced up and down to keep from getting colder, as she waited for the bus to come from Clones to ferry her to Dublin.

As she waited for the bus to pass by the gates of the convent, Sister Philomena met an employee of the convent, and the pair traded greetings. It was around 8.20 am.

Later on, the head nun peered from inside the convent out to the gates where she had left her old friend. Neither Sister Philomena nor her luggage was anywhere in sight so Sister Aloysius was certain her colleague had got the bus. She would later recount, however, that she also noticed someone acting "slightly suspicious" in the vicinity of the convent gates. It would emerge that someone else, other than the head nun, was watching Sister Philomena as she waited for her bus.

Kealen Herron was standing on the main street of Ballybay, ostensibly waiting for a lift to work, when he saw a young Lithuanian woman who worked locally pass down the street. He decided that he would attack the young woman. He got up from where he sat and slowly followed the young lady out the Clones Road of the town. The woman was walking in the direction of the convent of Our Lady of the Sacred Heart. Herron was walking about 200 metres behind her, planning his attack.

But as he attempted to catch up with the woman, a man clearing frost from a car windscreen distracted Herron. The youth feared that the man would notice him and later identify him. By the time Herron caught up with the young woman, she was taking a turn into the avenue leading up to the convent. The young Lithuanian woman greeted the friendly nun who was coming out with her suitcases to catch her bus.

The young woman had just evaded a possible sexual assault and perhaps even death. Sister Philomena Lyons was to become Kealen Herron's new target.

Earlier that morning, Herron had travelled from his girlfriend's home in Cootehill, County Cavan, where he had stayed the previous night. That morning, Herron's mother had rung the girl's house to be told that her son had stayed over for the night and that he was late for work. Herron's father drove to his son's girlfriend's house in Cootehill so the young man would not be too late. The father dropped the youth off on Main Street, Ballybay, where he was to get a lift on to work.

When he got to Main Street, Kealen Herron had gone into Quinn's shop, where he bought a soft drink. He went back into the shop a second time to buy cigarettes. CCTV cameras in the shop had recorded him making the purchases.

As Herron watched the two women, he paced slowly in

the direction of the gate, before appearing from around the side of one of the pillars and grabbing the nun. He dragged her behind him up the convent avenue. Then he pulled her further into a secluded field, hidden by a deep hedgerow.

What happened next remains clouded in some doubt, although the issues in question are matters of sequencing. Herron would later give contradictory accounts of what occurred after he dragged the nun into the field. The then Deputy State Pathologist, Professor Marie Cassidy, supported the view that Sister Philomena was unconscious at the time she was sexually assaulted. Investigators found no sign of a significant struggle between the woman and her attacker. It was concluded as highly probable that she may have lapsed into shock.

Herron needed no weapon, nor indeed had he any cause to bring such an item with him or worry about its disposal afterwards. He knew that he could do what he needed to do with his own hands, in what would be a bloodless slaying. He wrapped the scarf around the Sister's neck and pulled tightly.

Herron quickly fled the crime scene, running through adjoining fields and around the back of houses. When he finally made it to the Castleblayney Road, he had the intention of thumbing a lift in the direction of his work.

But instead of going to work he decided to turn back. He got a series of lifts to his home and when he got there he slept soundly. Later that evening Herron met up with his girlfriend and displayed no sign of the terrible crime that he had just committed.

When they were told that the nun's baggage had been left unattended at the roadside, outside the convent gates, Sister Philomena's colleagues became very worried for the welfare of their friend. After making a few enquiries, it emerged that Sister Philomena had not reached Blackrock, Co. Dublin, her intended destination. At 4 pm the convent alerted Gardaí that Sister Philomena was missing and a full-scale search was mounted.

Local CCTV footage was immediately seized, lest it would be needed at a later stage. It proved a wise move. The Garda team distributed questionnaires locally to ascertain what people had seen earlier in the day. They were hoping someone could provide useful information for the investigators.

On the following morning, Sunday, December 16, Kealen Herron filled in one of the questionnaires. He also volunteered to give a fingerprint sample, because he was one of the people sighted in the locality around the time of the murder.

The detectives spotted immediate discrepancies in his questionnaire. It raised their suspicions about the young man. But Gardaí had little to show that he was the killer. Then a breakthrough came in the form of tests carried out on the murdered nun's glasses, at the State Forensic Laboratory. On the evening of December 18, three-and-a-half days after Sister Philomena was sexually assaulted and killed, Herron's fingerprints were identified on her glasses. The following morning, at 6.15 am, Gardaí arrested Herron at his parent's home, six miles from where the nun had been sexually assaulted and murdered.

Further forensic evidence showed a DNA match between a sample of staining taken from the jeans that Herron had worn on December 15 and a sample of staining found on Sister Philomena's clothing.

Herron was charged and brought to trial for the nun's murder. The Central Criminal Court would later hear evidence from Superintendent Tom Long that Sister Philomena's body was found at 5.05 pm on December 15 by Gardaí, aided by the lights of a squad car, which had beamed into the hedge of a field on the periphery of the convent complex.

Professor Marie Cassidy would later conclude, after an examination of the body, that the woman had been strangled with her own scarf. This was still tied tightly around her neck when the body was found. Bruises around Sister Philomena's jaw and neck suggested to Dr Cassidy that the dead woman's assailant had forced his hands over her mouth, as he carried out his attack. The forensic expert concluded that the woman had been unconscious when she was subsequently attacked. Sister Philomena's clothing was found in a disturbed state. Her tights and underwear had been pulled down. Evidence of a sexual assault was discovered on the body. Investigators were certain that the assault had occurred in the vicinity of where the body was found.

After his arrest by Garda Detective Inspector Hugh Coll, Herron was placed under caution and it was at this point that he made a series of statements and admitted the murder.

In the Garda patrol car following his arrest, he had initially denied the sexual assault. But during the first formal statements that the youth gave to Gardaí, he claimed that he had sexually assaulted her after he had strangled her. In later statements he claimed that he had sexually assaulted the 68-year-old woman first and then strangled her afterwards because he was fearful that she would report him to Gardaí.

Herron's defence counsel, Patrick Gageby SC, said that his client wished to express his "profound sorrow, regret and remorse for his actions". He expressed "deep sympathy" to the nun's family, friends and religious colleagues.

The court heard that the youth, who lived with his parents six miles from Ballybay, had no prior convictions. He had worked at an assortment of jobs, including as a labourer, in an abattoir and in a plant hire business.

At his trial Herron pleaded guilty to the murder of Sister Philomena Lyons in the grounds of the Sacred Heart Convent,

Ballybay. On July 14, 2003, he was convicted of the nun's murder, for which he received a mandatory life sentence.

The murdered nun's family and former religious colleagues issued a statement: "Philomena would have forgiven Kealen Herron for this awful crime, which he must now deal with. We also forgive him and pray that he can reconcile whatever it was that led him to this terrible deed."

The statement was read to the media outside the Central Criminal Court by Sister Brigid Browne, Provincial of the Daughters of Our Lady of the Sacred Heart, on behalf of the Order and the relatives of Sister Philomena – the McCarthy and Lyons families.

The nun's family and colleagues did not omit from their sympathy the family of her young killer: "On this day, we also want to acknowledge how dreadful this tragedy has been for the entire Herron family, and we will keep you in our prayers at this most difficult time for all of you," Sister Brigid said.

"She was a friend, a colleague and a teacher who was dedicated to her own family and to the work of her congregation. She was a wonderful person and we miss her terribly. The circumstances of her tragic death devastated all of us who were privileged to experience her gentle, caring and helpful nature."

Sister Philomena would be "fondly remembered" in the prayers of her family and religious colleagues.

Like Sister Philomena Lyons, women who are strangled to death are victims of assaults by men physically stronger than they are. The strength differential between men and women explains the large difference in how each are killed – while the majority of men who are killed die after the use of a weapon, the majority of women are killed without the aid of weapons.

Strangulation accounts for almost one third of female killings, a statistic far in excess of its equivalent in male deaths. Over the first six years of the decade, just two men were strangled to death, which accounts for less than one per cent of the total. Indeed, just over 30% of men killed in Ireland die as a result of assault or strangulation, compared with over 55% of female victims of homicide.

Including the horrific case of Sister Philomena Lyons, there was a sexual motive behind the killing of six women in Ireland during the first six years of the decade and in each case it is believed the victim was strangled to death either prior to, or immediately after, a sexual assault.

While a greater proportion of women suffer death as a result of physical assault, the proportion of homicides that are caused by knives are similar for both men and women. Alongside the increasing availability of high-powered guns, the rise of a "knife culture" has been one of the largest contributory factors to Ireland's growing homicide rate. More people have been killed by knives over recent years in Ireland than by guns. There is a growing tendency, especially amongst young men, to reach for a knife during a dispute. It is a tendency that has resulted in much needless bloodshed.

In total, 35% of male homicide victims between 2000 and 2005 died as a result of stab wounds. Tellingly, almost half of those men were under the age of 30. For women, the figure is slightly lower but at 29% of all female homicides, knives have clearly ended too many lives.

Indeed, the number of people being killed by knives following minor verbal disputes has been addressed several times by members of the judiciary: in November 2005, Mr Justice Henry Abbot expressed his bewilderment at the fact that people are increasingly "thinking knives are natural and normal ways of resolving difficult social situations".

Judge Abbot was speaking at the sentencing of 22-year-old Mark Warner, from Donomore Avenue in Tallaght, who had been found guilty of the manslaughter of 17-year-old Jamie Keogh in July 2004. Keogh had been stabbed in the stomach after being embroiled in a physical confrontation, first with Mark Warner, and later with his brother, Kevin Warner.

Warner was charged with murder, with the prosecution claiming that he had retrieved a knife and brutally stabbed an unarmed man in the stomach: "What you have is Jamie Keogh, who is unarmed, facing someone who is heavily armed because he has a big knife with him," said prosecuting counsel Justin Dillon SC. "Mark Warner couldn't possibly have thought that he was under any threat."

Warner was found not guilty of murder but guilty of manslaughter. The jury's decision not to condemn Warner to life imprisonment for murder probably stemmed from Keogh's own behaviour on the night in question, which even Judge Abbot and Keogh's parents noted was far from acceptable.

The young father-of-one, still a child himself, had been drinking with friends in a local park before returning to his girlfriend's home. After he woke their child, Keogh's partner, Louise Cunningham, shouted at him and he responded by punching her. Christopher Cunningham Senior, the girl's father, intervened, but he, too, was assaulted by Keogh and was knocked unconscious during the incident.

Louise Cunningham's sister went to the Warner household, which was across the road, looking for her brother to come back and help restrain the violent Keogh. A fight broke out between Keogh and Mark Warner, although this was soon over. It was later that night when Keogh returned to the Warner house, looking for a re-match, that Kevin Warner became involved. A vicious fist-fight ensued. Eye-witnesses would recall how the pair were "kicking the heads off each other".

However, Keogh soon got the better of Warner. It was at this point that Mark Warner, a recovering heroin addict, produced a knife and fatally stabbed Keogh in the stomach, causing a 10-centimetre-deep wound that severed the lower part of his liver and punctured his portal vein. Keogh died at the scene.

Warner was sentenced to seven years' imprisonment, with the final year suspended. Judge Abbot said that while Keogh had behaved poorly on the night of his death, he did not deserve to die.

Just as Mr Justice Abbot had commented on the number of knife cases coming before his bench, so too, did Mr Justice Barry White when he was sentencing a Dublin youth for the stabbing to death of a party-goer outside a house in north Dublin in March 2001.

"Far too many are seen all too readily to resort to knives or other sharp instruments to settle conflicts," he told the court after Stephen Kelly, from Artane, had been found guilty of the manslaughter of 21-year-old Dundalk Institute of Technology graduate, Jonathan Guy.

Despite what Kelly initially told investigating Gardaí, Guy was defenceless and posing no danger when he was brutally stabbed with a kitchen knife.

The tragedy that would claim Guy's life all began when 17-year-old Jennifer O'Hara decided to throw a party. That it wasn't her house did not worry her. O'Hara had been thrown out of her own house after a blazing row with her parents that centred on her consumption of ecstasy tablets. She was staying with a friend who lived in the Newgrove Estate in Donaghmede on Dublin's northside, but the tenant of the house, Maura O'Reilly, had gone out and left O'Hara in charge for the night.

It didn't take long for her to start texting her friends, telling them that she was throwing an impromptu party. After texting and phoning a number of people, the crowd began to arrive.

The group spent the evening drinking alcohol, with some of those present consuming ecstasy too. The group present were mostly friends of O'Hara, although Maura O'Reilly's teenage son Michael had also brought friends over.

Amongst the group at the party was Stephen Kelly, from nearby Artane. As the party got into full swing, Kelly went upstairs to Michael O'Reilly's bedroom and exchanged words with one of O'Reilly's friends. Later on, as O'Reilly's friends were leaving the party, Kelly followed them outside and stole one of their mobile phones. A small scuffle broke out, the noise of which alerted three young men who were in an adjacent house.

Jonathan Guy, from Priorswood, was one of those young men. Hearing the commotion outside, Guy and his two friends went outside to try to break up the dispute. Kelly and his friends retreated back into the house, but Jennifer O'Hara was not happy with the turn the evening had taken.

"Jenny came in at around 2 am and asked us to leave," recalled Mark Larkin, who had attended the party with Stephen Kelly. "She said there was too many of us in the house and we had to leave."

The group decided to leave the party and Kelly, together with Larkin and a third friend, Karl Rheinisch, went into the kitchen of the house to look for weapons in case they were attacked outside. According to Larkin, the group went into the kitchen "to see if we could get a pole or something". He claimed that they looked for weapons in order to protect themselves.

As he entered the kitchen, Larkin saw Rheinisch open a drawer and take out a knife, which he handed to Stephen Kelly. Larkin left the house ahead of his two friends and was not assaulted by anybody. He told the court that he walked past the group and waited for his friends at the front gate of the house.

When the rest of his friends left, it wasn't so peaceful. When Stephen Kelly caught up with him, Larkin was shocked by his friend's disclosure. "He just said, 'I'm after stabbing a man' or something," he told the court. "I was in shock; I said 'you did in your bollocks'."

The two men parted ways, Larkin getting a taxi to his home in Finglas and Kelly getting into a separate taxi to the home of his friend David Cunningham, where he was staying that night.

Cunningham would later recall hearing from Kelly about the stabbing incident. "I hope that yer man's all right," he said to Cunningham, as the pair went to bed.

Jonathan Guy was far from all right. He was rushed to hospital, where doctors battled in vain to save his life. Guy had suffered one stab wound to the chest, which penetrated his heart. The victim had been stabbed with a downward swing of the knife, inflicted as Kelly left the party.

When Kelly heard that his victim had died, he spent the day travelling on the Dart from Howth to Dun Laoghaire considering what he could do. Eventually, he decided to hand himself in to Gardaí.

After he was arrested, Kelly admitted stabbing Guy but claimed to have done so in self-defence, after he was attacked by a group of men outside the house who were armed with poles or bars. He initially told Gardaí that Guy went to attack him and "the knife went into him". However, he later admitted that Guy had not approached him and was, in fact, totally unarmed at the time of the stabbing. The court heard

The headless body of Paiche Onyemaechi, daughter of the Malawian Chief Justice, was discovered in Co. Kilkenny in August 2004. Her killer has not been brought to justice.

Leader of the so-called 'Westies', Shane Coates was one of a new breed of Irish criminal – young, ruthless and fearless.
(© *Collins Photo Agency*)

Twenty-two-year-old Martin Kenny was shot as he lay in bed with his girlfriend at her home in Ballyfermot. His murder was related to a gang feud in the city.
(© *PA*)

The body of 26-year-old Darren Geoghegan after he was shot dead in Firhouse in November 2005. Geoghegan was shot dead alongside 30-year-old Gavin Byrne as they sat in a car. The double killing was part of a vicious feud between rival criminal gangs.

(© Colin Keegan, Collins Photo Agency)

Above: Geraldine Leamy holds the communion shoe of her murdered son, Eric. Liam Keane was charged with his murder but not convicted.
(© *Mark Condren*)

Left: Limerick woman Geraldine Leamy turned her house into a shrine for her murdered son, Eric.
(© *Mark Condren*)

David 'Frog Eyes' Stanners is serving life imprisonment for the murder of Limerick crime boss Kieran Keane. (© *Collins Photo Agency*)

Anthony McCarthy was convicted and sentenced to life in prison for Kieran Keane's murder. (© *Collins Photo Agency*)

Mayo farmer Padraig Nally's conviction for the manslaughter of John Ward was overturned by the Court of Criminal Appeal in October 2006. He now faces a retrial.
(© PA)

Left: Thirty-six-year-old bachelor Shaun Duffy died after a savage attack in his home in Co. Donegal. Duffy was beaten, stabbed and shot with a crossbow during the assault. His killer remains at large.
(© *Declan Doherty*)

Below: Kathleen Duffy-Ward standing outside the home of her murdered son, Shaun – "I don't think anyone will ever be caught for killing Shaun".
(© *Declan Doherty*)

Above: Popular actor Robbie Doolin died after a street altercation in August 2000. His coffin was draped in the Tricolour.
(© *Collins Photo Agency*)

Right: Gardaí at the scene of the killing of 17-year-old Jamie Keogh in Tallaght, in July 2004. Keogh was unarmed when he was stabbed to death during a street brawl.
(© *Collins Photo Agency*)

Felix McKenna, former Head of the Criminal Assets Bureau, has been at the forefront of the battle against organised crime in Ireland.
(© *Justin Farrelly*)

A sniffer dog at Dublin Airport – over €1 billion worth of illegal drugs are trafficked through Ireland every year.
(© *Mark Condren*)

that Guy was simply in the wrong place at the wrong time, as Kelly left the house armed with a knife.

Following a 13-day trial, Kelly was found guilty of the manslaughter of Jonathan Guy. Sentencing Kelly to 14 years imprisonment, Mr Justice Barry White took into account the defendant's previous good character and the fact that he had no prior convictions, but imposed a sentence at the higher end of the manslaughter scale. Mr Justice White said that deterrent sentences were necessary in order to call a halt to the knife culture that was causing so much death and injury in modern-day Ireland.

Speaking after her son's killer was jailed, Sheila Guy reiterated the judge's comments, saying that young people have to learn the repercussions of arming themselves with knives. "He didn't deserve to die, I do feel it's necessary to give strong sentences," she said. "It [the 14-year sentence] might put fear into the heart of any man out there who chooses to take a weapon and stick it into an unarmed man."

In April 2003, White again stated his desire to impose tough sentences in order to make young men think twice before picking up knives to settle disputes: A "loud and clear message must go forth," White said. "The use of knives for violence will not be tolerated," the Judge insisted.

In the dock on this occasion was 22-year-old John Dillon, from Carlow. Dillon admitted that he had attacked 17-year-old Warren Slater with a knife on May 13, 2001, but he claimed it was in self-defence. Not only did he believe his victim to be carrying a knife – a belief that proved false – but Dillon also claimed that the deceased had attempted to rape his mother some weeks before the fatal stabbing.

The court heard, during the nine-day trial, of bad blood between Dillon and Slater. The two men lived in the same house at Granby Row in Carlow town. Slater shared a downstairs bedsit with his girlfriend, Louise Heary. The couple had a six-month-old baby girl together. Above them lived the Dillon family: John, his sister Cathy, and his mother Noeleen.

Noeleen, John's mother would later tell the court that a few weeks previous to the stabbing incident, Slater had gone into her flat while she and her daughter were there, wearing just a pair of underpants. He had a duvet wrapped around his shoulders. The woman had been upset over an unrelated matter at the time and Slater was offering her some comfort when he lunged at her and knocked her off the couch and onto the floor. He then pounced down on top of her and tried to initiate a sexual encounter with her, Noeleen Dillon told the court. Her arms were "covered in bruises" the following day, she recalled. Her son had reacted with fury over the alleged incident, in which Slater had tried to sexually assault her.

In the hours preceding the fatal incident, Warren Slater and his girlfriend had a row. Later that day she asked John Dillon to accompany her across the road to a party where her boyfriend was drinking and relaxing with friends. Heary wanted Slater to come home but she did not want to go over to the party on her own. Dillon was hesitant at first but he eventually agreed. She, "insisted" he later told the court.

As John Dillon and Louise Heary crossed the street, Slater emerged from the house in which he was attending the party. A "shouting match" developed between him and his girlfriend. But when Warren Slater spotted Dillon he verbally attacked his neighbour. "He kind of started with me straight away then, because of what happened with my mother."

Dillon's mother told the court that she heard her son say: "You tried to rape my mother" and then heard Mr Slater say: "So what?" or words to that effect. Noeleen Dillon said her son "just flipped".

As they began to argue outside the house, Dillon said that Slater was, "kind of shoving me with his elbow". The accused man told the court that Slater blamed him for spreading stories about the alleged sexual assault on his mother.

Warren Slater and his girlfriend were, "still arguing" while the two men were having the initial verbal row. "Louise was telling him to stop and he didn't want to stop, he wanted to keep going at this stage, he wanted to get to me," Dillon said. Slater went to come at him but his girlfriend tried to block him. Dillon said it was then that he went into the house and picked up a knife.

"The reason I went for the knife was I thought he had a weapon. When he came at me, he had a hand behind his back, and I thought he had a knife," Dillon told the court.

Dillon had become enraged at this point. He vehemently denied that he had ever told any third party about the Slater's alleged attempted rape of his mother. "I got into an awful state of temper," Dillon recalled. He could remember going into the house and going as far as the kitchen. He could remember nothing after that moment. "I couldn't really recall what happened. I was in a rage at the time," he said. "I wasn't really thinking, I wasn't really thinking straight."

John Dillon's mother saw her son leaving the house with the knife and she made an attempt to take it from him. He resisted, leaving her with cuts across the inside of her fingers, and rushed past.

As he was leaving the house, Warren Slater was trying to come in after him. Slater broke loose from his girlfriend and went to lunge at Dillon. Dillon "swiped" at Slater with the knife. Slater was stabbed four times; the most significant wound was to cut through his jugular vein and carotid artery. Slater slowly choked on his own blood.

When Gardaí arrived to arrest John Dillon, he told them that he had believed that Slater had a knife behind his back and that he was going to stab him or his mother. "He came at me; I thought he was going to stab me. I didn't mean to stab him. I will go to jail, I did not mean to kill him," he said. The previous year, John Dillon had been on special medication for anger management. He had "a terrible temper," he would later tell Gardaí when they arrived at the scene.

Dillon was convicted of the youth's manslaughter, by a unanimous jury verdict. Mr Justice White said that while the minimum sentence he sought to impose was 20 years, he took into account Dillon's "relative youth," his low intellect and the remorse he had shown as mitigating factors. The Judge sentenced Dillon to 14 years in prison for the manslaughter of the teenage father-of-one. "As a result of your actions, a young infant girl is left bereft of the support, companionship and affection of her father," the Judge said.

Warren Slater's young partner and mother of his child was left deeply traumatised by what she saw on the night of May 13, 2001. Likewise, Mary McCarthy will never forget the day she saw her own son bleed to death in front of her, inside the hallway of their home at Spriggs Road in Gurranabraher, Cork.

Twenty-eight-year-old Noel McCarthy returned from Cork University Hospital on the night of May 2, 2000, at around 3.30 am. He had a large wrap-around bandage on his head and a plaster on his face. He had earlier been involved in a row with a neighbour, Keith O'Donovan.

Shortly after 3.30 am, Mary McCarthy was standing with Noel and one of his friends in her hallway when "a very loud bang came on the door. When Noel opened the latch of the door, the door was pushed in," Mary McCarthy later recalled. "I had my arm around Noel to support him." Keith O'Donovan and another man came in. "Keith called either Noel or me a 'cockroach'," she said.

Noel McCarthy said to the intruders: "In the name of God what are ye doing this to me for? What did I ever do to ye?" The young man's mother said she saw Keith O'Donovan's face filled with anger and rage. He was "grunting, he was really grunting, his face was distorted."

What she saw next was something no mother could bear to witness. Keith O'Donovan plunged a knife into her son's groin.

"When he came in I didn't see any knife. The knife was put into the left groin and when the knife was in there he twisted it. He twisted the knife in my son," Mary McCarthy later recalled. As O'Donovan withdrew the blade, Noel McCarthy's mother grabbed the knife. It was, "covered in blood," she said. "He said, 'let the knife go and I'll go', and I said no. He said, 'let the knife go and I'll go'," the jury was told.

What had led to the knife attack was clouded in some mystery, although it was established that the stabbing was not the first assault that Keith O'Donovan had committed that day. Nor indeed was it his first time to wield a knife in violent circumstances.

Mary McCarthy told the jury that she had gone to her bedroom at around 10 pm, having spent the evening watching television with Noel and her other son Peter and four friends of theirs. She was preparing to get into her bed when she heard a "tremendous loud bang" on the front sitting-room window. "I was going to come down but I heard Noel opening the door. I heard the voice of Keith O'Donovan and knowing him all my life I said, 'that's only Keith', and I got undressed and went to bed."

Mary McCarty told the court that she fell off to sleep. Some time later she was woken up by a further "disturbance". "I looked out the window and I saw a man who was banging someone's head on the steps," she recalled.

She got up from bed and put on a dressing gown and went down to the front door to see who was being hurt. When she got to her front door she saw Keith O'Donovan and another man assaulting her son Noel outside the house. "I was very angry, I cursed at him [Keith O'Donovan]," she said.

Mary McCarthy told the court how she grabbed hold of O'Donovan's jumper. She recalled how she "managed to throw him into the garden to give Noel a chance to get up". To her amazement, Noel's four friends looked on from inside, through the front window. "I got vexed with them because they didn't help Noel. They were looking out the window and they didn't help Noel, I was very annoyed at them," she recalled.

Noel McCarthy was visibly distressed after the attack. His mother said that her son was "shaking and very pale" after he returned inside to the house. Unwisely, Noel McCarthy then decided to go to Keith O'Donovan's house, just four doors away from the McCarthy home, to demand an apology for the assault. Noel McCarthy returned five minutes later with a head injury and was taken to hospital in a taxi, she said.

It was the second time in the evening that O'Donovan had assaulted Noel McCarthy, but worse was yet to come. Mary McCarthy told the court that while she was sitting downstairs in her house, with one of Noel's friends, waiting for him to return from hospital, they heard voices outside the house. "We're back Noel, Noel we're back", she heard. She recognised one of those voices as that of Keith O'Donovan. She was "frightened, very, very frightened" by them.

When her son returned from hospital, O'Donovan was waiting for him. He pushed in the door of the McCarthy's home and, within a few seconds, he had stabbed the 28-year-old man. The force of the knife attack was powerful. O'Donovan punctured the young man's bladder and cut through his femoral artery. Noel McCarthy was rushed to Cork University Hospital but, despite emergency surgery, he bled to death.

Thirty-one-year-old Keith O'Donovan, a single father of a 10-year-old son, was charged with his neighbour's murder. He was convicted at a June 2002 trial but this was overturned on appeal to the Court of Criminal Appeal. O'Donovan was re-tried in July 2004 and found guilty of manslaughter. It emerged after the court case that, up to that date, the guilty man had 18 previous convictions dating back to 1989. Among these were several convictions for assault, including assault with a knife and assault with intent to rob.

While many fatal stabbings see the killer or killers flying into a rage over a row or dispute, there is ample evidence that many involve no such provocation. Fifty-nine-year-old Patrick Clinton was a victim of just such an attack. He lived with his brother Noel in a caravan at the back of their parents' house in Ardee, County Louth.

Patrick Clinton had spent most of his life working in England, where he had laboured long and hard on the construction sites that dotted the UK in the 1970s and 1980s. He was a hard worker and had returned to Ireland to live in his retirement. He had moved into the caravan at the bottom of his elderly parents' garden.

Just six days before Christmas 2000, the brothers were visited by father-of-two Martin Myles (33) of Ferdia Park, Ardee, and his drinking buddy, 17-year-old Kevin Reilly, of Hurlestown a rural area outside Ardee. He had been drinking alcohol since the age of 11. By the time he cycled with Myles to the Clintons' caravan, he was drinking three flagons of cider a day and was also dependent on drugs.

Myles, too, had a chequered past. He had previous convictions in Ireland for assault, forgery and possession of a firearm but prior to the attack he had escaped detention in Loughnan House and fled to England. There, he gathered 21 convictions, including one for possession of an imitation firearm.

Reilly and Myles had been drinking since early on the evening before they called to the brothers. En route to the Clintons' caravan, the pair had eaten takeaway chicken and chips, washing their meal down with whiskey. At the caravan, they spent a while drinking more cider and lager with Noel and Patrick Clinton,.

The Clintons would not have suspected that their visitors had planned anything more than just a day of boozing and talking. But Kevin Reilly was in debt to a Dundalk drug dealer. He needed money and he planned to get it by taking it from the Clinton brothers.

When later interviewed by detectives from the Garda National Bureau of Criminal Investigation (NBCI), Martin Myles, admitted that he and Reilly had planned to rob the brothers. The pair were aware that both Clintons would have just recently been paid their Christmas double Social Welfare payment.

Reilly had a plan that he and Myles would each stab one of the brothers before they would take the men's social welfare payments. After a while spent drinking, Reilly took a knife and stabbed Patrick Clinton twice in the back. Gardaí would later be told that Myles was supposed to stab Noel Clinton, but he could not make himself do it. When interviewed later by Gardaí, Myles told them that he believed Noel Clinton would have given him money if he had asked for it.

The injured and bleeding man went to his parents' home at the other end of the garden. Here he woke his 84-year-old mother, Brigid. The elderly woman helped him dial the emergency services. In two of these calls to the emergency services, and later when he spoke with the first Garda at the scene, Garda Maurice Cullen, Patrick Clinton named Myles and Reilly as the men who had entered their caravan.

Patrick Clinton died from his injuries. The then Deputy State Pathologist, Professor Marie Cassidy, would later conclude that the knife wounds inflicted on Clinton would not normally have resulted in a fatality. However, the 59-year-old had a severe heart condition, rendering him less able to survive the assault and making cardiac resuscitation more difficult.

Following the conviction of both men in May 2003 for the manslaughter of Patrick Clinton, the dead man's daughter Barbara was highly critical of the office of the Director of Public Prosecutions (DPP) for accepting manslaughter pleas from the pair rather than trying them for murder. The Central Criminal Court handed down a 17-year jail sentence to Martin Myles and a 14-year jail sentence to Kevin Reilly.

Barbara Clinton told local newspaper, the *Drogheda Independent*, that she believed that if somebody takes a life then it is only right that their life is also taken. Her anger at the manslaughter convictions was palpable. Life in prison should mean life, not the opportunity to apply for parole after a few years, she insisted. She described Myles and Reilly as "scumbags" and predicted that the killers would "spend a few years in a prison-cum-hotel" and would ultimately walk free.

Her father, meanwhile, was in a graveyard – another victim of Ireland's new knife culture.

*   *   *   *   *

Discounting strangulations, physical assault, in which no weapons are used, account for 30% of all male homicides and 24% of all female killings. The vast majority of cases involving both men and women occur after a large quantity of alcohol has been consumed by either the victim, the aggressor or both. Many, although by no means all, fatal assaults take place late at night.

Not all fatal assaults involve sustained physical attacks,

however. It is a fact that is tragically ignored that it can take just one punch to kill a person, depending on that person's health, the amount of alcohol or drugs they have consumed and the force with which they hit the ground after the punch.

The elderly obviously stand the highest risk of dying after assault. Several cases involving elderly men killed by intruders have repulsed the country. Paddy Logan, an 81-year-old who lived with his brother in Castlejordan, Co. Meath, was one such victim. Logan died after being beaten with a sweeping brush by two men who called to his front door as he was listening to a GAA match on the radio.

Likewise, 82-year-old Mick Creighton – the oldest victim of homicide over the first six years of the decade – died after he was tied up and beaten by intruders at his home in Westmeath.

However, while the elderly are at a higher risk of death following assault, minor – or, at least, not sustained – physical attacks have also killed young and healthy men. And while there have been cases of people dying following savage beatings which, in some cases, have rendered them almost unrecognisable to their loved ones, it is equally as common for the deceased to have been on the receiving end of a far lighter beating. In some cases, the victim has died hours after the fight. They have already returned home before the level of injury to the brain has become clear.

Many of those who have found themselves in court charged in relation to a violent death have spoken of their shock and horror at learning of their victim's death the following morning.

Mark Donovan, from Ennis, Co. Clare, was one such accused. Donovan was charged with an assault that claimed the life of 20-year-old Alan O'Donnell, from Crusheen, also in Co. Clare. The court heard that the pair had collided on the dance floor of a nightclub in Ennis and that Donovan's reaction was to punch O'Donnell in the head. The young man fell to the ground due to the force of the punch, striking his head on the floor. He died some hours later. Donovan was sentenced to six months for assault.

* * * * *

There is one case that is recorded on the Gardaí's list of violent deaths which resulted in no prosecution after the DPP recommended not pressing charges. The case caused much comment in the media, not so much because of the incident itself, but because of the person involved and the unusual funeral it created.

It was a rare sight for a Dublin church – a coffin draped in the tricolour, flanked by a piper and four teenage boys dressed in full paramilitary regalia. This was no ordinary funeral. The 33-year-old man being buried at St Bernadette's Church on Clogher Road, in August 2000 was a member of the so-called "Real IRA", a hardcore group of Republicans disillusioned with the Northern Peace Process, who two years earlier had planted the bomb in Omagh that had killed 28 people. This was to be a funeral with full paramilitary honours, as evidenced by the four youths dressed in black berets, green khaki jumpers, black trousers and black shoes. Plainclothes Garda detectives from Crumlin station were joined by anti-terrorist officers based at Harcourt Square for the funeral, scanning the crowd for "Real IRA" suspects.

The dead man had been a member of the FCA but army chiefs had reportedly banned former reservist colleagues from attending the funeral service in uniform because of the dead man's suspected links with the outlawed terrorist group.

As the press photographers' cameras flashed, it was hard to believe that the man being honoured by the renegade terrorist group was, in fact, a well-known television actor who had starred in a number of television productions for RTÉ.

It was also hard to believe that despite the paramilitary treatment, the deceased had been the victim of little more than a street fight.

Dubliner Robbie Doolin had played roles in sit-coms including *Upwardly Mobile*. He met his death after being involved in a row outside a hackney office. An inquest a year after his death heard that the 33-year-old minor celebrity, and active Real IRA member, died of cardiac arrest after he was physically restrained by a security guard. His sensitivity to cocaine, the illicit drug in his system, was a major contributing factor in his death but the jury also heard that he had three times the legal drink-drive level of alcohol in his blood.

Doolin, of Clogher Road, Crumlin, Dublin, died in the early hours of August 21, 2000. State Pathologist Professor John Harbison told the inquest in June 2001 that there was cocaine in the actor's urine and cocaine byproducts were also found in his blood. The pathologist said that it was not uncommon for sudden death to occur among users of cocaine, although Harbison did not find signs of habitual use of the drug. Doolin inhaled blood that was created by an injury he received to his mouth, which had played a role in his inability to breathe.

His *Upwardly Mobile* co-star and fellow thespian, Joe Savino, would later tell the inquest that Doolin called to his apartment at 9 pm on August 20. Fifteen minutes later the two actors went to a pub for a drink and to play a game of darts. They both drank Jack Daniels and coke. It was later estimated that the pair had about six doubles each.

Just after midnight the two men left the bar. Savino had work commitments the following day and so he didn't stay out any later. The men parted company at the quays. "Robbie was in top form: we had been working on a script together," Savino said.

Pony Cabs security guard John O'Keeffe told the inquest that Doolin came into the premises at around 2 am. The actor was looking for a cab. Whether it was a consequence of having taken too much drink or not, Doolin rushed out of the cab office about 20 minutes later and vomited in the street. Upon his return, he was told that he would not be able to get a cab because there was a chance he would get sick again. Doolin then shouted at staff at the cab company. He claimed that he was being belittled. As staff tried to pacify the actor, Doolin swung a punch and put his two fists up in front of him.

Gardaí came along and calmed the situation. The officers asked the security man if he was going to get Doolin a cab, to which O'Keefe said he was not. Gardaí asked Doolin to move along and he did. It was around 2.20 am and up to that point all the actor had done was earn himself some bruises and an injured ego. But worse was to follow.

At the inquest, his mother Alice told how her son had arrived home at 4 am on the morning of the incident. He hugged her and said, "I love you Ma" just after arriving home by taxi. He needed £3 for the fare and she gave him £5. After hugging her son, she watched him go to the front door with his motorcycle helmet, saying that he was going to "get the person who beat me up". His mother pleaded with him not to go, advising her son that he had a few drinks on him. He revved up the bike and drove off. Three hours later she identified him in St James's Hospital morgue.

About an hour after the intial fracas at the Pony Cabs office, a motorcycle pulled up and a man in a motorcycle helmet came into the office, holding a telescopic baton and said: "I'm going to kill you," to the security guard.

It was the same man that O'Keefe had struggled with earlier. But this time Doolin seemed stronger and the security guard had to enlist the help of a hackney driver who happened to be in the office to restrain him. O'Keefe told the inquest that the man rolled around on the ground and kept struggling. O'Keefe tried to keep Doolin down by holding his own chest against the man's back.

The mêlée carried on outside the office, where Doolin struck the security man with the baton and also bit him. Cleaner Loretto Byrne, who was walking down South Great Georges Street at around 4.30 am on her way to work, told the inquest into Doolin's death that she saw the disturbance outside the Pony Cabs' office. She said that she saw a man lying on the ground and another man on top of him. The man on the ground was not moving.

Gardaí arrived on the scene and an ambulance was quickly dispatched. Doolin was rushed to St James's Hospital, where he was pronounced dead.

Robbie Doolin's name is listed by Gardaí as being among those who died violently in 2000. The circumstance of his death were just that – violent. It was also completely avoidable. To what extent Doolin was acting out of character, having consumed cocaine before he returned to pick a fight with the security guard, will remain in doubt. But while many people have died as a result of premeditated rows involving knives and other implements, Robbie Doolin's death arose from an act of his own aggression, whether drug-inspired or not.

Professor Harbison told the Dublin City Coroner's Court that Doolin died from myocardial hypersensitivity resulting in cardiac arrest, due to cocaine sensitivity in circumstances of physical restraint. He had in his system a level of 272 mg alcohol per 100 ml of blood, more than three times the legal limit for driving. After hearing the story of Robbie

Doolin's final hours, the jury returned a verdict of death by misadventure.

The inquest heard that Gardaí had sent a file to the Director of Public Prosecutions and the DPP directed that no prosecution be taken.

Just as the death of Robbie Doolin was not the result of a violent assault on his person, the killing of Kilkenny man James Healy was by no means the result of a "normal" shooting incident.

A fatal shooting almost immediately stirs up images of a drug-related slaying. That is not always the case, however. There were 11 cases of people being shot to death by a legally owned firearm following disputes over the first six years of the decade. The reasons behind each dispute were different – some were domestic incidents, others involving rows between friends. Perhaps the most intriguing case, however, involved that most Irish of disputes – a row over land.

Thirty-nine-year-old Michael Kehoe was a man typical of many rural areas of Ireland. He was a bachelor and though a young man, he was unlikely ever to find a mate: he rarely socialised and when he did his conversational skills were limited. He was dedicated to an ideal – his existence was inextricably linked to the land. His solitary interest was in retaining his association with the farm on which he was born, at Coolyhune in County Carlow.

That farm was the place in which he and his two siblings – his elder sister Catherine and his younger brother John – were born in the 1960s. At just over 55 acres, it was not a large farm and was insufficient to provide any substantial income, particularly as it was only of average quality land. It was partly boggy and during the 1980s and 90s it had never been modernised to maximise its profitability. Anyone who would work on the farm would have to supplement their living by working elsewhere as well.

The three Kehoe siblings all lived on the small farm with their parents for their early adult years. Catherine, the eldest, was a catering assistant and gave much of her spare time to minding her ailing elderly parents. Michael did the principal farming work and his brother John was a farm labourer. Their parents became less active and the father died in 1988. Michael then emerged as the principal manager of the small farm. He assumed a position of seniority over his two siblings because of his aggression and a temper, which he did not keep in check.

His temper would ultimately play a defining role in his attitude towards anyone who crossed him or who challenged his uncompromising belief in his claim to the land of his birth.

The relationship between the siblings was not an equal one. Michael, though rash and illogical in relation to his supposed entitlement, was not a fool. Believing that he could annex the land for himself solely by force of character, Michael took total control of the farm's affairs.

When his mother became ill and died in 1993, she left no will or testament to say which of her children would inherit the farm. Sensing the implications of a property intestate, Michael reportedly expelled his sister from the farm. He had taken what was rightly his, in his own mind at least. The law would ultimately be called upon to determine the validity of Michael's sole claim to the land – but Michael Kehoe placed no faith in the claims of law. In his mind, he was naturally entitled to a farm that he had worked himself.

Michael Kehoe continued to live off the sale of sheep he reared on the small rough farm. He also drew unemployment assistance from the Department of Social Welfare. He worked briefly in a local meat plant to supplement his meagre income. For a time he also worked as a trainee on a FÁS local-employment scheme at Saint Mullin's graveyard. This allowed him to retain his social welfare payments while receiving a small amount extra for community-based work refurbishing the cemetery.

John had remained as a labourer, working on and off, but he posed no challenge to Michael over the land. Michael lived a solitary existence in the two storey house that had formerly been the family home, located down a quiet and lonely avenue. Catherine and John Kehoe were entitled to one third each of the estate of their parents, arising out of the absence of a final will and testament. But their brother Michael continued to lay claim to the land by virtue of his occupation of the property. He failed to offer any settlement proposal.

In 1998, Catherine Kehoe went to a solicitor and took out legal administration of the estate, forcing Michael to concede to a deal a year later. Michael Kehoe and his sister both signed papers agreeing that he would raise a sum of around €65,000 to pay for her portion of the farm.

How he would raise this money was another issue altogether. He did not have access to capital or cash of any great amount. He reportedly applied to Carlow Council for planning permission for a property on a section of the land with road frontage. He could then sell the land with an enhanced value, but the application failed.

Michael Kehoe delayed and showed little further interest in meeting his side of the 1999 agreement. As the estate's administrator, Catherine took further legal action, which culminated in a High Court order in April 2002. The outcome of that action was that a section of the farm was to be sold off to meet the terms of the deal.

Michael Kehoe bitterly resented the court's interference in his affairs. He is believed to have consulted a number of lawyers, adamant in the view that having a part of the farm sold was unacceptable and should be stopped. But he was told that the facts were simple. He had acknowledged his sister's proper legal entitlement to the share of their deceased parents' estate and had done so in writing. He had then failed, in the three years since, to live up to this agreement in any substantial way whatsoever.

The sale of 26.75 acres of land was to be handled by Kilkenny-based estate agent David Hughes who was from Graiguenamanagh, a few miles from the farm. The local newspaper, the *Kilkenny People*, carried advertisements for the sale over a couple of weeks leading up to the December 12, 2003 auction, at the Club House Hotel in Kilkenny.

Less than a dozen people were in attendance at the opening stages of the auction when a number of local farmers spoke up. One told the attendance: "This is not a free sale of land and no neighbour is going to bid on it and noone will be welcome in the area if they buy it." Hughes told the men that it was none of their business and that they simply did not know the facts leading up to the auction.

The auction failed to reach the €80,000 reserve. Two months later, on February 6, 2004, a further advertisement appeared offering the land for sale by private treaty. It was at this point that James Healy, a young man from Gowran in Kilkenny, took an interest in buying the property.

On February 11, 2004, Healy bought the 27 acres for in excess of €100,000, as an investment. Healy was a totally different character to Michael Kehoe. The 30-year-old was a massive Liverpool football supporter, he loved movies and he considered himself to be something of an expert on 1980s music. He had studied Science at NUI Maynooth and worked in Dublin for years before returning to Kilkenny to manage pharmacies owned by his brother Pierce. In 2003 he married Yvonne, whom he met in Maynooth. He lived a happy life with his new bride and "little James", Yvonne's eight-year-old son from a previous relationship.

The dispute over the land continued and Michael became more troublesome for his sister as the sale was being completed. Catherine obtained an interlocutory injunction at Kilkenny Circuit Court in May 2005, preventing her brother Michael from entering or interfering with the land.

James Healy had also been compelled to take out an injunction against disruption by Michael Kehoe. Kehoe had made efforts at intimidating the young man to prevent him from making use of the land which he had fairly bought.

Gardaí at Thomastown in Kilkenny reportedly received a number of complaints from the Healy family, alleging threats and intimidation from Michael Kehoe. Things were getting worse and Michael Kehoe's determination to prevent the land being used by anyone other than himself, coupled with his aggressive nature, would reap horrifying dividends for both the Healy and Kehoe families. James Healy was aware that Kehoe appeared to be growing increasingly volatile but he could not have imagined what was to happen next.

Healy put down fencing around the perimeter of his newly acquired land in late August 2005, but it was torn up and damaged. He could guess who had done it. He went back to the property along with another brother, Brian, to re-erect the fencing on his next day off, Saturday, September 3. Beforehand, James Healy took the wise step of telephoning Gardaí at Graiguenamanagh to tell them he was going out to the farm.

James and Brian Healy arrived early that morning. At 10 am, Michael Kehoe and James Healy met at the site where the brothers were fencing and a brief and seemingly meaningless discussion ensued over tractor access.

Kehoe returned to the farmyard. He went into the house and fetched his legally-licensed shotgun. He returned again to where the two young men were working away, fencing the boundary of James Healy's land. The Healy brothers could not have understood the seriousness of the situation when they spotted Kehoe re-emerging through the fields. The armed man fired one gunshot at the men but it missed. He then aimed to fire a further shot.

What happened next would be recalled by Brian Healy at an inquest weeks later. "The second shot came quickly. I was in utter terror and I feared both of us were going to be killed. I was already through the gate into the next field when the second shot came. I heard James roaring," Brian Healy later recalled. He saw Michael Kehoe take aim a third time and hit his brother James in the back.

Brian Healy went over to his brother: "I asked him was he okay. James shook his head, there was blood coming from his mouth and on his face."

Local farmer, Lar Cushen told how he heard a shot, but only became concerned when he heard the second shot: "Then I heard a shout and a scream. I recognised Mick's voice and heard him shout, 'Get the fuck out of here and don't come back.' I then heard a third shot – I was very anxious."

Kehoe walked away from the bloody attack, as James Healy lay dying. Gardaí rushed to the scene and at 4 pm Kehoe was located in a nearby farmyard shed. As they awaited the arrival of a qualified police negotiator, detectives at the scene attempted to persuade him to leave the gun down and come out to them. Detective Sergeants John Hunt and Jim Lyng approached the armed man in the shed. The experienced Gardaí spent over two hours trying to engage him in conversation. They offered him an opportunity to talk to family, a priest, a doctor, a solicitor or anyone else he wished to. "There were long periods where he remained totally silent with his head in his hands as if in troubled contemplation," Detective Sergeant Hunt later recalled.

Shortly before 6 pm, Michael Kehoe killed himself with a gunshot to the head.

At the inquest, on November 15, the jury issued an unusual although interesting statement, pointing out the anomaly that Michael Kehoe had been at the centre of a contentious and, at times, aggressive campaign of intimidation over disputed land, but he nonetheless was allowed to retain possession of his firearm.

They were echoing a point raised by James Healy's brother Pierce, who questioned why a person wishing to obtain a certificate to possess a deadly weapon was not obliged to first of all get a certificate from a doctor confirming their suitability, or otherwise, to get a gun licence. The law in relation to the licensing of firearms, notwithstanding proposed changes in the Criminal Justice Bill 2004, substantially dates to 1925.

"We call on the Minister for Justice, Equality and Law Reform to carry out a comprehensive review of the law on firearms and offensive weapons, particularly in the area of revoking licences, and bring forward necessary amendments and adequate resources for enforcement as soon as possible," said the jury.

Afterwards the Healy family issued a statement in which they welcomed the jury's recommendation calling for a review of firearms legislation.

Eight

The Most Dangerous County in Ireland

On July 16, 2005, a terrorist bomb ripped through a tourist bus in the Turkish resort of Kusadasi, shattering the peace in what for years had been a popular holiday spot for Irish travellers. Amongst the five victims of the atrocity was 17-year-old Waterford girl, Tara Whelan.

The pretty young Irish girl had boarded the bus to make the short journey into the local town. Her holiday with friends was nearing an end and she hoped to buy some presents for family members at home.

When news of the tragedy reached Waterford, people were devastated at the needless waste of a young life. Whelan's body was flown home to be buried close to her house in the village of Kilmeaden. There was a sense of unprecedented mourning in the village as the body of one of their own was returned from foreign soil.

Amongst the large crowd of mourners at the funeral was Dick Forristal, a 68-year-old who was well known, both locally and nationally, as a horse-breeder. Forristal made the journey to the funeral from his home at the Carrigavantry Stud. He was joined by Louis Murphy, a friend who he had known for over 50 years and who lived with him at the isolated stud farm. Like so many others, Forristal was outraged that a local girl could go on holidays only to be murdered in a senseless terrorist attack. He did not know Tara personally, but felt compelled to attend the funeral.

Forristal and Murphy paid their respects to young Tara Whelan on July 21 and made their way home to the Carrigavantry Stud. Murphy was driving and he dropped his friend off at the house. From there, he drove to the home of John Kent, who had arranged to join them for lunch. The plan was for Forristal to start cooking while Murphy collected their friend.

Forristal entered his house but soon discovered that he was not alone. Twenty-year-old Anthony Barnes and 21-year-old Andrew Halligan, two young thugs from Ballybeg in Waterford City, had broken into his home in the hope of robbing him while he was out.

It was not the first time Forristal had seen the two thieves. Two days previously the horse breeder had spotted the two youths acting suspiciously in the area. Forristal had met them at the entrance to his three-bedroomed home and knew straight away that they were up to no good. The bachelor had been broken into on five occasions over recent years and he told the two youths in no uncertain terms not to return to his property.

He would have recognised Anthony Barnes and Andrew Halligan instantly when he saw them inside his house on July 21. He confronted the youths but this time Barnes and Halligan would not be moved on so easily. A scuffle broke out. Forristal was a big man, weighing 17 stone, but he was no match for the youth of Barnes. The younger man got hold of a nine-inch knife and plunged it into the body of Forristal. The blade entered the upper left side of Forristal's chest, fatally penetrating his aorta along with his windpipe. Barnes stabbed the man a further three times. Within seconds, the popular Waterford horse-breeder was lying dead in a pool of blood in his own home.

Barnes and Halligan fled the scene and made their way

back into Waterford City, leaving Forristal's dead body in the hallway of his isolated house. It was not until Louis Murphy returned to the farm, that the gruesome discovery was made. Murphy tried to gain entry into the house but, although the door was unlocked, he was unable to open it. Something was blocking his path. He pushed hard into the door and managed to squeeze into the house. He let out a scream of terror.

The object that had blocked his path was, in fact, the body of his old friend. Dick Forristal was lying dead on the ground, his feet up against the door. Murphy looked for any glimmer of life inside his friend and tried to talk to him, but he soon realised that his friend was dead. Forristal had a large wound and the floor was covered in blood.

Murphy ran back to the car, and screamed at John Kent to call the Gardaí. "Dick is dead," he told him hysterically. Kent telephoned the Gardaí. But the two men were in such a state of shock and panic that they couldn't wait at the scene. Instead, they drove to a neighbour's house, where they knocked on the door but there was no answer, and so they got back into the car and drove to Tramore, to the house of Eamon Keating, an old friend. There, they met retired Garda Sergeant Oliver St John. The four men sped back to Carrigavantry. By the time they arrived, Gardaí were already at the scene. A murder investigation was launched immediately.

After killing Dick Forristal, Anthony Barnes returned to his home in Ballybeg. He took off his clothes and burnt them, telling his mother that they had been destroyed by muck. Barnes had taken a measly €50 during the burglary and he went down to a local shop and used it to purchase cigarettes, a bottle of Coke and some sweets. As he contemplated his next move, Barnes was unaware whether the man he had stabbed was alive or dead. It was not long before this question was answered, however. Sitting down in front of the television news that evening, he felt the blood drain from his body as the bulletin declared that an elderly man had been stabbed to death at his home near Tramore.

That same evening, Anthony Barnes made a shocking revelation to his father: that he had killed Dick Forristal. Alex Barnes advised his son to contact Gardaí and the two men drove to Waterford Garda station the following day. Anthony Barnes walked into the station and stunned Gardaí by confessing to the killing. "I killed the man in Tramore yesterday," he told Gardaí.

Barnes was arrested immediately and charged with murder. His accomplice, Andrew Halligan, was charged with trespass.

At his trial one year later, Barnes claimed that he had not intended to kill Forristal but had done so out of self-defence. He outlined how he had broken into the house and was just about to leave when Forristal returned home. Barnes claimed that he had tried to escape but Forristal had come at him with a knife. The two men struggled for a few seconds but Barnes got the better of the older man and took the knife from him. He didn't know how many times he had stabbed him, he said, but it was more than once.

"It was either him or me," he claimed. "I broke into the house to commit burglary and I know I will pay for this. I dropped the knife and ran through the fields. I thought he was going to kill me. He was in a rage and he shouted: 'I will kill you.' I did not know the man had died until I saw it on the news later."

A jury of nine men and three women found Barnes guilty of murder, following almost four hours of deliberation. Justice Paul Carney handed down the mandatory life sentence, backdating it to when Barnes was first taken into custody. Barnes' mother, Anna Le Blanche, broke down in tears in court when the guilty verdict was handed down. "It couldn't be," she screamed. "Murder, oh no." He was later handed down a further three-year sentence for trespass, to run concurrently with the life sentence.

Andrew Halligan was found guilty of trespass. After the verdict was delivered, it was revealed that he had 150 previous convictions for serious offences. While counsel for Halligan stated that he had attempted to mend his ways since his last conviction, Justice Carney said that the short-term sentences he had received in the past clearly had not encouraged him to live his life by the rule of law. Carney sentenced Halligan to seven years' imprisonment. "There is a great deal of preying on elderly people which causes acute distress, and the nature of the crime was a prepared one," said Carney. "He [Halligan] has 150 previous convictions on extremely serious matters. Over the past he has received moderate sentences which have not done him any good or deterred him. Now he is going to face [that] gravity."

As if to prove his point for him, Halligan screamed out in court that Justice Carney was "a grey-haired bastard". His sentence was not back-dated.

Terry Keane, sister of the dead man, was too distressed to comment following the sentencing process. Louis Murphy, too, declined to comment, merely telling waiting reporters that "more discipline is needed" in society.

* * * * *

The trial of Anthony Barnes and Andrew Halligan made history – it was the first time the Central Criminal Court had sat in Waterford since the foundation of the State. It is, perhaps, a growing indication of the increasing lawlessness in County Waterford that the judiciary now travel south to hear cases relating to horrific, violent crime.

With a per capita homicide rate of 1: 5,312, Limerick

is the most dangerous county in Ireland. However, by removing gangland deaths from the figures, Waterford takes that position. Whereas Limerick struggles with a culture of violence brought on by the presence of hardened criminal gangs who have spilled blood in bitter feuds over recent years, Waterford struggles to contain 'ordinary' violent crime.

Waterford's place at the top of the Irish murder rate table was ensured during 12 bloody months in 2002, when a person was killed every ten weeks in the county. Nine more people fell victim to homicide in Waterford before the end of 2005. These senseless killings, which have often involved the consumption of alcohol or other drugs, together with the killing of Thomas McAuley in 2001, leaves the county with a total of 15 killings. With a population of just 101,546 in 2002, the deaths give the county a higher per capita homicide rate – 1: 6,770 – of non-gangland deaths than any other county in Ireland.

It is important to note that Waterford's record may well be worse than this. The remains of the Malawian woman Paiche Onyemaechi were discovered in July 2005 in neighbouring Kilkenny, wrapped in a black plastic bag. However, Gardaí suspect that she was killed in Waterford, where she lived, before being taken into Kilkenny, but her death is recorded in the Kilkenny figures. To record the killing in Waterford would further cement the county's place as the most violent in Ireland.

Indeed, given that many of those 15 killings took place in Waterford City itself – a small city of less than 45,000 people – the level of violence becomes clear.

The first 19 months of the decade did not see any killings taking place in Waterford. That was to change, however, in August 2001, following a vicious fight on a city street. The case was unusual insofar as neither the victim nor the killer were locals – one hailed from Belfast, the other from Albania.

Tragically, the other details of the case remain familiar – a dispute, a knife and a victim lying in a pool of blood.

Thirty-year-old Isuf Kryzi, also known as Ismet Ceka, had been living in Ireland for a year and a half when he murdered Thomas McAuley in full view of over two dozen eye-witnesses on Manor Street, Waterford. At his trial for murder in 2003, counsel for Kryzi claimed their client had been acting in self-defence when he stabbed Ardoyne-born McAuley. He had recently begun a relationship with a former partner of McAuley's, with whom the Belfast man had a child. The two men had clashed on several occasions as a result of this.

McAuley had previously threatened Kryzi and had claimed to be a member of the IRA. The threats were taken seriously, so much so that on the afternoon of August 13, 2001, the Albanian man visited a shop in Waterford City where he purchased a diving knife. The shopkeeper would later recall how Kryzi ran his fingers over the blade to check its sharpness, before strapping it to his leg under his jeans.

Earlier that day, McAuley had visited the home of Samantha O'Brien and their daughter, Dineke. In fact, McAuley should not have been anywhere near the house. He was a violent man and his relationship with O'Brien had been marked with vicious outbursts. So unpredictable was he that O'Brien had successfully applied for a barring order against her former partner. When McAuley came to the house that afternoon, he was furious. He had become convinced that Kryzi was abusing young Dineke and made several threats to O'Brien that he would "sort out" her new partner. After he left the house, O'Brien sent a text message to Kryzi warning him that McAuley was looking for him and was going to attack him.

Kryzi was living in a hostel on Manor Street and it was here that McAuley would find him shortly before 8 pm that evening. James Geary would later tell the court that he was walking along Manor Street when he saw McAuley running towards Kryzi and shouting aggressively. As Kryzi left the hostel building, McAuley ran at him and struck him. A struggle ensued, with the two men grabbing at each other's clothes and jostling.

"[They were] dragging out of one another, tussling with one another," eye-witness James Geary would tell the court. "Dragging one another's clothes, trying to push one another away."

The fighting was taking place on the footpath of Manor Street, but Kryzi soon got the upper hand in the struggle and McAuley was forced onto the road. McAuley was lying on his back on the road with Kryzi standing over him, kicking him several times in the body. Several eye-witnesses recalled that as he lay on the ground, McAuley held out his hands in a defensive manner and shouted: "please don't, please don't" at Kryzi. The reason for McAuley's sudden pacifism was that Kryzi had produced the knife from underneath his jeans. Ignoring his victim's cries for help, Kryzi proceeded to lunge at McAuley, stabbing him six times in the body and chest.

At his trial for murder in 2003, Kryzi insisted that he was acting in self-defence and recalled the threats made by McAuley, a man with a history of violence, earlier that day. The jury rejected the plea, however. They found that Kryzi had acted in self-defence during the initial fight but had already won the fight when he produced a knife and stabbed the defenceless McAuley.

Isuf Kryzi was sentenced to life imprisonment.

In the four years that followed McAuley's murder, a further 14 people were killed in Waterford. For a region with such a small population, to suffer one killing almost every three months over a four-year period, is quite remarkable within the context of Irish society. Seven of these killings

– including those of McAuley and Forristal – were inflicted by knives. This compares with just two gun killings in the county.

Keith Doyle had a history of violence with his brother, Gary. In 1999 a dispute between the two had led to Keith, the oldest of the pair, losing an eye after Gary struck him in the face with a glass. Despite this, the brothers had mended their relationship and were on good terms.

To celebrate the dawn of 2003, the two brothers went to a pub near their Ballybeg homes to ring in the New Year together. They consumed up to eight pints each and also several vodka drinks and were quite drunk by the time they left the pub in the early hours of January 1, 2003. According to eye-witnesses, Gary and Keith Doyle had their arms around each other as they left the pub shortly before 2 am.

On the walk home, however, a row developed between the pair. Angry words were exchanged. Friends attempted to calm the brothers down, but to no avail. The two brothers traded insults, calling each other a variety of names. When Keith Doyle reached his house at Priory Lawn in Ballybeg he walked away from his brother and invited two friends inside. Twenty-eight-year-old Gary Doyle did not want to drop the argument, however, and continued knocking on his older brother's front door. He punched the door and shouted at his brother to come outside. Referring to the incident four years previously, Gary Doyle shouted at his brother that he would knock his other eye out if he came outside.

"He was calling me a one-eyed bastard [and saying] that this fella and that fella was riding my girlfriend," Keith Doyle would tell Gardaí later that morning.

Keith wanted to avoid confrontation but he soon lost his temper. He picked up a baseball bat and went after his brother outside the house, where a fight ensued. He got the better of his brother and Gary soon retreated from the garden.

Keith went back inside his house, but only to find another weapon. Then he got into his car and chased his brother down the street.

He caught up with Gary Doyle on Ballybeg Drive and another scuffle ensued. This time Gary would not be able to get back up. Keith Doyle produced a blade and stabbed his brother in the neck. With Gary lying on the ground and bleeding heavily from the stab wound, Keith drove back home and went to bed. Hours later Doyle's girlfriend informed him that his younger brother had died. "What am I after doing?" he shouted, as his girlfriend attempted to calm him down.

Keith Doyle was arrested and charged with the murder of his younger brother. At his trial, he claimed that Gary's taunts had made him lose control – "it was blind rage," he told the court. Lucy Doyle, mother of both the accused and the deceased, told the court that the two men were great friends, as well as being brothers. She wept in the witness box as she told the court how the incident on New Year's morning 2003 had devastated the family. "Gary is in heaven and Keith is in hell," she said. "He [Keith] doesn't have a life any more. His life is sitting at his brother's grave."

Her third son, Mark, told the court that to lose Keith to a murder sentence would only compound the family's grief. Having already lost one member of the family, they could not bear to lose a second, he said. "It's ruining all our lives, including Keith's," he said. "He's doing a life sentence as it is." Mark Doyle testified that his brother now left his house only to visit the graveyard – "he goes out every night and spends hours with Gary at the grave. Sometimes he goes over two or three times a night". The court heard that Keith Doyle had not touched alcohol since his brother's death and was unable to work due to depression.

A jury of seven women and five men cleared the defendant of murder but found him guilty of manslaughter.

After the guilty verdict was read out, it was revealed that Keith Doyle had a string of previous convictions for offences such as larceny, burglary and malicious damage, as well as for drugs and firearms offences. He was sentenced to four years' imprisonment for the killing of his brother.

Gary Doyle's death was brought about by a lethal combination of alcohol abuse and a willingness to use weapons in order to resolve disputes. It is a deadly combination that has resulted in misery throughout the island of Ireland over recent years, and one that is becoming more prevalent.

The Ballybeg area of the city where the Doyle brothers lived – and also Anthony Barnes, the killer of Dick Forristal – was also home to Anthony Stone. The 20-year-old father-of-one had a history of brushes with the law. He had a number of previous convictions for driving and drugs offences.

On the evening of September 7, 2004, Stone was drinking and smoking cannabis in Simon Carton's flat on Barrack Street in Waterford City.

Originally from Gorey, Co. Wexford, 33-year-old Carton had spent much of his life travelling. When he was seven years old, he had moved with his family to Dublin. Later on, he moved to England, the Netherlands and Gibraltar, spending time working in each country. Carton settled in Waterford when he was in his mid-20s and had been living in the area for eight years.

As Carton, Stone and others sat in the Barrack Street flat, one of those present, James Halligan, asked whether he could borrow a UB40 CD that belonged to Carton. Carton refused to loan the CD to Halligan but offered to make him a copy of it that he could keep. A tussle broke out between Halligan and Carton over the CD. Carton could not have known it, but he was in the wrong company for getting into fights.

Two weeks earlier, Anthony Stone had been attacked and knocked unconscious by a group of Travellers. He had spent a few days in hospital as a result. Vowing that he would never again be beaten up, Stone decided to carry a knife with him at all times. He had also celebrated his release from hospital by going on a two-week drinking binge. Now, Stone produced the kitchen knife that he had been carrying down his sock and stabbed Simon Carton seven times in the neck, shoulder and body.

A witness to the incident, Rossa Blackmore, recalled how Stone grinned, as he repeatedly plunged the knife into the defenceless Carton. He was screaming on the ground as blood gushed from his body.

At his trial, Stone pleaded not guilty to the murder of Simon Carton, claiming that he acted in self-defence after the deceased began to choke James Halligan. He used the knife, he said, only because he had consumed too much alcohol to be able to take Carton on without the use of a weapon. "I think James swung for him, gave him a dig in the chest and then Simon hit James and James fell back on the floor," he told the court. "He was a big young fella. I was probably too drunk to tackle him myself. I tried to stab him in the shoulder just so he'd leave go."

Prosecution counsel Edward Comyn SC described the assault as a "horrific attack without warning", and Stone's defence was rejected by the jury.

He was found guilty of murder and given the mandatory life sentence behind bars.

Mr Justice Eamon de Valera told the court that it was clear that alcohol and drugs had played a significant role in the events of the evening. De Valera stated that he had sat through three rape trials and a murder trial over the preceding 14 days, none of which would have arisen were it not for the consumption of "serious amounts of drink".

Peter Carton, father of Simon, urged friends and family of his son to forgive Stone for his actions on the night. "Simon was a free spirit, gentle and forgiving," he said. "We asked ourselves, 'What would Simon do?' We believe Simon would have wanted us to forgive."

* * * * *

Between January 1, 2000, and December 31, 2005, a total of 336 people were victims of violent death in Ireland – more than one a week over a six-year period. Out of this total, 152 were killed in the capital city. Yet Dublin is not the murder capital of Ireland. As a result of unequal population distribution in Ireland, counties with far fewer violent deaths actually have higher per capita homicide rates.

County Limerick, with a population of just 175,304, has the highest per capita homicide rate in Ireland. The west-of-Ireland county experienced a massive 33 violent deaths during the first six years of the decade. That figure gives Limerick a per capita homicide rate of 1: 5,312, although that figure is reduced to 1: 7,012 when the 8 gangland-related killings are left aside.

With 15 violent deaths to its name, Waterford comes next, with a per capita rate of 1: 6,770. The south-eastern county is closely followed by Louth, with 14 homicides out of a population of just 101,546. Those figures give the border county a per-capita homicide rate of 1: 7,272, although that figure, too, is reduced if gangland 'hits', of which there were two in Louth, are taken out of the equation.

Dublin, with its population of over one million people, does not feature on the table until fourth spot. Kilkenny has the fifth highest homicide rate in Ireland. Its high position can be partly explained by one horrific event in September 2000, when 41-year-old Stephen Byrne killed his wife and two children. Although the two young boys, Alan (10) and Shane (6), were actually killed in Wexford, they lived in

Kilkenny, alongside their mother, Maeve, who was stabbed to death at her home in Cuffesgrange immediately prior to the boy's deaths. As was previously mentioned, the Kilkenny figures may be potentially distorted by the inclusion of Paiche Onyemaechi in the county's figures.

Like Kilkenny, Westmeath also suffered a triple killing, which brings to eight the number of homicides in that county. Greg Fox was sentenced to life imprisonment for the murder of his wife Deborah Fox (31), and their two young children, Cillian (7) and Trevor (9). The Fox family lived in Castledaly, Co. Westmeath.

The only county not to record a homicide between 2000 and 2005 was Longford. The midlands county, with a population of just over 31,000 people, is Ireland's safest.

As may be expected, homicide rates are highest in counties with large urban centres – Waterford, Limerick, Louth and Dublin are the four most dangerous counties in Ireland; Longford, Donegal, Mayo and Offaly have the lowest per-capita homicide rates. Cork, however, is unusual in that it has a per-capita homicide rate lower than many rural centres such as Kerry, Clare and Wicklow. With a population of close to half a million – almost 130,000 of whom live in Cork City – and having recorded 21 homicides during the timeframe, Cork has a per-capita homicide rate of 1: 21,325, significantly lower than several predominately rural counties.

Louth is one of the counties that shows a surprisingly high homicide rate. While paramilitaries have long been known to operate in the county, the vast majority of killings in Louth were, in fact, unconnected to militant Republican organisations.

Two notorious murders, however, were directly linked to paramilitary activity.

Stephen Connolly locked the door to the Carlton Bar in Dundalk and walked out onto Bridge Street. The publican was young, just 26 years of age, but he was already a successful businessman. Aside from the Carlton Bar, of which he was the proprietor, Connolly was also a partner in a car sales business.

However, as Connolly walked down Bridge Street that night, March 31, 2000, he fell victim to a pre-planned assault. He was struck with an iron bar by two men who had been waiting for him. As they struck the young publican with the bar, they put forward their own business plans to him. Their demand was a simple one – he would pay them £500 a month and, in return, they would never harm him nor his businesses again.

Connolly broke free from the men and ran down Bridge Street to escape. As he ran, one of the men pulled out a gun and fired twice at Connolly. The publican was lucky, both bullets missed their intended target. They didn't catch up with him, but they had made their point – do business with them or pay the consequences.

Protection rackets are nothing new to Dundalk. The practice had been introduced to the town decades before by paramilitaries operating on both sides of the border. The men who attacked Stephen Connolly were members of the INLA and had been operating protection rackets in the town for many years. Pubs had always been a favoured target. As well as being profitable businesses, to control a pub gave the paramilitaries a meeting space, as well as control over an area's nightlife. This was particularly useful if the group was also involved, or at least complicit, in the sale of illegal drugs. The Louth INLA had targeted a number of pubs in Dundalk and throughout the county.

Stephen Connolly, however, was not going to play ball. He refused to pay money to the INLA. As a result, he would pay the ultimate price.

On July 27, almost four months after Connolly had

been assaulted and almost killed outside his pub, he was out socialising with friends in Dundalk town centre. He had left his home in Jonesboro and arrived in Oscars Bar at 10 pm. He stayed in the bar until 12.30 am, when, together with a couple of friends, he left for Ridley's Nite Club. The group stayed there until roughly 3.30 am.

After leaving the nightclub, Connolly and a female companion drove a friend to the Knocksbridge area. After dropping her off at her house, they drove back into Dundalk Town. Connolly's Mercedes car had been parked near Williamson Place, and so his friend pulled up alongside the vehicle in order to let Connolly drive his own car home. As they pulled in, the pair sat in the car talking. Connolly was in the front passenger seat.

Little did they know that the INLA were lying in wait. The gang, led by Nicholas O'Hare, had been looking for Connolly. They had spotted his car parked at Williamson Place. There, they had sat and waited for their target to return.

As Connolly and his friend sat in the Toyota Yaris talking, O'Hare and his accomplice crept towards the vehicle. The street was deserted, so the killers managed to creep towards the car unnoticed. Connolly would not have seen O'Hare and his fellow INLA thug until it was too late.

Standing in front of the vehicle, O'Hare pulled out a gun and fired two shots through the windscreen of the car. Both shots hit Connolly. The young publican moaned in agony as his female companion screamed. Connolly managed to open the car door and made a bid to scramble away from the scene. He was badly wounded, however, and was unable to run. His assassins casually walked behind him and fired one more shot into his body. Stephen Connolly collapsed dead on the street. The INLA members escaped on foot, down Williamson Place and onto The Ramparts, where a getaway car was waiting.

The murder of Stephen Connolly heightened the fearsome reputation of Nicky O'Hare, known as 'Mad Nicky' due to his violent and unpredictable nature. Born in Belfast, O'Hare had moved to Louth where he had risen to the top of the INLA, a paramilitary group renowned for criminality and extreme violence, and for its involvement in drugs and extortion rackets throughout Ireland. O'Hare's gang ran rackets throughout Louth and also in Dublin. They were also involved in the security business, providing bouncers to well-known nightspots in the capital city. O'Hare was the prime suspect in a rash of armed robberies on both sides of the border and had also been convicted of trying to extort over £40,000 from a Dublin businessman. 'Mad Nicky' was more than just a Republican terrorist – he was a violent thug, well-known in criminal circles and much despised by his rivals. He had already spent time in Portlaoise prison for firearms offences in the 1980s.

Weeks after the killing of Connolly, O'Hare was brought in for questioning in connection with a second murder, that of Pat Neville, who was shot dead in April 2000, outside his flat in Dublin. Thirty-one-year-old Neville had been shot dead in apparent retaliation for the killing of young INLA member Patrick Campbell.

In what was later dubbed "the Ballymount bloodbath", 22-year-old Campbell had died during a shoot-out between INLA members and a criminal gang in the Ballymount Industrial Estate in Dublin, in October 1999. The INLA had been offering "protection" to a businessman who had been threatened by criminals in the area. Paramilitaries had tortured six people associated with the criminal gang and ordered them to leave the country. However, 12 associates of the criminals appeared and attacked the paramilitaries, resulting in the death of Campbell.

O'Hare was not charged in relation to the murder of Pat Neville, although Gardaí believe he ordered the killing.

The killing of Stephen Connolly, however, was to prove one step too far for the volatile terrorist leader. Just three weeks after the brutal slaying of the young businessman, O'Hare was talking to an acquaintance on Church Street in Dundalk Town centre. The fact that O'Hare was freely walking around the town showed his arrogance and his belief that he would never be harmed. But Mad Nicky's reign of terror was nearing a bloody end. As he stood on Church Street, two men approached him. They walked calmly and did not stand out from the crowds of people spilling in and out of the town's pubs.

As they reached their target, the two men pulled out pistols and fired eight shots into O'Hare's body. It was a professional hit, carried out by men who remained calm throughout. As passers-by let out screams of terror, the men took the time to purposely fire a bullet through each of Nicky O'Hare's eyes. The paramilitary leader lay dead on the street, his arms outstretched and blood pouring from his body. Ironically, O'Hare died just yards from the site from where he had cruelly snatched Stephen Connolly's life, just three weeks earlier.

The main suspects in the killing of Nicky O'Hare are local Provisional IRA members, believed to have finally lost their patience with O'Hare's reckless ways.

The killings of Connolly and O'Hare would not be the last time Republican groups based in Louth would murder. In February 2001, the body of 39-year-old Ciaran Smyth was discovered in a field outside Ashbourne, Co. Meath. He had been shot in the back and head.

Smyth was later named by British customs officials as one of the principle organisers of an international gang believed to have smuggled millions of euro worth of cigarettes across the border. Gardaí believe the killing of Smyth may have been carried out by elements connected to the so-called Real IRA, whose members are suspected of raking in millions from cigarette smuggling. Crucially, Smyth's killing is recorded as a Co. Meath death as that is where his body was located, but, even leaving out the killing of Ciaran Smyth, Louth has proven its place as one of Ireland's most dangerous counties.

* * * * *

While murder rates in counties such as Louth, Waterford and Limerick have spiralled, violent death remains extremely rare in many other corners of the country. Yet, even counties that have experienced very low levels of violent crime have seen some of the most horrific and talked-about homicides.

The north-western counties of Mayo and Donegal are amongst Ireland's safest. Despite the fact that both counties boast populations significantly larger than Waterford's and Louth's, they have recorded just two violent deaths each. With per capita homicide rates of 1: 58,723 and 1: 68,787 respectively, Mayo and Donegal are statistically up to ten times safer than Waterford or Louth. However, while the number of killings remains small, the murders that did take place in Mayo and Donegal rocked the entire country.

One such brutal killing was that of 35-year-old mother-of-four, Dolores McCrea. When her marriage collapsed in April 2003, she left the marital home in Ballybulgin, Co. Donegal and took her four children with her. Her relationship with husband Gary McCrea had reached a level of such bitterness that the pair could no longer contemplate life together. Dolores won full custody of her four children, then aged 18, 14, 7 and 5.

Before long, Gary McCrea's hatred of his former wife

began to turn into an obsession. She was all he talked about, only he refused to refer to her by her name. Instead he labelled her with a string of profanities. He was furious that his children were living with their mother, limiting him to one day a week with them. Unforgivably, he dragged his children into his bitter world: when he saw them, as he did every Saturday, he would fill their heads with rumours about their mother.

"He would tell me if I moved with him, I would have a better life," his second-eldest child, who was not named for legal reasons, would later recall. "He used to go on about other men, that she was a whore. He used to call her names, that she was a tramp and a walking disease."

The teenager became so upset by her father's relentless tirades against her mother that she sought psychiatric help. Gary McCrea named a man from Co. Fermanagh as being his wife's new partner and told his children that he had discussed the possibility of getting someone to, "badly beat up" the man.

His obsession with his former wife soon saw Gary McCrea threaten violence against her, too. "He always maintained that Mum didn't care about any of the children," his oldest daughter, Sharon, told the court. "He said that he was going to keep fighting in the courts for full custody, he said he'd fight and that if he didn't get it, he'd kill her. He'd be able to do time for her, that he'd be out in no time and that he'd get his family back."

At McCrea's trial for the murder of his wife, his second eldest daughter told the court: "he told me he was going to kill my mother, he told me he was going to stab my mother and rip her guts out."

These threats were also made to Dolores's mother, Kathleen McGrory. He telephoned the elderly woman in August 2003, just four months after the relationship had collapsed, and threatened to kill her daughter. McGrory would later tell the court that her son-in-law had said that Dolores "wasn't a fit mother" and said, "if he had it his way he would fucking kill her and that he would stab her."

Gary McCrea followed through on his threats in January 2004.

On the evening of January 20, Dolores McCrea called up to her estranged husband's home. They had previously arranged that he would purchase her car off her. As much as she hated going near him, Dolores wanted to discuss the sale. She was due to play a game of darts in Donegal Town at 7.25 pm that evening and so the visit to Gary McCrea's house was to be a quick one.

She would never make it to the game of darts.

Whatever happened between Dolores and her husband on that evening, Gary McCrea decided to brutally end her life, before making a macabre attempt to dispose of her body.

At 10 am the following morning, Sharon McCrea telephoned her aunt. Her mother had not returned to the house and she was worried. Carmel McGrory, the missing woman's sister, drove to Dolores's house and the two women began to search for her. They drove around the local area looking for the missing mother-of-four. McGrory also telephoned one of the women on her sister's darts team, who confirmed that she had not made it to the match the night before. Carmel knew that Dolores had intended to call in to her estranged husband's home and so they drove to Gary McCrea's house to ask whether he had seen his wife the previous evening.

When they pulled up in front of the house, they saw that Dolores's car was parked outside. They asked him to explain why the car was still there. Gary McCrea told the women that she had left the car there and had travelled into town by hitching a lift from a passing car. In a parting shot, he told the women not to worry about Dolores because she was most likely "whoring around" with somebody. As Gary McCrea launched further insults at his absent wife, only he knew that she was already dead.

As the women left the area, they didn't realise that Dolores's body was just yards away. Yet, the women were suspicious. Even Sharon McCrea did not feel comfortable with her father's explanation for why her mother's car was parked outside his house. After all, he had a history of threatening to kill the woman and now she was missing and he was the last person they knew who had come into contact with her. "After we left Ballybulgin, I rang Mammy and said I felt there was something wrong," Carmel McGrory later recalled.

At 5.30 pm that evening, less than 24 hours after Dolores left home, the women rang the local Garda Station to report her missing. It didn't take long for Gardaí to track down Dolores McCrea, although few could have expected the nature of their discovery.

Just hours after the woman had been reported missing, Gardaí arrived at the home of Gary McCrea. There, at the back of the house, Garda Brendan McMonagle found a large fire smouldering. He approached the smoky remains of the blaze and in the midst of the old tyres that had been used to begin the fire, he saw what appeared to be human bone. The bones found at the scene were immediately brought for testing and it was confirmed that they were human. Using dental records, the remains were identified as those of Dolores McCrea.

Her estranged husband was arrested on the morning of January 30 and charged with murder at a special court sitting in Donegal town that evening.

At his trial in October 2005, the State's Forensic Dental Surgeon, Dr Paul Keogh identified the remains found burning at the rear of McCrea's home as those of the missing mother.

State Pathologist Professor Marie Cassidy said that it was not possible to prove conclusively how Dolores McCrea had died, due to the level of fire damage. Although it could not be said how the woman had met her death, the evidence against her husband was overwhelming. Friends and family members queued up to recall how he had threatened to kill his wife, even saying how he was prepared to go to jail for a number of years just to ensure she was no longer around. The court also heard that the woman was last seen on her way to Gary McCrea's home.

Alister McClay, friend of both the accused and the deceased, recalled a conversation with Gary McCrea in a pub one year prior to the disappearance of Dolores McCrea. "He was having a conversation about Dolores and the children," he said. "He was very bitter. He never used her name, it was 'bitch' or 'whore'… He made a comment that he was going to sort it out. He more or less said he was going to take matters into his own hands." After he told the accused to "cop himself on," McClay said that his friend said: "I'll do time for her".

After a trial that lasted ten days, a jury found Gary McCrea guilty of murder, with four hours and 37 minutes of deliberation. Justice Michael Hanna told the guilty man: "There is but one sentence that I can impose on you", and handed down the compulsory sentence of life imprisonment.

McCrea stood holding onto the wooden bench in front of him, separated from his parents by two prison officers, as the verdict was read out. He was shaking visibly.

His children sat three rows behind him, alongside other members of Dolores's family. They let out a collective sigh of relief after hearing the word "guilty". Sharon McCrea made a brief statement to the media afterwards, expressing her belief that "justice has been done". She paid a simple tribute to her beloved mother, calling her "a wonderful mother, daughter, sister and friend to all of us".

Donegal was shocked by the gruesome murder of Dolores McCrea. However, an equally horrific murder was to bring fresh tragedy to the county one year later.

Shaun Duffy was well-known in the Dungloe area, a peaceful and sparsely populated peninsula with a tight-knit farming community. It would have been hard to ignore Duffy, due to his many business interests, which ranged from property to security to under-taking.

The 36-year-old was well known, although he was not always well liked. Described by local TD Pat "The Cope" Gallagher as a "larger-than-life character," Duffy had an explosive temper and had been in trouble with Gardaí before. At the time of his death Duffy was awaiting trial in relation to an assault charge.

On Friday, January 28, Duffy went to his local pub, the Strand View Bar in Maghery, for a few drinks, as he often did at the weekends. After a few hours, Duffy left the pub and made his way to his mother's house. It was only a short walk from his own home, just outside the village of Meenacross.

Gardaí believe that, while Duffy was at his mother's house, intruders broke into his home. Theft was not their motive, however. Instead they lay in wait for their target to return. When Duffy entered his home shortly after 2.30 am, on the morning of January 29, he was brutally attacked. His attackers used a knife on their unarmed victim, before shooting him in the arm with a crossbow. They then hacked at his head with an axe. The sustained assault was horrifically violent and left Duffy dead on the floor with blood seeping from the many wounds to his body and head. Satisfied that their victim was dead, the intruders left the house and fled the scene.

The body of Shaun Duffy was discovered the following

morning by his 18-year-old brother, who called into the house and made the horrific find. A murder investigation was launched immediately, with a team of 45 Gardaí assigned to tracking down the killer or killers.

Gardaí began door-to-door enquires but nobody in the area could help them with their search. A forensic examination of the house offered no clues, either.

For the family of Shaun Duffy, there was the worry that they may accidentally have impeded the Garda investigation by disturbing the scene.

"We were in a terrible state and I have wondered since did we do something or move anything that would have damaged whatever evidence the killers left behind," the victim's mother, Kathleen Duffy-Ward, told the *Sunday Tribune* on the first anniversary of her son's murder. "When the guards came on the scene, one of them ran us out and said we were doing terrible damage to the crime scene, but we didn't think of it. We were in terrible shock."

Kathleen cannot forget what she saw after entering her son's house that day.

"Shaun was lying on the floor in a room that was being used as a living-room," she recalled. "His head was sideways against the couch and his body was twisted. There was blood everywhere between the kitchen and the room. You can't imagine what it's like having a picture of your child's murdered body in your mind. It's something so bad, I can't really describe it."

Of the several murder weapons believed to have been used on Duffy, only the crossbow was discovered. Contrary to media reports at the time, the crossbow did not belong to the victim.

That was not the only media inaccuracy that caused unnecessary hurt to the Duffy family, however. In the absence of facts surrounding his case, some newspapers resorted to printing local rumours. One such rumour was that Duffy had been a Garda informant, while another suggested that he had been killed after making homosexual advances towards another male. The family deny both runours.

"When it was written that he might have been gay, it made the younger ones in the family very angry," says Kathleen. "They found it hard to accept that someone would write that without some evidence, just because he wasn't around to defend his name."

The only advance Gardaí could make in the case was to rule out robbery as a motive, after it was confirmed that there was nothing missing from the house. Investigating officers remain convinced that Duffy was murdered by somebody who sat and waited for him to return. Gardaí have so far failed to establish a motive for the killing.

The local area was completely stunned by the murder of Shaun Duffy and has not yet recovered from it. Locals remain nervous due to the fact that Gardaí have yet to charge anyone in connection with one of Ireland's most horrific crimes of recent years. Speaking at the funeral, Fr John Joe Duffy, a cousin of the deceased, pleaded with anybody who had information to go to Gardaí.

"Somebody wanted Shaun dead; somebody wanted to play God," he told mourners. "I urge you to hand yourself over to Gardaí. Whoever did this will not be able to live with themselves; it will eat you up and your conscience will only be cleared by a confession. There is a fearful state of mind in the town due to the horror that took place. Do not allow fear to eat up this community."

So far, the priest's words have fallen on deaf ears.

For Shaun Duffy's family, the pain continues. "I hope it never turns out to be someone local," says his mother, Kathleen. "If it was, I don't think it would ever end with the younger ones in the family. They'd be very angry if it turned out to be someone that they know. But I don't think anyone will ever be caught for killing Shaun."

The killing of Shaun Duffy in an isolated area of Donegal sent shockwaves through the entire country, both because of the rarity of violent death in Donegal and the horrific nature of the attack. The case also re-focused attention on the safety of bachelors living alone in isolated areas, an issue that had been raised following a killing elsewhere in the north-western corner of Ireland three months before Duffy met his death.

Few cases have provoked as much debate and argument as the killing of John Ward, a 43-year-old member of the traveller community, by Mayo farmer Padraig Nally. The killing of Ward, together with the trial and subsequent conviction of Nally, whipped up a storm of controversy, leading to claims that Ireland's politicians, media and judiciary were all inherently biased against the traveller community.

Like Donegal, Mayo is a county where killing is extremely rare. Prior to 2004, it had been many years since anyone had met a violent end there. That year, homicide would strike twice.

In March 2004, Liam McDonnell was found dead in an unoccupied house in Castlebar, Co. Mayo. It was the first homicide in the county this decade and McDonnell's brother, Frank McDonnell, was later charged in relation to the killing but a jury cleared him of any wrongdoing. Although people in Mayo were shocked at the violent nature of McDonnell's death, events in October of that year would stun the western county.

Padraig Nally arrived at his home in Funshinagh, Co. Mayo at 2 pm on October 14 to find an unfamiliar car parked outside. The engine was running and a man could be seen sitting in the driver's seat of the vehicle. Nally approached the car and asked the man what he was doing.

Tom Ward and his father, John, had been driving around the area that afternoon looking for old cars to buy. Tom Ward himself was driving a car that he had purchased a few days earlier for the sum of €180. He was driving despite later admitting that he had neither insurance nor a driver's licence. When Nally asked why he was sitting outside his house with the engine running, Tom Ward replied that his father had spotted a white Nissan on the premises and was looking to purchase the vehicle. "I said my father was looking for the owner of the car and he said to me that he won't be coming out," recalled Ward.

Nally didn't buy the story. He recognised the man in the car from an earlier incident. A few weeks previously, Nally had been in his home when there was a knock at the door. He answered it and found two men – Tom Ward and his father, John Ward – in his garden, claiming to be lost and needing directions to the lake so that they could go fishing. Nally would later tell the court that he was suspicious of the two men on that occasion because they did not appear to have any fishing equipment with them.

In truth, Nally was suspicious of all strangers. He had recently suffered two break-ins at his isolated farm and his mental stability was slipping. On one of those occasions, the legally held shotgun which he stored under his bed had been disturbed. He moved the weapon to the shed for fear that he would be shot by intruders, as he lay sleeping.

The bachelor farmer had taken to writing down the registration plates of any unfamiliar cars in the area. He was growing more paranoid by the day. The court would later hear that he had spotted cars driven by the Wards in the area several times in the weeks leading up to October 14. "He'd have the [registration] numbers ready when you'd pull up," said Michael Mellett, a neighbour. "They were written all over the house."

On one occasion a car had entered and left Nally's yard at speed and the farmer had written down the registration plate. A few weeks later Nally was with a friend, Joe Concannon, and he had seen the car in the area again. Concannon later identified Ward as the driver of that vehicle. Tom Ward agreed that he had driven ten to 15 different cars in the previous six months but denied that he switched cars so they could not be traced back to him.

As well as noting down the movements of strangers, Nally was showing increasing reluctance to leave his farm for any amount of time. When he did leave, he threw water over the soil at the entrance to his property in the hope that the mud would record footprints of anybody entering the land in his absence.

The paranoia over his own safety resulted in Nally spending up to five hours a day in his shed. He sat there clutching his loaded shotgun, ready to tackle any intruders. His growing instability was affecting him financially as well as mentally. He was neglecting his farm – sheep were not being sheared and he was yet to bring in turf. "I felt that something was going to happen," he would recall in court a year later. "If it didn't, I'd have to shoot myself the following weekend. The pressure had got to me."

For elderly farmers, such as 60-year-old Padraig Nally, the threat of being attacked in your home, far from the nearest neighbour, was a very real one. Elderly farmers living in isolated areas had been targeted by criminals in the past. In June 2000, 81-year-old Paddy Logan had been beaten to death at his farm in Co. Meath by two brothers from a settled Traveller family who proceeded to steal £45 from the house. The two brothers, John and Christopher Doyle, were sentenced to 15 and 12 years respectively for their roles in Logan's death. The two thugs had repeatedly targeted the elderly, and John Doyle had a conviction for stabbing an elderly man to death in Dublin in 1984.

Having been informed by Tom Ward that there was a man lurking at the rear of the house, Nally went to his shed and retrieved his shotgun. At the rear of the house, he came into confrontation with John Ward, the man who weeks earlier had asked directions to the lake.

When Padraig Nally confronted John Ward at the back of his farm in Funshinagh, it was essentially the meeting of two disturbed minds. While Nally's mental condition was somewhat unstable at the time, so was Ward's. The father-of-eleven had a history of violence and had a number of convictions for larceny. He had once left a man in need of 18 stitches to the face, after assaulting him with a cup. At the time of calling to Nally's farm, Ward was waiting for another court appearance, this time for threatening a Garda with a slash-hook.

Ward was receiving psychiatric care for his problems. Two weeks prior to the confrontation with Padraig Nally he had been re-admitted as an emergency patient to the psychiatric unit at University College Hospital, Galway. He had a history of impulsive aggressive outbursts and auditory hallucinations, including a man's voice telling him to kill himself and his wife. A consultant psychiatrist who had treated Ward, Sheila O'Sullivan, noted that he was afraid, "he would attack before he was attacked."

Psychiatric treatment had left Ward on a cocktail of drugs. He mixed these with other illegal drugs, such as opiates and cannabis, which he consumed in conjunction with his prescribed medication.

Nally would later testify that his paranoia was so bad that he had slept for just one hour on the night before the incident. Nally threatened Ward with the shotgun and told him to get off his land. A struggle between the two men ensued. The shotgun discharged and the bullet fragmented, hitting Ward in the hand and thigh. Ward fell to the ground and screamed out in agony. The shock of having shot the intruder did not stop Nally, however. He began to beat the injured man. He hit him up to ten times. Nally would later tell the court that striking Ward was "like hitting a badger".

Nally went back into his shed as Ward attempted to escape the scene. However, Nally re-emerged from the shed having reloaded his weapon. He followed Ward, who was on the ground and struggling to escape. Nally stood over his victim, aimed, and shot him once more. This gunshot wound proved fatal. John Ward lay dead, his arms outstretched.

Nally would later tell the court that he had meant the second shot as a warning but that his hand was shaking so much with nerves that he had accidentally hit the wounded and unarmed man. The State Pathologist Professor Marie Cassidy said that, from the angle the bullet entered Ward, it could be seen that Nally was standing over his victim at the time of the shooting. "The trajectory [of the shot] suggested that the gunman was above him…and that [the victim] may have been bent over or was crouching down," said Professor Cassidy.

The picture painted in court was of Nally standing over an unarmed and defenceless man, lying on the ground and ruthlessly shooting him, having minutes earlier reloaded his weapon with the intention of killing the man. The seemingly pre-meditated nature of the act led to a murder charge against Padraig Nally.

Nally's defence team argued that while it was undisputed that the farmer had fired the shot that killed John Ward, he could not be found guilty of murder because of the level of provocation. Nally was presented to the court as an elderly farmer, driven to the edge of suicide, by fears for his own safety.

The case caused unprecedented public debate. On one hand, there was the right of a landowner to protect his property. On the other hand, however, was the fact that Padraig Nally had stood over his victim and cruelly shot him as he lay wounded.

A jury found Nally not guilty of murder but guilty of manslaughter. Justice Paul Carney sentenced the Mayo farmer to six years' imprisonment. Sentencing Nally, Mr Justice Carney described the case as "undoubtedly the most socially divisive case I've had to try and the most difficult case I've had to sentence." It was a remarkable admission from the country's most experienced criminal judge.

The sentencing of Padraig Nally to six years behind bars caused huge controversy, with Traveller groups arguing that the verdict showed the huge prejudice against members of their community, and supporters of Nally arguing that a home-owner should have the right to protect his/her land against unwanted intruders. Counsel for Nally had called on Justice Carney to suspend "all or most of any sentence" but the court opted not to do so.

Speaking after sentencing, the victim's brother-in-law, Martin Reilly, argued that the case should not have been held in Mayo but should have been heard in Dublin. He said the jury's verdict reflected the prejudice against travellers in rural Ireland. "A man's life is worth more than six years," he said.

Nally's supporters, on the other hand, had strongly believed that the Judge would impose a partially suspended sentence, but Mr Justice Carney declined.

This was, however, not the end of the Padraig Nally case. In October 2006, the Court of Criminal Appeal dramatically quashed the Mayo farmer's manslaughter conviction. Counsel for Nally had argued that the trial judge, Mr Justice Carney, had erred in law by not allowing the jury to consider an acquittal. At the trial, Carney had told the jury that it could only bring in a verdict of guilty of manslaughter or guilty of murder. In an 18-page-ruling, the appeal court of three judges, headed by Mr Justice Nicholas Kearns, ruled that Nally's conviction be overturned.

The 62-year-old now faces a retrial. If the original trial polarised the country and dominated public debate for weeks, the retrial is set to be explosive.

Nine

Justice, But Not For All

Twenty-two-year-old Cork man, Ian Horgan, showed no sign of emotion as he sat in the Central Criminal Court in Dublin. On the afternoon of March 10, 2006, the young man awaited a decision that could see him set free from jail, if he was lucky. He showed no sign of nervousness or distress and sat comfortably.

Horgan might have considered himself to be fortunate to be awaiting what could be positive news, in light of the crime of which he had earlier been convicted – the brutal defilement and murder of 22-year-old Rachel Kiely, whose body was found in a local park in Ballincollig in Cork on October 26, 2000.

Horgan had spent all of his adult life to date vilified in public as a man who had carried out a most despicable act against a popular and much loved young woman. Four-and-a-half years earlier Horgan had been sentenced to life for the murder and rape of the young beautician near her Ballincollig home. But Horgan had brought his case to the Court of Criminal Appeal (CCA) and the conviction was overturned and retrial ordered by the CCA.

Prosecution lawyers claimed that, in the June 2002 murder trial, DNA evidence linked Horgan directly to the crime: DNA in semen taken from the body of Rachel Kiely was a match with DNA from saliva samples taken from Horgan.

The former State Pathologist, Dr John Harbison, had

said at that trial that the young woman had been strangled after she was raped. But prosecutors on behalf of Horgan argued in the CCA six months later that the trial judge had failed to direct the jury adequately on the DNA evidence and failed to deal with the "circumstantial evidence" in the case. The prosecution said that it was known that science could make mistakes and that semen could be found days after being discharged. But the jury in Horgan's initial trial had not adequately been informed that DNA evidence may in itself be misleading.

In its judgement, the CCA said that there was a strong case to be made against Horgan in relation to Rachel Kiely's killing. But they added that there were clear grounds for concern about certain aspects of the trial, including the trial judge's charge to the jury relating to the DNA evidence. Interestingly, the CCA also noted that they had operated their appeal hearing on the basis of a transcript of the evidence in the 2002 trial that had been certified by the judge at the end of the trial, but which was clearly not satisfactory. Portions of the transcript appeared to be attributed incorrectly, the CCA stated.

Thus, for the family of 22-year-old Rachel Kiely, the wait on March 10, 2006 for the jury in the retrial to bring back its decision was doubtlessly almost impossible to endure. Just days beforehand, the court heard the harrowing details of how the young woman met her death and of the depraved attack that preceded her killing. For Rachel's mother, Rose, it was a disturbing replay of a story that she had endured once already but now had to face again. Even more difficult for the Kiely family was the fact that Horgan, who had initially pleaded not guilty in 2002 but had been convicted of raping and murdering Rachel Kiely, was now admitting manslaughter but was denying both rape and murder.

The events of the day in which her daughter was killed

were ingrained in Rose Kiely's mind. The dead woman's mother told the court that she became increasingly worried after one of the family dogs that her daughter had been walking arrived home without her on the evening of October 26, 2000.

Rose Kiely told prosecuting counsel for the State, Patrick J. McCarthy SC, that her daughter Rachel walked the family's two dogs in the nearby park in Ballincollig most days of the week. On the evening of October 26, Rose Kiely said that she watched her daughter leave through a gap in the fence into the park with the animals.

Rose Kiely was busy in her kitchen as Rachel left the house. Rose's husband had been due back to the family home at around 5 p.m. that evening and she was busily preparing the evening meal. She had asked Rachel to stop and have dinner with them but the young woman told her mother that she would have it when she got back after bringing the dogs for their stroll.

Just before 6 p.m. that evening, Rose Kiely heard a noise. It was the sound of one of the dogs scratching on the front door of the family home. "Normally she would bring them in the back way. Rachel wasn't there and I began to get worried," Rose Kiely told the court.

She became anxious and she wanted to go out and look for Rachel. It was unusual that the young woman had not returned with the dogs and Rose feared that something may have waylaid Rachel during the stroll. Rose Kiely waited just until her husband returned home from work before she set off to the park with her youngest daughter, Elizabeth.

While Rose and Elizabeth Kiely looked around the area where Rachel would have walked the pets, the youngest girl said she had heard a scream or a cry and suggested that it might have come from the nearby playing field. Time was already running out for the pair as they looked around for

Rachel. The late-autumn evening was beginning to close in on the two women as they looked for her. The pale grey sky was becoming swiftly darker as the minutes passed.

The pair decided to go back to get more help. Rose Kiely was going back to her home the way she had come when she met then 16-year-old local lad Ian Horgan. "I said 'hi' and then he said 'hi'," she told the court. Horgan was known locally in the Ballincollig area as a promising young athlete. He had won all-Ireland medals for athletics and running. He had dropped out of school a year earlier, at the age of 15.

When Rose Kiely returned to the family home her husband suggested they call the Gardaí. The couple had become particularly nervous. It was not like Rachel to just disappear without any notice or to wander off without telling them where she may be going. A group of people also began searching for Rachel after Rose and her husband raised the alarm. Rose bought "four or five or six torches" from a local shop to help the searchers to see their way around the dark evening, she told the jury of five women and seven men at the 2006 retrial.

Asked by Brendan Grehan SC, defending counsel for Horgan, whether she had given evidence to Gardaí about her daughter, Elizabeth, saying she had heard a scream, Rose Kiely replied: "I did. That was in my statement. I'm sure it was."

However, defence counsel put it to Rose Kiely that in the statement her youngest daughter Elizabeth had given to Gardaí she did not mention this matter. The mother replied: "We were in such a state of shock that night we just put it out of our minds."

She admitted it was a week or a fortnight later that her daughter had claimed the scream was Rachel's. "That's why I stood and called Rachel's name," she said, alluding to having called out to her missing child in the park that evening.

Opening the case before the jury, the prosecuting counsel for the state said that, despite the fact that Horgan was now entering a plea of guilty to manslaughter, he would still be calling on the same evidence as if he had pleaded not guilty to the crime.

He told the jury that both Rachel Kiely and Ian Horgan had lived very close to the regional park in Ballincollig. They would have known each other to see even if they did not know each other's names.

Horgan, along with a large number of other people, had filled out a Garda questionnaire about his movements that night and had told a number of lies, the prosecution said. Counsel for the State told the jury that they would also hear forensic evidence that was compelling in relation to Horgan's role in the young woman's horrific final moments of life.

There was other damning evidence in the 2006 retrial. A neighbour of Horgan's told the jury that the young man told them that Rachel Kiely had been "beaten and raped" on the evening her body was found. This was before the post-mortem results were carried out and at a time when not even investigators were certain of the detail of the young woman's final suffering.

Local woman Josephine McCoy said in answers to the counsel for the prosecution that she had seen an ambulance in the park at around 8:30 p.m. on the evening of October 26, 2000. Sometime between then and 8:45 p.m., McCoy said that she met Ian Horgan and she had asked him if he knew what was going on and why there was an ambulance at the park. "He just said Rachel Kiely was beaten and raped," McCoy testified. McCoy said that she had not made a statement to Gardaí about this alleged comment until November 13, 2000, after Horgan had been charged.

"I take it from that, that it [Horgan's comment] didn't strike you as particularly odd or sinister at the time. Otherwise you would have brought it to the attention of Gardaí?" counsel for Horgan asked the local woman. "At the time we were just in complete shock," she answered.

The forensic evidence presented in court was compelling. Two leading forensic experts told the court that DNA taken from Rachel Kiely's body matched that of Ian Horgan. Dr Maureen Smyth, from the State Forensic Science Office, told the retrial that she had conducted a series of tests on samples of DNA taken from the victim's body. Smyth told prosecuting counsel that semen was found on three of the swabs. Traces were also detected on a fourth swab. A DNA profile of the semen was carried out and this matched Horgan. The forensic specialist said the chance of the DNA of the material found on the dead woman's body belonging to anyone who was not a blood relative of the accused was one in a billion. Horgan had voluntarily provided samples of his DNA in the days following Rachel Kiely's death, the court heard.

The doctor had also examined items of clothing that Rachel Kiely was wearing when she died, along with items recovered from the home of Ian Horgan. Smyth told the jury that she found acrylic fibres on a fleece jacket worn by Rachel Kiely that compared with fibres from a jumper that belonged to Horgan. That indicated there was close contact between the garments.

In statements that he gave to investigating Gardaí, the young man had denied causing harm to Rachel Kiely. Chief State Pathologist, Professor Marie Cassidy, said in her report to the court that the young woman had died as a result of pressure being applied to her neck.

The state prosecutors hoped that retrial would see Horgan sent down for a second time on a charge of murder and there should be no reason for this case to be overturned. It would carry the mandatory sentence of life behind bars –the tariff of which is decided at the discretion of the Minister for Justice.

If found guilty of the heinous act of raping and murdering the 22-year-old woman, Horgan could expect to remain in jail for a long time into his adult life.

However, by pleading not guilty to rape but guilty to manslaughter Horgan hoped that, while he faced an almost certain prison sentence, he could at least see a light at the end of that tunnel. If he received a sentence for manslaughter and he kept his nose clean in jail he could realistically expect to be free from incarceration while still in his early 30s or even his late 20s if the retrial went his way.

Now, on March 10, the jury was returning with its verdict, as Horgan waited patiently in the court. They had to decide on whether he was guilty of murdering Rachel Kiely or whether he had solely committed an act of manslaughter, as he admitted.

The family of the dead woman could not have expected a worse outcome to the retrial. The jury returned a verdict of guilty on the count of rape but not guilty of having murdered the young woman. He was convicted of manslaughter in accordance with his plea of guilt to that charge.

Mr Justice Barry White, who presided in the case, warned the Kiely family that they may not like the sentence which he would have to hand down to Horgan arising out of the circumstances of the retrial and conviction. For the rape and unlawful killing of Rachel Kiely, White sentenced Ian Horgan to eight years in prison. The judge instructed that six of these years be suspended. The sentences for rape and manslaughter were to run concurrently, the judge said.

Judge White acknowledged that Ian Horgan had spent four-and-a-half years in custody since November 2000. The judge said that this term was the equivalent of a six-year sentence. As a result the judge suspended the last six years of the term and ordered that Horgan's sentence begin on the following day. Explaining the sentence, Mr Justice White said that he had to take into account that the killer was just 16 years old at the time of the offences. White said that it was also important that Horgan had no previous convictions. The judge said he knew all too well that the Kiely family would not be pleased with the sentence, but hoped they could appreciate the position he was in.

White then turned to the guilty man. He told Ian Horgan that his conduct had, "devastated the Kiely family and their wider circle of friends".

The fact that former State Pathologist Professor John Harbison, became ill and was not able to give evidence was perhaps to Horgan's benefit, the judge said. He added that the pathological evidence given by Professor Marie Cassidy based on photographs alone was "less forceful".

After the sentence was handed down, David Dunlea, who is married to Rachel Kiely's sister, Roselyn, said that the Kiely family were disappointed with what they considered a lenient sentence.

The young man, who made a surprise attack on the young beautician while she was on an evening's walk, dragging her to a secluded place and raping her, and who then strangled her to death, will be eligible for release on or before March 11, 2008.

However, Horgan's case is not unique: a sample analysis carried out by the authors of three years of violent deaths, from 2000 to 2002, shows that there were 58 homicides in which a murder conviction was secured. This represents over 34% of all violent deaths that occurred. But four of these cases, including Ian Horgan's, were successfully appealed to the Court of Criminal Appeal (CCA), resulting in the murder convictions being overturned. All of the four murder convictions that were overturned by the CCA from 2000 to 2002 resulted in a subsequent retrial at which the accused was found guilty of manslaughter.

On the evening of September 22, 2001, Gordon Farrell and Michelle Donnelly returned after drinking at a pub in Wexford Town with Nicholas Donnelly, who was the woman's brother.

The evening started off pleasantly and there was no sign of trouble. But later an argument began in which Gordon Farrell and Nicholas Donnelly exchanged harsh words. A lot of alcohol had been consumed and within a short period of time the dispute turned violent.

Gordon Farrell picked up a coffee table and looked like he was about to throw it at Michelle Donnelly during the row, it would later be told in court. Her brother Nicholas would also explain that he had a knife in his hand at the time but not with any intention of using it for violence: he had been using it to cut up hash. As the verbal altercation progressed into something altogether more serious, Nicholas Donnelly found himself fighting physically with Gordon Farrell, whom he stabbed 10 times. Nicholas Donnelly claimed the first injury occurred after Farrell fell on top of him on to the sofa. Donnelly insisted that the remainder of the injuries were inflicted after Gordon Farrell bit down on his ear.

A small section of Donnelly's ear, containing three earrings, was found lying beside Gordon Farrell's body when later examined by forensic experts.

Nicholas Donnelly, who was 24 years old at the time of the fatal stabbing, was charged with Farrell's murder. In March 2004, a Central Criminal Court jury, returning a majority verdict, found Donnelly guilty of the murder of 20-year-old Gordon Farrell. Donnelly had denied the charge.

But Donnelly's lawyers believed that their client had grounds to have the conviction overturned. The CCA decided in 2005 that the trial judge had erred in law in refusing to allow the defence of self-defence to be taken into consideration by the jury. The trial judge had only allowed the defence of provocation to go to the jury, which clearly rejected it and convicted Donnelly.

The CCA said that as a matter of fairness one had to take into account in particular the statements of Donnelly and of his sister and other minor witnesses and the general description of what evolved in the house at the time of the fatal stabbing and beforehand. Having referred to the evidence, the appeal court noted the fact that the fight arose out of an attack by Gordon Farrell against Nicholas Donnelly's sister seemed significant.

During the initial murder trial, Michelle Donnelly had given evidence that her relationship with Gordon Farrell had been "kind of up and down" in the immediate seven days or so just before the fatal incident.

She said her boyfriend had gone to the dentist earlier and had had a tooth removed on the day before the dispute occurred. Gordon Farrell was in some pain and later got painkillers from a doctor but he proceeded to drink a large amount of alcohol when the three went to a local hostelry.

Michelle Donnelly told the court that her boyfriend had quite a lot to drink, "because he thought the drink would take away the pain in his mouth".

When they returned to his home, he became abusive, she said. "Gordon was looking for his drugs and he just started shouting at me because I wouldn't give them to him." He demanded cannabis and some Valium that she had and he became abusive and "started firing stuff at me," Michelle Donnelly said. Gordon Farrell "fired a pint glass and was screaming and shouting," she added. Her partner then picked up a coffee table and held it above her, which was when the physical fight between Farrell and her brother Nicholas began, she said.

Gordon Farrell's sister Amy was allowed, at the judge's

discretion, to read to the court her victim impact statement in which she said her family hoped that "justice is served" in relation to her brother's killing.

"The morning of September 23, 2001, when Gardaí called to our house to tell us Gordon was dead will haunt us forever," she said. "Gordon was only 20 years old when he had his life cruelly taken from him. He had his whole life ahead of him still, but Gordon missed out on everything because of Nicholas Donnelly."

"He missed his daughter's first day of school; he won't see her First Communion, walk her down the aisle or ever become a grandparent. Gordon was just an ordinary boy. He was very family orientated and he loved his family, especially his daughter Nicole," she told the court.

Nicholas Donnelly was found not guilty of murder but guilty of manslaughter. At the subsequent sentencing of Donnelly, presiding judge, Mr Justice Barry White delivered some strong words on the nature of violent murders to which a strong "deterrent" sentence should in some cases apply.

Mr Justice White said that there is little or no respect for human life among a certain element of society. "We live in an increasingly more and more violent society. Less than fifty years ago, you could count the number of unlawful killings in this country on one hand. Now, it's almost a daily occurrence." He added: "It seems to me that steps have to be taken to bring change towards the respect of life and human dignity. I am not saying that no one has shouted stop but to date such shouts have appeared to have fallen on deaf ears."

One can only guess what was going through Nicholas Donnelly's mind as White said the following words: "A sentence of life imprisonment for manslaughter can be imposed and in appropriate cases, a life sentence should be imposed. Deterrence is a factor that a judge is entitled to consider when imposing sentences. It is high time the courts started to impose deterrent sentences for manslaughter."

However, Judge White said Donnelly's case "does not merit a deterrent sentence". The judge noted that Nicholas Donnelly had not armed himself with a knife for the purpose of killing his sister's boyfriend.

He sentenced Donnelly to seven years in prison with 15 months suspended, to take into consideration the time he had already served.

Few types of violent death are more difficult for a victim's family to bear than those in which there is no likelihood that justice can ever be done in court. This harrowing situation arises when a perpetrator takes his or her own life at the same time as killing the other person. Almost six percent of all violent deaths that occurred in the three years studied by the authors were cases of homicide-suicide.

Such cases rarely involve a victim and perpetrator who are strangers to each other or two persons whose families are unconnected by any means. The data shows that the person who takes a life before also committing suicide is invariably a member of the same family as the victim. In fact, in most cases it is a parent acting under considerable mental strain, which leads them to kill.

The ten cases of homicide-suicide examined by the authors have been among the most controversial killings of all, with bitter recriminations emerging in public over whether some of the deaths could have been prevented.

Little Deirdre Crowley had not been seen since she had been collected from her mother's house by her father, Christopher, on December 4, 1999. Garda Sergeant Brian Fitzgerald was based at Douglas Garda station in August 2001 when he was interviewed as part of an RTÉ programme dealing with the case of the missing child. In words that were to have a prophetic significance, Fitzgerald offered the opinion that people were wrong to see the disappearance of the little girl as a domestic situation rather than a criminal act. "If a four-year-old girl was taken by a stranger, the whole country would be up in arms. But because it was her father, people don't seem to be as concerned. They say that the case is sad but tend to think that she is safe with her father," the Garda said.

Sergeant Fitzgerald's comment was more prescient and sensible than most people with a passing knowledge of the case realised. But even the experienced Garda could not have known just how serious the case was about to become. Talking on the *Would you Believe?* documentary, Gardaí appealed for students of the former maths teacher, who may have seen Christopher Crowley, to come forward.

"Mr Crowley would have taught maybe 14,000 - 16,000 students over the years in Fermoy, Co. Cork. We are hoping that one of these people may have spotted him on their travels," a Garda spokesman said.

Up to that time there had been alleged sightings of the man and his daughter in both Ireland and the UK but the information never yielded any definite location for the pair. Christopher Crowley's car had been discovered by Gardaí in Co. Wexford shortly after he abducted his daughter, which suggested that he may have taken the ferry from Rosslare.

Gardaí described the man as being meticulous and possessing good organisational skills but they added that the abduction could not have been carried out without assistance from others and that he could not have acted alone. "It seems as if they walked off the face of the earth," the Garda spokesman said.

Deirdre Crowley's mother, Christine O'Sullivan, and Christopher Crowley broke up in December 1998 but the couple remained on reasonably good terms. The girl lived with her mother in the Cork suburb of Douglas. He mother described Deirdre as a "real girlie girl" who loved Barbie dolls.

Christopher Crowley had clearly taken major steps to ensure that neither he nor Deirdre was found. He had managed to effectively disappear for two years. The girl's mother was deeply distressed for her daughter's welfare and was desperate for her return.

What Gardaí did not know was that since November 2000, Christopher Crowley had rented a house in Clonmel town, on Cloville Road, using the name of 'Mr Allen'. That accommodation had been arranged by a woman who would later plead guilty to aiding the abduction of the little girl.

Regina Nelligan was 29 years old when she bumped into her former teacher, Christopher Crowley, at a supermarket in the midlands in 1999. The pair had not met for some time but they had been connected in the past by more than just a student-teacher relationship.

Nelligan was just 16 years old when she began an affair with Crowley while she was a student at Loreto Convent in Fermoy. The alliance lasted until she sat her Leaving Certificate, but when they later went to Italy on a holiday, the romance ended badly. Nelligan went to Dublin to study at the National College of Art and Design (NCAD). Crowley visited her on a number of occasions while she was living as a student in the capital but the relationship petered out. A considerable time elapsed before they met again in 1999, just months before Crowley would abduct his daughter with the assistance of his former girlfriend.

The psychological hold that Crowley held over his former student and partner was later described in court as not unlike the relationship between a child abuser and his victim.

Nelligan organised the rental of the Clonmel house after Crowley had returned with the girl, having spent some time in

Wales prior to November 2000. There was nothing to suggest that Nelligan was ever aware that the abduction would turn into something far more serious.

After the Garda appeal on the RTÉ programme, new leads seemed to emerge in relation to the location of the missing father and daughter. Christopher Crowley would almost certainly have been aware of the intensive search for Deirdre.

He had managed to keep the child almost completely hidden from any public view. Neighbours would later say how they did not see a young girl at the rented house and at times the property seemed to be so quiet that they believed it to be unoccupied. The milkman who called to deliver at the house later said that he had never seen the girl once.

But the pair did leave the rented property on occasion, albeit highly infrequently, as was evidenced by a local shopkeeper who had spotted the man and his daughter at Hearn's Hotel in Clonmel in the week after the programme's broadcast.

Eddie Kelly had no idea that the man was in fact being sought by Gardaí for abducting the girl but something odd about their situation stuck in his mind.

Kelly was having breakfast in the hotel when he noticed the man and the little girl at a nearby table. "What caught my attention was that they only had one cup of coffee, which he was drinking, and there was nothing else placed on the table. They were talking away," Kelly later told *The Irish Times*.

"He was smiling at her with a very soft smile. I found it extraordinary the way he kept smiling at her. I found it unusual as well that she was not having anything to eat, but then I thought she had probably had breakfast at home and they had just called in because he wanted a coffee."

When he next looked up, the girl had the coffee and drank it down in gulps. She then counted some money from her purse and in response to a question from the man, she shook her head.

"When I saw that, I wondered if they had no money and should I offer to buy them breakfast. It certainly seemed as if she needed that coffee," Kelly said.

"I didn't know if they would be offended, but just when I was going to get up and offer, they got up and left. Mister Crowley walked ahead of his daughter and she did not appear to be in any distress," the local shopkeeper said.

But there was "something that wasn't quite right" about the pair, which was why the incident had stuck in his mind. There was nothing one could pinpoint to suggest there was anything untoward about the relationship. It was only in the days after the girl's killing and her father's suicide that he realised just whom he had seen.

Just eleven days later, on August 30, 2001, local Gardaí in Clonmel called to the home in which Crowley and his daughter were staying. They left with the intention to return, acting on information in relation to the occupants of the house. What they found on their return was a gruesome discovery for which they could not have been prepared. The child lay in a pool of blood and beside her was her father's body.

The former State Pathologist Professor John Harbison later described the horrific scene in the house.

Before conducting an examination of the bodies, Harbison observed a "clean and tidy" kitchen. Food had only recently been prepared. In the living room of the house there were boxes and toy teddy bears and dolls lay on the floor. A large collection of crayons and pastels was placed beside the television in the corner of the room.

In the bathroom-cum-laundry, the blood-soaked bodies of Deirdre Crowley and her father lay on the floor. The little girl's left leg was underneath her father's right leg and her right arm was in a pool of blood. A shotgun was clutched firmly in Christopher Crowley's hand.

Harbison would later tell an inquest into the deaths that Christopher Crowley had shot himself in the side of the neck and cheek but it appeared he had not died instantaneously.

Deirdre Crowley had suffered massive damage to her head. Harbison said that there was no part of the child's face that remained recognisable as a result of gunshot at almost point blank range. She had been shot with a single cartridge. Her father, too, had suffered a single shot to the head but it was discharged at a point between the neck and cheek. He was not killed instantly but died from shock and hemorrhage caused by the gunshot wound. His death was consistent with self-infliction, Harbison said.

Christine O'Sullivan had made numerous public appeals during the two years that her daughter remained missing after the abduction, but after Deirdre was fatally shot her mother could only await the inquest, for the bare facts of how that killing occurred. There would be no explanation of why her child's life was taken away.

Like many parents just like her whose child was killed by a person who subsequently, or indeed simultaneously, took their own life, Christine O'Sullivan was left with countless unanswered questions. Regina Nelligan was sentenced in February 2002 to two years in prison for her role in assisting the child's abduction, with six months of that term suspended. But the little girl's mother has always maintained that other people also had knowledge of where her daughter was and did not inform Gardaí.

Twelve months after Regina Nelligan's sentencing, Christine O'Sullivan repeated her belief that her daughter's life could have been spared had Gardaí been told of Christopher Crowley's secret Tipperary hideout sooner. "I have absolutely no doubt whatever that if she [Nelligan], and indeed all the others who were involved in concealing Deirdre's whereabouts, if any one of them, even one person, had told the truth, Deirdre would be alive today," she insisted.

*****

Cases of homicide-suicide will forever leave the victims' families without any recourse to courtroom justice. But a detailed study of the rate of convictions, acquittals and other charges arising from violent killings in Ireland conducted for this book shows that the State is very successful in investigating and prosecuting homicide cases.

The authors examined all the violent deaths that occurred over three sample years – from the start of 2000 to the end of 2002. These years were chosen to allow adequate time for Garda investigations to have progressed to the criminal courts or, where appropriate, to have failed to yield any criminal charge at all.

The authors have excluded nine of the cases in particular, due to important considerations such as pending legal issues before the courts and so forth. Of the remaining 167 homicides, analysis shows that 32% resulted in a successful murder conviction in the courts (discounting murder convictions overturned at the CCA). In a further 42 cases, the state brought a successful manslaughter conviction or secured a conviction on this charge after having failed to make a case for murder. This shows that one quarter of all homicides result in a conviction for manslaughter being handed down in the Irish criminal courts. A further seven people were found guilty of murder but insane and were committed in most instances to the indefinite care of the Central Mental Hospital in Dundrum in Dublin. These cases represent just over four per cent of all violent deaths over the three-year study.

When all the convictions for murder, manslaughter and the conviction of guilty of murder but insane are combined, it shows that a significant majority of all killings result in a homicide conviction. In total, 103 cases resulted in such charges being successfully brought by the state – showing that just over 61% of all violent deaths result in a murder or manslaughter conviction.

The remaining convictions that were brought include reckless endangerment and assault.

Although there were 54 homicides in which a murder conviction was achieved, in fact, 57 killers were given life sentences for the act of murder. In three of these violent deaths, more than one person was convicted for murder.

Likewise, while 42 violent deaths resulted in successful manslaughter convictions by the state, 50 people were convicted on manslaughter charges. In the case of two murders, manslaughter convictions were handed down to an additional three men for their part in these deaths. In five other cases of homicide, two men were convicted of manslaughter for their roles in taking a life in a violent attack.

But while the state has a high rate of success in bringing a conviction for homicide in relation to violent deaths, it is still the case that, over one fifth of all killings result in no-one being charged. Out of the 167 homicides surveyed analysis shows that in 36 cases there has been no charge brought, meaning that in 21% of all violent deaths, no-one has ever been charged.

On further analysis there is a noticeable trend among these violent deaths in which no charge is brought by the State. Fatal shootings account for almost half – 47% – of these cases, a statistic which is completely out of proportion with the number of violent killings committed by people using guns. The vast majority of fatal shootings which have resulted in no charges being brought to date are killings which are linked by Garda sources to the criminal underworld – so-called 'gangland-style' murders. The low rate of charges in this category of homicide shows just how difficult gangland-related gun murders in particular are to investigate. Compared to most other types of killing, it would appear that so-called gang "hits" are considerably more premeditated than any other type of violent death. The killer or killers clearly make an effort to carry out the murder with the intention of leaving scant physical evidence in their wake, that could see them prosecuted.

While around one third of all homicides involve the use of a knife, just over one quarter of the cases that resulted in no charge were fatal stabbings. Deaths arising out of a fatal assault account for a further seven violent killings in which no charges have been brought – 19% of the total. A further handful of cases related to death as a result of trauma arising from an altercation or violent encounter.

Looking at the various types of killing, it would be accurate to conclude that a significant proportion of those not involving firearms are much easier to successfully investigate. It is highly unlikely that someone who drinks a large amount of alcohol, and then engages in a violent row which results in a fatal assault, would possess sufficient composure or control of their faculties to then clean the crime scene of damning forensic evidence.

Likewise, crimes of passion, such as the killing of a former lover by a rejected ex-partner, seem far more likely to be done suddenly and without planning, anecdotal evidence suggests. Killers who act on a spur of sudden anger or rage, inspired by what they unreasonably believe to be provocation by their victim, are also far less unlikely to evade some connection to the crime.

Indeed, the killing of Dublin man John Waters by his son Gary shows just how unplanned such deaths are. Thirty-four-year-old Gary Waters stabbed his father 19 times in a "frenzied" attack, the Central Criminal Court heard during the January 2004 trial.

The court was told that Waters had "snapped" on December 29, 2001, after he heard his father John talking in a "cavalier" fashion about allegations that he had sexually abused his daughters.

During the trial, Gary Waters' sisters told the court that their father John had, in fact, sexually abused them when they were small children. The accused man told investigating Gardaí that his father said to him on the night of his death that he had "just fondled them, never penetrated them". Hearing this, Gary Waters became enraged and he lost control.

The presiding judge in the case, Mr Justice O'Higgins, summed up precisely the type of rage that fits the profile of so many other killers who acted in similar circumstances. "It would appear that you simply lost the use of yourself after certain things were said by your father and that there were allegations made against him," the judge said.

"The allegations have been supported by other people, and there's no doubt you lost control of yourself in circumstances where you believed your father was dealing in an absolutely uncaring and cavalier fashion towards matters of the utmost seriousness." After he stabbed his father repeatedly, Waters called Gardaí and admitted what he had just done. Gary Waters pleaded not guilty to the charge that he had murdered his father at the dead man's home in Oliver Bond Street.

The jury in the case returned a verdict of not guilty of murder but found him guilty of manslaughter in relation to his father's death.

It is highly unlikely that an organised criminal would make such a call to Gardaí after carrying out a gangland assassination nor indeed would the killing have occurred in such an unplanned fashion. However, there has been much political debate over the issue of the low conviction rates in relation to gangland-style murders, with the government coming in for some criticism. But it is nonetheless accurate to say that police forces all over the world find such killings more difficult to detect than other categories of homicide. This is a point that has been made on a number of occasions by the Minister for Justice Michael McDowell, with little public acknowledgement.

Figures published by McDowell's own department show just how low the conviction rate is among gun murders, the majority of which are related to organised crime activity. Just one in six – 17% – of all fatal shootings result in a criminal conviction in the Irish courts. That compares dramatically with conviction rates of 60% for other categories of homicide, in analysis conducted for this book.

There is significant anecdotal evidence to suggest that many of the actual gunmen who pull the trigger in gangland-style shootings frequently become victims of homicide themselves within a short period of time. This makes it even more difficult to secure a conviction in relation to an assassination. The fatal shootings of many of the shooters' criminal conspirators is also damaging to the likelihood of a successful homicide prosecution.

There are several examples of just such cases, based on information provided to the authors by Garda sources. The murder of criminal John Roche in 2005 is highly illustrative of this trend.

Roche was embroiled in a feud between two southside Dublin gangs, one of which he was an active member. On March 9, 2005, he was shot dead by rival gang members